PERSONAL LETTERS THAT MEAN BUSINESS

Linda Braxton Sturgeon

Anne Russell Hagler

PRENTICE HALL
Paramus, New Jersey 07652

Library of Congress Cataloging-in-Publication Data

Sturgeon, Linda B. (Linda Braxton).
   Personal letters that mean business / by Linda B. Sturgeon and
Anne R. Hagler.
     p. cm.
   Includes index.
   ISBN 0-13-126178-9
   1. Letter-writing. 2. Commercial correspondence. I. Hagler,
Anne R. (Anne Russell). II. Title.
PE1483.S75 1991   91-16097
808.6   CIP

Printed in the United States of America

10 9 8 7 6   10 9 8

ISBN 0-13-656307-4   ISBN 0-13-656299-X(PBK)

PRENTICE HALL
Career & Personal Development
Paramus, NJ 07652
A Simon & Schuster Company

On the World Wide Web at http://www.phdirect.com

Prentice-Hall International (UK) Limited, *London*
Prentice-Hall of Australia Pty. Limited, *Sydney*
Prentice-Hall Canada Inc., *Toronto*
Prentice-Hall Hispanoamericana, S.A., *Mexico*
Prentice-Hall of India Private Limited, *New Delhi*
Prentice-Hall of Japan, Inc., *Tokyo*
Simon & Schuster Asia Pte. Ltd., *Singapore*
Editora Prentice-Hall do Brasil, Ltda., *Rio de Janeiro*

For
Walter Sturgeon and Paul Hagler,
whose patience, encouragement, and unfailing good humor
supported this effort so admirably

What This Book Will Do for You

Throughout our lifetime we encounter many situations that make it necessary to step outside our comfortable circle of family and friends and communicate with strangers about matters that affect our personal well-being.

If you have experienced the frustration of attempting to compose a personal business letter, or agonized over an expression of sympathy to an acquaintance or coworker, you know that the task of presenting a clear and concise accounting of your situation, or offering an appropriate demonstration of caring and concern, can be far more difficult than you imagined.

The problem of communicating effectively in writing is common to all of us. The "blank page syndrome" strikes without regard to age, interests, education, vocation, profession, or position.

Often our attempts falter because we cannot find the words to express our needs adequately; our letters do not contain sufficient information to enable the recipient to recognize the problem and offer a solution; and we fail to direct our messages to the appropriate individuals or departments; thus creating confusion and delays in obtaining a response.

Personal Letters That Mean Business virtually eliminates the obstacles that have hampered your efforts in the past. As you examine the hundreds of model letters contained in the twenty-one business chapters and sixteen personal ones, you will quickly discover what makes this letter book unique.

The key is simplicity. The proper style and formatting of your personal business letters are shown in the example featured in "Styling and Formatting the Business Letter" at the openings of Parts I and II. The salutation or greeting preceding each model letter suggests the appropriate individual or organization to whom you should direct your correspondence. Once you have substituted your own personal information where it is indicated in bold print in the model letter, the message you have chosen becomes your very own. Simply sign your letter, provide any additional identifying information needed, enclose the documents, if any, that you have indicated accompany your letter, and dispatch it to your intended recipient.

Throughout the book and the appendix are numerous aids that will help you

- Select the proper form of address (see Forms of Address in the appendix)
- Guide you to the best methods to mail your correspondence (see U.S. Postal Service in the appendix)

- Provide you with commonly used business terms (see "What They Mean When They Say . . ." in the appendix)
- Give you quick access to a comprehensive listing of addresses and telephone numbers of selected federal, national, and state agencies and organizations to whom you may write (see Information Please . . . also in the appendix)

Whether you are writing to express interest in an employment opportunity or to investigate a credit problem, terminate a lease, inquire about health, education, or Medicare services, request reduction of an insurance rate, dispute a claim, apply for Social Security benefits, or ask for a determination of eligibility for veterans' entitlements, you will find these letters and many more in Part I: Business Letters.

If your messages are of a more personal nature, the examples in Part II: Personal Letters will enable you to offer congratulations and condolences, mend a broken friendship, offer a helping hand, or, when necessary, say "No," in a sincere and forthright manner.

Personal Letters That Mean Business addresses situations most common to everyday living, and we are confident that you will find just the example that best suits your needs. Whether you use the letters as they are written or adapt them to formulate one of your own, this book will enable you to produce clear and concise business and personal messages in a direct, no-nonsense manner that will elicit a quick response and positive results.

Acknowledgments

It is appropriate that our first message is a personal one, acknowledging the efforts of a special group of individuals whose expertise, encouragement, and response to our endless requests for information helped to transform an idea into a startling reality.

We are grateful to the U. S. Office of Consumer Affairs for permission to use resources from the 1990 edition of the *Consumer's Resource Handbook*; Attorney Sandra M. McClean, Office of the Federal Register, Washington, D.C., who responded so generously to our request to utilize resources from *The United States Government Manual*; Paul Williams, U. S. Department of Labor, Washington, D.C.; Richard P. Cook, statistician, U. S. Department of Education, Washington, D.C.; Thomas R. Margenau, deputy director, Office of Information, Social Security Administration, Baltimore, Maryland; Fred Young, Office of Information, Social Security Administration, Baltimore, Maryland; Marty Hudspeth, assistant district manager, Social Security Administration, Clearwater, Florida; Paula De Smith, Office of the Clerk of Circuit Court, Pinellas County, Florida; Joyce Kliebert, Federal Information Center, St. Petersburg, Florida; Susan D. McDonnell, assistant vice president, Florida Federal Savings Bank, Dunedin, Florida; Sharon Ellison, taxpayer service representative, Internal Revenue Service; Larry Garren, real estate broker-contractor, Palm Harbor, Florida; those anonymous individuals who responded to our queries from The Health Care Financing Administration, Washington, D.C., and The Office of the State Insurance Commissioner, Tallahassee, Florida; Barbara Skubish, reference librarian, Dunedin Public Library, Dunedin, Florida; Mimi Krystal, Clearwater, Florida, for research assistance; Louise B. Young, Educator, Belleair Bluffs, Florida, for research assistance; Patricia Thorbin-Hancock, R.N., Largo, Florida, for research assistance; Rita Freudenthal, R.N., Largo, Florida, for research assistance; Mary T. Holmes, income property manager, Clearwater Beach, Florida, for research assistance; and finally, our special thanks and appreciation to Ellen Schneid Coleman, senior editor, Prentice Hall Business Information & Publishing Division, who provided opportunity and motivation, and, simply put, made it all possible.

Contents

Chapter 9   Government   69

PART II
PERSONAL LETTERS

APPENDIX

Part I

Business Letters

HOW TO WRITE BUSINESS LETTERS THAT GET RESULTS

The model letters featured in Part I are designed to help you open the channels of communication and establish a mutually beneficial dialogue with the organizations, businesses, and government agencies to which you may have to write. In addition to providing the means to obtain information or assistance, clarify a misunderstanding, or seek a resolution to a problem, your letter serves as a permanent record of your effort to address your particular situation in a reasonable and forthright manner.

Whether you rely solely upon the contents of the model letters or use them to formulate your own original one, following a few simple rules will enable you to capture your recipient's attention and aid him or her in formulating a prompt response.

First Impressions

How important is the overall appearance of your letter? Put yourself in your recipient's place. Imagine that you arrive at your office to find a stack of letters on your desk. A quick inspection reveals that more than half are illegible and that some are addressed only "To Whom It May Concern." The majority do not indicate at first glance what the letter is about, and abusive and threatening phrases leap from the pages of others.

However, among this questionable collection one stands out. It is typed or neatly handwritten and properly formatted, the message is clear and concise, and it is addressed to you personally. Which one would you be most likely to attend to first? Although we live and work in an advanced technological environment, it is important to recognize that the human aspect remains the predominant force to contend with in the workplace. To discount its importance is to court disappointment.

Return Address

It is surprising how often this vital bit of information is inadvertently omitted from letters. If you use personal preprinted stationery, repeating your address is unnecessary. If not, you must provide an address to which your correspondent may respond. If you prefer to have a reply sent to an alternate address, indicate this desire in the body of your letter.

Dates

The date your letter is written should be shown directly beneath your return address. If subsequent follow-up correspondence is necessary, you should indicate the exact date on which you initiated your original inquiry in order to justify why you have found it necessary to write again, or to address your situation to another individual who may be more inclined to provide a timely response.

Dates are especially important if you are referencing an occurrence such as an insurance claim or insurance policy term. Dates and numbers should always be rechecked for accuracy. Incorrect information can result in a delay of several days, perhaps weeks, before you receive a response.

Reference or Subject Lines (Optional)

Though not as widely used today as in the past, reference or subject lines that follow directly below the recipient's name and address quickly identify the purpose of your letter and enable the recipient to pinpoint the problem before reading the content of your letter. Reference and subject lines usually identify account, policy and claim numbers, dated events or indicate that you are responding to a previous correspondence.

The Importance of Targeting Your Source

Such greetings as "To Whom It May Concern," "Dear Sir," or "Gentlemen" seldom produce quick results and should be used only when it is impossible to obtain the name of an individual to whom you must address your correspondence. Indeed, some consider "Dear Sir" or "Gentlemen" to be sexist and, instead, use the salutation "Dear" followed by the name of the organization or department or the title of the person to whom they are writing. Targeting a specific person almost always ensures prompt personal attention to your situation. If you are faced with a critical deadline or if previous efforts to resolve a problem have gone unanswered, telephone the business or organization in question to determine the name, title, department, and correct mailing address of the individual who can help you. It is always advantageous to obtain the name of the person's supervisor and copy your correspondence to him or her. Should you be required to address the matter again, you will almost certainly want to take it a step higher.

You may also lend added weight to your need for expediency by utilizing one of the special methods of mailing described in the appendix under U.S. Postal Service.

Salutation or Greeting

Your recipient's name should always be preceded by his or her appropriate title. The use of first names is not recommended unless you are personally acquainted with the individual to whom you are writing, or if, after a period of time, your recipient indicates that this is acceptable.

Content

Letters that are concise, factual, and to the point are more likely to receive a quick response than are those that ramble and state opinions in lieu of facts. Abusive or threatening messages greatly reduce your chances for a prompt response and may actually harm your prospects for a positive resolution.

Conclusion

By concluding your letter with an expression of appreciation for the reader's assistance and anticipated response, you convey your recognition of his or her efforts as well as your willingness to cooperate to achieve a mutually beneficial solution to the problem.

Closing

Your signature should reflect your current name. If you have obtained an account or contract under another name, indicate your previous or alternate name directly beneath your correct one. Directly below your name you may wish to indicate any identifying information such as position, title, Social Security number, service number, or Medicare number, to name a few.

Signing off with only your first name should be restricted to correspondence with those individuals with whom you have established a good working relationship and who you are reasonably certain will not mistake you for someone else. "First name only" closings are not considered appropriate when addressing persons previously unknown to you. As a matter of professional courtesy, always give your full name below your written signature, whether you are signing *only* your given name or your full name.

The closing preceding your signature enhances the overall tone of your letter. "Very truly yours" is generally considered a formal closing, "Sincerely" is direct and acceptable in most all situations, while "Cordially," "Best regards," and "Warmest regards" are reserved for those persons with whom you have developed a mutually pleasing or beneficial relationship. While "Sincerely" is used most often throughout this book, common sense and your personal knowledge of your situation will dictate the appropriate choice.

Supporting Materials (Enclosures and Attachments)

Directly below your name, indicate what materials you plan to include with your correspondence, listing each item individually if you have not done so in the body of your letter. Unless specifically required, do not send original documents. If you must send an original document or a monetary instrument, check with your postal or courier service for the best method to ensure safe delivery to the individual for whom it is intended.

Copies to Others

If you plan to send a copy of the original letter and documents to other interested parties, indicate who they are at the bottom of the original letter.

"Blind copies," those sent to other interested parties without your correspondent's knowledge, are not shown on the original letter. However, they should be noted on your personal copy.

Failure to Respond

If you fail to receive a response to your initial contact within a reasonable period of time, send a copy of your original letter marked "Second Request" at the top. If you still do not receive a response, or you have not been advised that your letter has been forwarded to another individual or department for handling, direct your next letter to someone in a supervisory capacity or an administrative position. Many businesses have set policies regarding acceptable response times. Failure on the part of their employees to adhere to this policy will result in an immediate inquiry.

Return to the Source

As a rule, it is more expedient to initiate your inquiry or grievance locally, or at the original source, as opposed to contacting a regional or national office. The closer your contact, the more likely you are to conclude the matter quickly. Only after you have attempted resolution at this level should you request district, regional, or national intervention.

Response to certain inquiries or requests for action may result in your *having* to complete required forms or supply additional documentation, particularly in the areas of finance, personal credit accounts, insurance, and most government departments and agencies.*

Millions of pieces of business mail travel through our postal and courier systems daily. The greater percentages are letters from people like you and me. No business or organization is immune to mistakes. In spite of the impressive lengths they employ to reduce the potential for disputes, sooner or later you are going to come face to face with a situation that should not have happened. At that point it becomes your responsibility to, first, make the manufacturer, vendor, credit department, insurance claims representative, or government official aware of the problem, and, second, give them the opportunity to correct it.

This can be accomplished most effectively through your personal business letter. A carefully researched and clearly stated accounting of the situation, addressed to the appropriate individual in a reasonable and cooperative manner, is your guarantee of a quick resolution.

As a consumer, yours is the most powerful voice in the corporate sector. Use it prudently, and it will work for you. Abuse it, and it will lose its effectiveness.

STYLING AND FORMATTING THE BUSINESS LETTER

First impressions are as important in letter writing as they are in face-to-face meetings. When you meet someone, no matter what the occasion, you form a first impression based on his or her appearance. The same is true for a letter. The recipient of your letter also forms an initial impression based on the appearance of your letter. Since you want your recipient's first impression to be a favorable one, your choice of style and format is critical.

We recommend full-block style because it looks good on the page, and it is easy to set up and type (see the accompanying sample). In full-block style, all parts of the letter, from the inside address to the complimentary close, begin flush with the left margin. If there are enclosures or carbon copies to other persons, these entries begin at the left margin as well. If you are using your own personal letterhead, your letter will begin with the date, starting at the left margin. Although it is best to type (or print on a word

---

* Forms listed in many of the model letters are subject to periodic revision or substitution. However, each letter is constructed in such a manner as to identify readily the information being requested.

processor) business letters, if you do not have a typewriter or word processor, a legible, handwritten letter is acceptable.

Your business letter should be formatted based on what you want your letter to accomplish. However, there are some basic guidelines to follow when writing to someone in business, government, education, or other organization:

1. Direct your letter to the appropriate person. Sometimes a phone call will be necessary to determine who that person is; however, that time will be well spent because it will increase your chances of a prompt response to your request.

2. State your reason for writing in a clear and concise manner near the beginning of your letter.

3. Include specific information that will allow your recipient to identify who you are (e.g., account number, claim number, Social Security number, etc.). Remember: Your name is not always enough for someone to process your letter quickly.

4. If you are responding to correspondence (or items) received, be sure to refer to that correspondence (or items) accurately so that your recipient will be able to identify it quickly.

5. Be clear about what you want your recipient to do. If your recipient knows precisely what you want the result of your letter to be, it is easier for him or her to decide how to respond.

6. Be sure to include all the available information about your request (e.g., dates, invoice numbers, check numbers, addresses, etc.). The more specific information you can give your recipient, the more likely you will be to get a prompt response. If your recipient has to search for the information, his or her response will be delayed.

7. Keep your letter short and to the point. Your recipient will not want to wade through a lot of unessential information in order to sort out what you want.

8. Include your phone number if you think that might speed up the process of getting a response.

9. The golden rule is as applicable to correspondence as it is to daily personal contacts. If you are reasonable, straightforward, clear, and courteous in your letters, you are more likely to receive timely and responsive replies.

GUIDE TO LETTER LAYOUT

Your Post Office Box or Street Address City, State, Zip Code	2 spaces between inside address and date
Current Date	4 spaces between date and inside address
Name of Contact Person (if known) Title of Contact Person (if applicable) Name of Company, Organization, or Department Post Office Box and/or Street Address City, State, Zip Code	
Reference or Subject (if included)	2 spaces if reference line is used

| Salutation or Greeting: | 2 spaces between inside address and greeting or reference line |

BODY OF LETTER

Complimentary Close, Your signature	4 spaces between complimentary close and your name (signature goes in this space)
Your name	
CC: (to whom sent)	2 spaces before copy identification
Enclosure/Attachment	2 spaces before enclosure identification

---

| BCC: | indicates (blind) copy—used only if copy sent to another person without knowledge of original addressee—not indicated on original letter |

SAMPLE LETTER

2349 Rosemary Court
Any Town, NE 09834

June 24, 1991

William S. Banker
Branch Manager
Hometown Savings and Loan
32 Main Street
Any Town, NE 09834

Dear **(name of organization or department)**:

On **May 30, 1991,** * I opened a **savings** account, **#092001837,** at your branch. At that time, I was told that if I kept my balance above **$500.00,** there would be no service charge on my account.

I just received my first statement, dated **June 20, 1991,** which includes a service charge of **$5.61.** I do not understand the reason for this charge since the statement clearly indicates that my balance never went below **$500.00.**

Please credit my account in the amount of **$5.61** and notify me of the date when my account is credited. If there is a reason for the charge that I am not aware of, please call me at **453-9271.**

Thank you for your prompt attention to this matter.

Sincerely,

---

* Boldfaced words and numbers indicate the areas where you would usually insert your own information.

Chapter 1

BUSINESS CLUBS AND ORGANIZATIONS

Invitation to Join
Welcoming New Member
Rejecting a Membership Application
Requesting Payment of Membership Dues
Refusing a Donation
Announcing a Special Event
Recruiting Volunteers—Blanket Letter
Thanking Volunteer

As a new member of a business club or organization, you may be surprised to discover that, unlike their purely social counterparts, these groups generally confine their membership rosters to individuals who share similar business interests and lend themselves to a variety of civic, governmental, and charitable works. Being accepted into such an organization carries with it such responsibilities as screening potential applicants, rejecting others who are deemed inappropriate, actively participating in events to benefit special causes, and undertaking the inevitable chore of searching out elusive volunteers.

How well you communicate within, and outside, the perimeters of your club or organization lends credibility to their goals and influences their opinion of your contributions as a whole.

The model letters featured in this chapter address a variety of situations you are likely to encounter either as a committee chairperson or as an elected officer.

INVITATION TO JOIN

Dear (**name of applicant or selected candidate**):

Each year the members of (**club/organization**) offer a select group of individuals the opportunity to join our organization.

We have reviewed the recommendation submitted on your behalf by (**name of sponsor**) and feel that your dedication and outstanding accomplishments in the area of (**nature of recognition**) make you an ideal candidate for membership in (**club/organization**).

We would like to invite you to join us at our next meeting, which will be held at (**location**), on (**day/date**), at (**time**).

Please contact our (**function coordinator/membership chairman/other**), (**name**), at (**telephone number**), if you plan to attend, or if you wish to decline in favor of an alternate candidate.

We look forward to hearing from you at your earliest convenience.

Sincerely,

WELCOMING A NEW MEMBER

Dear (**name of new member**):

On behalf of the (**club/organization**), permit me to extend a personal welcome to you and tell you how gratified we are that you have chosen to place your membership with us.

As you know, we are primarily a (**type of club/organization**), involved in many worthwhile projects in the community. We are particularly supportive of (**special project**) and work throughout the year to sponsor (**nature of assistance/aid**).

Your (**volunteer work/profession**) will lend additional insight and expertise to this program, and we look forward to hearing your ideas at our next meeting on (**date**).

Again, welcome!

Sincerely,

REJECTING A MEMBERSHIP APPLICATION

Dear (**name of applicant**):

As (**title**) of the (**club/organization**), it is my unfortunate duty to inform you of your ineligibility for membership in this organization.

Our bylaws stipulate (**give reason for denial, for example, does not reside within specific area for that particular chapter/does not meet academic requirements/does not have sufficient experience to qualify**).

Your credentials are indeed impressive; however, we are unable to give favorable consideration to your application based upon this technicality. Should your situation change, please resubmit your application. We would welcome the opportunity to reconsider your membership at that time.

We appreciate your interest in (**club/organization**) and look forward to hearing from you again.

Cordially,

REQUESTING PAYMENT OF MEMBERSHIP DUES

Dear (**name of member**):

Please be reminded that (**club / organization**)'s annual membership fee for (**year**) is now due.

If you have not done so, please mail your payment of (**$ amount**) to our (**treasurer/ business office/club/other**) at the address shown above, or stop by (**office/club**), weekdays, between (**hour**) and (**hour**).

Any account (**number of days/weeks/months**) in arrears will be considered a VOLUN-TARY LAPSE and will result in a loss of membership privileges. Your timely attention to this matter will be greatly appreciated.

Cordially,

REFUSING A DONATION

Dear (**name of donor, benefactor, or sponsor**):

On behalf of the (**club/organization**), I wish to express our appreciation for your generous donation. However, it is with great regret, since we are in need of additional funds, that we must decline your offer as it stands.

Our organization sponsors many worthwhile projects throughout the (**city/county/state**), and according to our established (**charter/bylaws/rules/other**), disbursement of funds must be equal and nondiscriminatory.

Your stipulation to utilize your donation for one specific (**project/group**) would be in violation of our policy and could possibly discredit our claim of impartial benefits to all our recipients.

If you would be willing to remove the restrictions accompanying your gift, we would be very pleased to accept the donation and extend the thanks of our membership for your generosity.

May we hear from you at your earliest convenience?

Cordially,

ANNOUNCING A SPECIAL EVENT

Dear (**name of member**):

We recently learned (**special guest**) will be visiting (**town/city**) on (**date**) to deliver (**lecture/commencement address/or consult**) to/with (**other organization/school/business**). (**He/she**) has graciously agreed to extend (**his/her**) stay to speak to our (**group/club/organization**) at our meeting on (**date**).

We are indeed fortunate to have this opportunity to meet a renowned expert in the field of (**guest's expertise**), and we are urging all members to attend this meeting as we are certain everyone will be interested in (**name**)'s message.

The meeting will be held at (**alternate location**) to accommodate the expected turnout.

Sincerely,

RECRUITING VOLUNTEERS—BLANKET LETTER

TO ALL MEMBERS:

On (**day/date**) the (**neighborhood/city/organization**) will host its annual (**event**) to raise money for (**project**). As you all know, this event has earned (**local/state/national**) recognition for its fine work on behalf of (**recipients**).

This year's (**event**) promises to be bigger and better than ever, enabling us to serve the growing needs of (**sponsored individuals/groups/activities**). The planning committee is issuing an urgent appeal for all civic and professional organizations throughout the area to pledge a 100% effort to this cause.

Volunteers are needed to (**list duties**). A list of volunteer positions has been posted at (**location**). Please stop by at your earliest convenience and sign up for one of these committees.

Thanks for your support. Let's make this a unanimous effort on behalf of (**group/ project**).

Best regards,

THANKING VOLUNTEER

Dear (**name of volunteer**):

On behalf of (**club/organization**), I would like to express our appreciation for the fine program you presented at our meeting on (**day/date**).

Your excellent approach to (**subject**) enhanced our understanding of (**related circumstances**) and helped us recognize the seriousness of the problems faced by (**individuals/ groups/other**).

Thank you for so generously volunteering your time and knowledge to bring us this important message.

Sincerely,

Chapter 2

CONSUMER PRODUCTS AND SERVICES

Potential Hazard—Notifying Manufacturer
Ordering by Mail
Follow-up—Product Not Received
Misrepresentation of a Product
Product Damaged in Shipment
Defective Product—Request for Refund
Returning a Substituted Item
Product Under Warranty
Canceling Order—Product
Requesting Return of Deposit
Canceling Unsatisfactory Service
Service Complaint

Technology, ingenuity, and mass production have made available an unprecedented abundance of goods and services to consumers worldwide today. However, with so much to choose from, how do we determine the best quality for our money, or recognize a genuine bargain as opposed to a scam or gimmick? In spite of safeguards offered by manufacturers, and the vigilance of quality assurance teams and consumer protection advocates, mistakes occur, and impostors surface all too frequently.

If you purchase a product that fails to measure up to the manufacturer's or merchant's usual standards, contact their quality assurance team or customer service department. Customer satisfaction is the mainstay of the free enterprise system. Reputable manufacturers and merchants want to know when you have a problem.

If you suspect you have been, or could become, the victim of dishonest business practices, contact your local Better Business Bureau or Consumer Protection Agency to verify credentials or check for complaints lodged by other consumers. Exposing unscrupulous practices is a proved deterrent against consumer fraud.*

POTENTIAL HAZARD— NOTIFYING MANUFACTURER

Dear (name of quality assurance supervisor or risk manager):

I am writing to alert you to a potential hazard with your (name of product). On (date) I purchased (item) as a gift for my (age) (child/other). Within moments (he/she) began choking. Fortunately, I was able to extricate the enclosed object, enabling (him/her) to breath normally once again.

It appears this object was not (attached correctly/sufficiently researched prior to marketing/suitable for age group/other).

This was a very frightening experience, and I am certain you will want to take immediate steps to ensure that it does not occur again, with possibly far more serious consequences.

Sincerely,

NOTE: You may wish to send a blind copy of this letter to the appropriate consumer advocate group.

---

* See "Information Please . . ." in the appendix for addresses and telephone numbers of national, state, and area Better Business Bureaus and Consumer Protection Agencies.

ORDERING BY MAIL

Dear (**name of manufacturer, distributor, or representative**):

Enclosed please find my personal check in the amount of (**$ amount**) to cover the cost and shipping charges for (**number**) (**item/s**) that (**was/were**) featured on page (**number**) of (**catalog/other**).

Please ship (**number**) in (**size**), in the color (**. . .**). If (**item/s**) (**is/are**) no longer available, or there has been an increase in the cost since this (**catalog/flyer**) was issued, please cancel this order and return the enclosed check. *NO SUBSTITUTION, PLEASE.*

I look forward to receiving (**item**), at the address shown above, within (**length of time stipulated in the advertisement**).

Sincerely,

FOLLOW-UP—PRODUCT NOT RECEIVED

Dear (**name of manufacturer, distributor, or customer service supervisor**):

On (**date**) I submitted an order for (**number and item**), accompanied by my personal check in the amount of (**$ amount**).

(**Length of time**) has elapsed since I mailed the order to you, sufficient time for it to have arrived. I have the canceled check showing you did receive the order and deposited my check, which cleared my bank on (**date**).

I have not received notification of (**cancellation of offer/out of stock/back order**) and must assume this is an oversight.

Please advise when you intend to ship. If you are no longer featuring this item, issue a refund to me in the amount of (**$ amount**).

Thank you for your prompt attention to this matter.

Sincerely,

NOTE: You should enclose a copy, front and back, of canceled check.

MISREPRESENTATION OF A PRODUCT

Dear (**name of distributor or customer service supervisor**):

On (**date**) I submitted an order for (**item**), along with my personal check in the amount of (**$ amount**) to cover the cost, plus handling and shipping charges.

I have just received (item) and am dismayed to find it is actually (smaller/different color/inferior quality/other) than portrayed in your (catalog/flyer/advertisement). I do not feel the quality justifies the cost, so I am returning this item, and requesting a refund in the amount of ($ amount).

Thank you for your attention and prompt response.

Sincerely,

PRODUCT DAMAGED IN SHIPMENT

Dear (name of district supervisor or regional manager):

On (date) I purchased (item) from a floor model featured at your (location) showroom. This item was not in stock at the time of purchase, and I agreed to accept shipment of an identical model from your (warehouse/supplier).

On (date), (name of commercial carrier) delivered the item, obtained my signature, and departed before I had an opportunity to unpack it. I discovered (state extent of damage) and immediately telephoned (place of purchase). I was informed by (name) that (name of seller) was not responsible for damage in shipment, and I must settle this matter with the carrier directly.

I contracted to purchase this (item) from you, and (name of seller) contracted with this particular carrier to deliver it. Therefore, in my opinion, it is your responsibility to settle the matter with (carrier).

I would appreciate your effort to resolve this matter promptly and arrange for a replacement to be delivered to me.

Thank you for your assistance.

Sincerely,

DEFECTIVE PRODUCT—REQUEST FOR REFUND

Dear (name of customer service supervisor):

On (date) I purchased (item) from your (specialty/area) section, at a sale price of ($ amount). After the very first use, it quite literally began to fall apart. (Give a brief explanation of what happened.) As you can see, aside from the obvious structural defects, this item shows no signs of misuse.

I am aware of your "no refund" policy on sale items, and normally one might expect some minor problem with a clearance item. However, this (item) falls far short of the quality of merchandise I am accustomed to finding in your store. I hope that this is an isolated incident and that such inferior products will not be offered in the future.

I am enclosing the sales receipt and requesting that a full refund of (**$ amount**) be credited to my account.

Thank you for your consideration.

Sincerely,

RETURNING SUBSTITUTED ITEM

Dear (**name of customer service representative**):

I have just received the order I placed with you on (**date**) and, to my surprise, discovered the (**item**) I received is not the one I originally ordered.

In spite of your assurance the (**substituted item**) is equal in value and quality to the one I selected, I cannot accept it. I specifically chose (**color/size/materials**) to compliment similar items I had purchased earlier. The one you sent is unsuitable.

I am returning the (**item**) to you and am asking that you credit my account (**number**) for the amount of this order.

Sincerely,

PRODUCT UNDER WARRANTY

Dear (**name of manager, designated service center**):

On (**date**) I purchased the enclosed (**item**), which carried a (**length of time**) warranty. Recently, I noticed it (**state problem**). As you can see, the (**item**) shows no evidence of neglect, nor have I attempted repairs myself.

I would like to have it repaired under the provisions of the existing warranty or [**be given a replacement of equal value/credit my account or issue a refund in the amount of ($ amount)**].

I am enclosing a copy of the sales receipt as proof of purchase, a copy of the warranty, ￫nd the amount of postage (**if required**) to have this item returned to the above address once it has been repaired.

Sincerely,

CANCELING ORDER—PRODUCT

Dear (**name of circulation supervisor or manager**):

On (**date**) I purchased a (**length of time**) subscription to your (**magazine/paper**), (**title**). Although I was unfamiliar with your format, the title led me to believe it would be of interest to me. Instead, I found the content, quite frankly, objectionable.

I am requesting cancellation of (**account/subscription number**) and a refund of the balance of the subscription price.

Sincerely,

REQUESTING RETURN OF DEPOSIT

Dear (**name of sales representative or general manager**):

On (**date**) I placed a deposit of (**$ amount**) on (**item**) to be (**shipped/delivered**) to me on (**date**). On (**date**) I discovered (**identical item**) at (**company/store/other**) for (**$ amount**), (**$ amount**) *less* than your advertised "sale" price. The (**owner/manager/sales representative**) admitted it was the full manufacturer's suggested retail price!

I can only conclude your company misrepresented this (**item**) as a sale item by increasing the alleged price and reducing it to make it appear as if you were giving a (**%**) discount.

I am quite distressed to find myself a victim of such practices and insist that you return my full deposit and cancel this order immediately. I will expect to receive my refund within (**length of time**).

Sincerely,

CANCELING UNSATISFACTORY SERVICE

Dear (**name of owner or general manager**):

In (**month/year**) I contracted with your (**type of service**) to take care of my (**lawn/pool/other**) at (**address**). In the beginning I was very pleased with the work performed by your (**crew/representative**), (**name**). However, in the past several weeks (**his/her/their**) lack of attention to detail is becoming more obvious with each visit.

I spoke with (name), who disagreed with my observations, stating most emphatically that my (lawn/pool/other) was in excellent condition. That, of course, is a matter of opinion. (Name) may be satisfied with (his/her/their) work, but I am not.

Since we are unable to agree on this matter, and (he/she/they) (is/are) clearly unconcerned about the condition of the property, or my complaint, I believe it would be to our mutual benefit to terminate our agreement.

Please issue a final statement for services as of (date).

Sincerely,

SERVICE COMPLAINT

Dear (name of owner or general manager):

On (date) I arranged to have one of your representatives, (name), come to my home to (install/repair/service/clean) (item) while I was at work. When I returned I found (state nature of damage or inferior workmanship). I must tell you that I find (results) totally unsatisfactory and invite your inspection. Please contact me at (telephone number) as soon as possible to arrange a time.

I am withholding payment on this account pending a satisfactory resolution of this problem.

Sincerely,

Chapter 3

CREDIT

Hundreds of thousands of individual credit transactions occur in this country daily. Satisfying an obligation in a timely manner will enable you to enjoy other credit opportunities in the future, while abusing credit privileges may make it difficult to persuade a lender, merchant, landlord, employer, health care institution, school, or college that you are a worthy credit risk.

Your personal credit record is a statement of your financial credibility. If you discover that it contains incorrect information, through another person's error, or your own, it should be dealt with immediately and aggressively. Such problems cannot be wished away and should never be ignored.

The letters contained in this chapter address some of the most common problems that affect personal credit.*

RESPONDING TO DENIAL OF PERSONAL CHARGE ACCOUNT

Dear (name of store or company credit manager):

On (date you applied) I applied to your (company/store) for a personal charge account. I received your letter of (date denial was written), denying my request based upon credit information obtained through an inquiry to (name of credit reporting agency).

I immediately asked them for an explanation of their unfavorable response to your inquiry, stating that I have maintained an excellent rating on all of my past and current accounts. An investigation revealed (state agency's findings), and they issued a letter verifying my correct payment history.

I am enclosing a copy of the letter and ask that you reconsider my application.

Thank you for your personal attention to this matter.

Sincerely,

TRANSFERRING ACCOUNT DUE TO RELOCATION

Dear (name of customer accounts manager):

This letter is to advise you that on (date) I moved from (previous address—city/state) to (new address—city/state).

I would like to transfer my account (number) to your store located (new area, or nearest facility—city/state).

All statements and correspondence pertaining to this account should be directed to my new address in (city).

---

* Listings of addresses and telephone numbers of banking authorities, Consumer Protection Agencies, and the Federal Trade Commission can be found in the appendix, "Information Please . . .".

Should you need to contact me personally, I may be reached by telephone at (**new telephone number**).

Thank you for your assistance.

Sincerely,

REQUEST TO INCREASE CREDIT LIMIT

Dear (**name of customer accounts or credit manager**):

In (**month/year**) I opened an account, (**number**), with your (**company/store**) with a credit limit of (**$ amount**).

Your records will reflect that I have maintained an excellent payment history on the account, and I would like to increase my credit limit to (**$ amount**).

I anticipate no difficulty meeting the monthly obligation this increase would generate and ask your favorable consideration of my request.

Thank you for your consideration and assistance.

Sincerely,

ADDING PERSON TO YOUR ACCOUNT

Dear (**name of customer accounts or credit manager**):

I would like to add (**spouse/child/other**) to my (**type of account and account number**) and ask that you issue a charge card to:

(**Name of person being added**)
(**Social Security number**)
(**Date of birth**)
(**Residence: if different from your own**)
(**Telephone: if different from your own**)

I agree to be responsible only for charges incurred by me and (**person who is being added to account**). No other person is authorized to use this account.

All statements and inquiries should be directed to my attention at (**address you wish information to be sent**).

If you have any questions, or require additional information, please contact me at (**telephone number**).

Sincerely,

DELETING PERSON FROM ACCOUNT

Dear (**name of customer accounts or credit manager**):

Please be advised that effective this date, I am requesting the deletion of (**name of person being removed**) from my (**type of account and account number**).

Pursuant to this notification, and return of the enclosed credit card, which I obtained from (**Mr./Ms.**) (**Name**), I will no longer be responsible for charges incurred by anyone other than myself. Please adjust your records accordingly.

Thank you for your *prompt* attention to this matter.

Sincerely,

CLOSING ACCOUNT—UNSATISFACTORY SERVICE

Dear (**name of credit department manager**):

Enclosed please find (**number**) credit cards and my personal check in the amount of (**$ amount**) for the entire balance due on my (**type of account and account number**).

In spite of repeated requests for assistance from your accounting department, I continue to receive incorrect statements; specifically (**state nature of grievance**). My payment history has been excellent; however, the confusion created by the billing errors is such that I am concerned it may adversely affect my credit rating. Therefore, I feel I have no choice but to close this account.

Sincerely,

PAYMENT NOT CREDITED TO ACCOUNT

Dear (**name of manager, accounts receivable**):

My recent payment of (**$ amount**) is not reflected on the statement I have just received. My records show payment was mailed (**date**).

Enclosed please find a photocopy, front and back, of my canceled check. You will note by the cancellation date that it cleared my bank on (**date**).

Please credit this payment to my account, (**number**), and issue a revised statement.

Thank you for your prompt attention to this matter.

Sincerely,

RESPONDING TO COLLECTION AGENCY

Dear (name of collection agency representative):

I have received your notification that my account (number) has been turned over to your agency for collection.

The attached photocopy, front and back, of my canceled check, made payable to (original creditor), is proof that this obligation was satisfied (number of days/weeks/months) *prior* to the date of your letter.

By way of a copy of this letter to (original creditor), I am advising them of this error and requesting an adjustment of their records, and a recall of this account from (name of agency).

I will expect a prompt response from either you or (original creditor) verifying that this account has been withdrawn and that I do not, in fact, owe this amount to either (original creditor) or (collection agency).

Sincerely,

BANKRUPTCY REBUTTAL

Dear (name of manager, collection agency):

I have received your letter of (date), demanding payment in the amount of ($ amount) on behalf of (original creditor).

Apparently you are unaware that this particular creditor was notified of a petition of (personal/business) bankruptcy filed on my behalf in (city/state), on (date), under Docket Number (number).

All creditors, once advised such an action has been initiated, are prohibited from pursuing collection of a debt through their own efforts or those of a second party. The penalties for violating this provision are serious indeed.

All subsequent correspondence should be directed to my personal attorney, (name), (address).

Sincerely,

REPORTING LOST OR STOLEN CREDIT CARD

Dear (name of bank/branch office customer accounts or credit manager):

This letter is submitted pursuant to a verbal report to (name) on (date), regarding (type of account(s) and account number(s)).

(Give brief accounting of circumstances surrounding your discovery that card, or cards, were missing.)

The last purchase, prior to the disappearance of the card(s), was for (item) on (date). It must be assumed any charges occurring after that day would be unauthorized, and I will not be responsible for payment.

Please issue a new account number and card to me.

Thank you for your assistance.

Sincerely,

REVISING PERSONAL INFORMATION—
EXISTING BANK ACCOUNTS

Dear (name of bank/branch office customer accounts manager):

Please send the forms necessary to change the name(s) on (personal/joint, type) account(s). Due to (state reason for the change—marriage, divorce, death of spouse, termination of relationship), the original information is no longer accurate.

The account(s) are currently in the name(s) of (name(s) under which account was originally opened), and the address is listed as (previous address, if you have moved).

Effective (date), all statements and correspondence pertaining to the above account(s) should be forwarded to my new address (new address).

Thank you for your prompt attention to this request.

Sincerely,

NOTE: If your name has changed, sign your correct name and below it indicate your name as it appeared on the account(s).

REQUESTING PERSONAL CREDIT REPORT

Dear (**name of manager, credit reporting agency**):

On (**date**) I applied for, and was denied, credit privileges with (**bank/store/other**), based upon a report obtained from your agency. Since (**30, or less**) days have elapsed, I understand I may obtain a personal credit report from you at no charge.

My full name is (**include maiden name, if married, and/or other name in which credit was established**). My Social Security number is (**. . – . . – . . . .**). I have resided at (**address**) for the past (**number**) years. (**If less than two years, also give previous address.**) My legal signature is affixed below.

Thank you for your prompt attention and response to this request.

Sincerely,

APPEAL TO FEDERAL TRADE COMMISSION—CREDIT BUREAU

Gentlemen:

For the past several (**weeks/months**) I have attempted to have an incorrect entry on my personal credit file amended by (**name of credit reporting agency**) in (**city/state**). Thus far, I have been unable to convince them the entry in question, a (**$ amount**) charge, has been erroneously attributed to me.

I first learned of this problem when I applied for a credit account and the application was denied based upon this entry. I have never had an account with (**creditor listed on report**) and have obtained a letter confirming this fact. I submitted a copy of this letter to (**name of credit reporting agency**) on (**date**), and asked that this entry be removed from my file.

I am enclosing a copy of my personal credit report showing the entry is still reflected on my record, (**length of time**) after my request to have it deleted. Also enclosed are copies of all correspondence I have sent to (**name of credit reporting agency**) attempting to resolve this matter.

I believe I have exhausted my options to obtain their cooperation, and I would appreciate your assistance in helping to conclude this matter.

If you have any questions or require additional information, please contact me at the address above, or by telephone at (**area code/telephone number**).

Sincerely,

NOTE: This letter should be addressed to the nearest Federal Trade Commission Office. See "Information Please . . . ." Below the signature line, include your Social Security number.

Chapter 4

EDUCATION

Perhaps in no other area of our society is change more evident than the American education system. Emphasis on "the basics" has long since given way to the urgency to keep pace with advancements in research, technology, and professional and scientific specialization. Educational institutions, from grade school through college, must constantly strive to provide more diverse curriculum, accommodate changing family structures, and find solutions to escalating costs.

The model letters featured in this chapter are examples of situations we are most likely to encounter in our pursuit of higher learning. Current information regarding tuition costs, legislative rulings, and financial aid programs is available through district, county, and state education offices.*

REQUEST FOR ADMISSION AND FINANCIAL AID INFORMATION

Dear (name of registrar or director of admissions):

I (or my son/daughter) plan to pursue (my/his/her) studies in (scheduled term/semester), and I would appreciate your sending me an application and a copy of your current catalog at your earliest convenience. Please also include any information pertaining to scholarships, grants, or other financial aid programs that are available.

Thank you for your prompt attention to this matter.

Sincerely,

REQUESTING COPY OF TRANSCRIPT

Dear (name of registrar):

I have recently applied (for employment/licensure/to attend another school), and I must furnish a copy of my transcript to complete my application. Please send a copy of this document to (employer/licensing board/registrar's office) at (address) by (date).

I (attended/graduated) from (school, college, or university you are writing to) in (month/year), with a (certificate/degree) in (major). My student identification number (or Social Security number) is (number).

I am enclosing a (check/money order/other) to cover the cost of this service.

Thank you for your assistance and prompt response.

Sincerely,

* See the appendix, "Information Please . . . ," for addresses and telephone numbers of federal and state departments of education.

NOTICE OF INTENT TO WITHDRAW
FROM SCHOOL OR PROGRAM

Dear (name of department head):

I regret to inform you that I must withdraw from (class/program/school) because (state reason). After exploring my options I can find no immediate solution to this (problem/situation), yet I am hopeful I will be able to return (give approximate time).

I sincerely appreciate your (concern/encouragement/guidance) during the past several (weeks/months), and hope that I may rely upon you for a favorable recommendation when I reapply to (name of school) to complete my studies.

Sincerely,

NOTE: *A copy of this letter should also be sent to the Office of the Registrar and the Dean of Admissions.*

REQUEST FOR REINSTATEMENT

Dear (name of registrar, dean of admissions, or department head):

In (month/year) I found it necessary to withdraw from (school/program) due to (state reason). This (problem/situation) has now been resolved, and I am requesting reinstatement to (school/program) beginning (specific term/semester).

My original application dated (date) and transcript are on file under student number (number). Please advise if additional forms must be submitted to reenter the program. If an interview is required, I will be pleased to meet with you at your convenience.

Thank you for your consideration and assistance.

Sincerely,

NOTE: *Copies of this letter should also be sent to the appropriate department head, other instructors, and the finance office.*

PROTESTING INCORRECT GRADE

Dear (name of dean of academic affairs or department head):

I have just completed (subject/course), taught by (instructor's name), and I believe my final grade of (grade) is incorrect. According to the grading scale, an overall average of (number) points is equivalent to a (grade).

I discussed this matter with (**name of instructor**) who verified I had indeed earned a (**number of points**) average for the term, but declined to adjust my grade from (**grade awarded**) to (**grade earned**). While the difference may seem insignificant, it could affect my ability to qualify for (**advanced studies**) in the future.

I would appreciate your assistance to help resolve this matter as I seem unable to persuade (**name of instructor**) to correct (**his/her**) error.

If you have any questions, or require additional information, please telephone me at (**number**).

Sincerely,

NOTE: Below the signature line, include your student number.

HONORING A STUDENT OR TEACHER

Gentlemen: (**office of alumni affairs**):

I would like to present the enclosed check of (**$ amount**) to (**department/program**) to be used for (**special interest of person you are honoring/worthy project he or she would have endorsed**). This gift is (**in memory of/in honor of/given on behalf of**) (**name of person you are honoring**), a close personal friend and a member of the (**year**) graduating class at (**name of school**).

(**His/her**) support and dedication for (**program/school**) (**is/was**) recognized and appreciated by those who (**know/knew**) (**him/her**), and I can think of no better way to (**remember/honor**) (**him/her**) (**on the anniversary of his or her passing/on the occasion of his or her birthday/other**) than to offer this gift in (**his/her**) name.

Respectfully,

NOTE: Send a blind copy of this letter to the person you are honoring or next of kin.

GUARDIANSHIP OF STUDENT

Dear (**name of principal, headmaster, or headmistress**):

This is to advise that, as a result of a recent court ruling, I have been (**awarded sole custody/appointed legal guardian**) of (**name of student**), who is enrolled in (**class**) at (**name of school**).

No one other than myself and those individuals listed below are authorized to remove (**name**) from school or exercise any authority regarding (**his/her**) attendance, curriculum, or participation in school activities.

If you are unable to reach me in an emergency situation, (**name of other individual(s)**, (relationship to student), may be reached at (address and telephone number).

Thank you for your cooperation.

Sincerely,

NOTE: Copies of this letter should be sent to the student's teacher(s), school office personnel, and others responsible for the student.

DISCIPLINARY ACTION

Dear (name of principal, headmaster, headmistress, teacher):

On (date), my (son/daughter/other), (name), was (state nature of punishment) for (reason given). While I am not opposed to reasonable disciplinary measures, I feel the nature of this offense hardly warrants such a severe (punishment/reprimand).

Surely there are more appropriate ways to address this situation, and I would like to meet with you as soon as possible to discuss this matter.

Please call me at (telephone number) at your earliest convenience to arrange a mutually convenient time for this conference.

Sincerely,

PHYSICAL LIMITATIONS

Dear (name of principal, guidance counselor, or teacher):

This letter is to advise you that my (son/daughter/other), (name of student), suffers from (nature of injury/illness), a condition that precludes (his/her) participation in physical education.

Enclosed is a statement from (name of student)'s physician, (name of doctor), verifying this information, and requesting that (he/she) be exempted from any form of strenuous physical activities.

I am requesting that (name of student) be assigned to an alternate class to obtain the necessary credits to complete the school's requirements for promotion to (next grade level).

If you have any questions, or require additional information, please contact me at (telephone number).

Thank you for your cooperation.

Sincerely,

NOTE: A copy of this letter should be sent to the student's physical education instructor.

Chapter 5

EMPLOYMENT

It is estimated that by the year 2000 the American labor force will reach 141 million workers, with service-producing industries leading the way, and manufacturing employment experiencing a decline even though factory output is projected to rise. Clearly, competition in the workplace is unlikely to abate.

Whether you are seeking employment; establishing yourself in your workplace, vocation, or profession; attending to the requirements of your job; or taking advantage of the benefits offered by your employer—how effectively you communicate your needs and desires will determine how quickly they are recognized and acted upon.

The letters in this chapter address the majority of situations that may require written communication, and are designed to give you the means to secure your position in the work force.*

BLANKET INQUIRY—EMPLOYMENT OPPORTUNITIES

Dear (name of personnel director or department manager):

I recently spoke with (name) regarding employment with (name of company). (He/she) suggested I direct my inquiry to you, expressing my interest in available positions in your department.

I am currently employed by (company), as (title), in the (name of department). I have (number) (years/months) experience in (type of work), and I am confident I would be able to adapt that experience readily to a similar environment with your company.

I am enclosing a current resume outlining my professional experience, educational background, and references for your review. If you have, or anticipate, an opening compatible with my qualifications, I would like to meet with you personally at your convenience.

Thank you for your time and consideration.

Respectfully,

NOTE: A blind copy should be sent to the person who referred you.

---

* See "Information Please..." in the appendix, for listings of addresses and telephone numbers for federal, regional, and state offices of the Occupational Safety and Health Administration, the U.S. Department of Labor, and the Social Security Administration.

EMPLOYMENT OPPORTUNITIES—RELOCATION

Dear (**name of personnel director or department manager**):

Recently I spoke with (**name**) concerning employment opportunities available in the (**location**) area, and (**he/she**) suggested I contact you regarding a possible opening at (**company**) for a (**position**).

For the past (**length of employment**) I have been employed as a (**position/title**) at (**company**) in (**city/state**). During that time I have acquired substantial experience in (**areas of expertise**), and feel I have much to offer a prospective employer in (**this/these**) area(s). In addition, I have been rated consistently superior in performance evaluations, compliance with departmental policies and standards, and interaction with supervisors and other staff members.

I am enclosing a current resume for your review. If you have an opening, or anticipate one in the near future, I would appreciate the opportunity to meet with you personally, at your convenience.

I am in the process of relocating from (**city/state**) to (**city/state**) and will be in (**city**) on (**date**). In the interim, I may be contacted at the address above, or by telephone in (**city**) at (**number**), or (**city**) at (**number**).

Thank you for your time and consideration.

Respectfully,

RESPONDING TO A CLASSIFIED ADVERTISEMENT

Dear (**name of contact person or "Gentlemen" if no name given**):

I am submitting a copy of my resume in response to your advertisement for a (**position**) that appeared in the (**date**) edition of (**name of publication**).

I believe that my qualifications are compatible with the requirements of this position and would like to meet with you, at your convenience, to discuss the possibility of employment with your (**company/firm**).

I may be reached at the address above or by telephone at (**number**).

Thank you for your interest and response to my inquiry.

Sincerely,

COVER LETTER ACCOMPANYING REQUESTED RESUME

Dear (**name of department manager or supervisor**):

Thank you for taking time to speak with me by phone on (**date**) regarding the opening in your department.

As promised, I am enclosing a copy of my resume, outlining my professional experience, as well as references.

I believe I can make a meaningful contribution to (**company**), and I would appreciate an opportunity to discuss the matter with you further, at your convenience.

Again, my thanks for your courtesy and your interest in my qualifications.

Sincerely,

HOMEMAKER'S REENTRY INTO JOB MARKET

Dear (**name of personnel director or suggested contact**):

I am planning to reenter the work force after an absence of (**number**) of years, during which time I (**cared for elderly relative/raised children/pursued other interests**). Prior to that time, I was employed as (**title/department**) with the (**name of company/firm**) and was considered an excellent employee.

I have retained my skills through my work with (**volunteer groups/work with children's school activities/interest in political affairs/offices held in various organizations/worked part-time with husband in family business, etc.**). I am seeking a job that would allow me to use my organizational skills, ability to establish priorities, flexibility to work on multiple projects, and accomplish the tasks in a timely manner.

If applicable, include the following paragraph:

My former employer, (**name**), has kindly offered to discuss my previous work history and qualifications with a prospective employer. (**He/she**) may be reached at (**company**), (**telephone number**).

I would appreciate an opportunity to speak with you personally if you have an opening for which I may qualify.

Thank you for your time and interest in my inquiry.

Sincerely,

NOTE: If optional paragraph used, send a blind copy to your former employer.

THANKING AN INTERVIEWER

Dear (name of interviewer):

Thank you for taking time from your busy schedule to meet with me on (date) to discuss the position of (title).

I was quite impressed with the programs that are currently in place, and feel that I would be able to make a genuine contribution, as well as promote my personal and professional growth in the field.

I am very interested in the position of (title) and look forward to hearing from you regarding the results of my interview.

Thank you again for your courtesy and interest in my qualifications.

Sincerely,

THANK YOU FOR FAVORABLE REFERENCE

Dear (name of former employer, clergyman, colleague, friend):

I would like to thank you for your favorable recommendation on my behalf to (Mr./Ms.) (name) of (company).

Based upon your response to (his/her) inquiry, I was offered the position of (title) over several other well-qualified applicants.

I am grateful for your confidence in my ability, and assure you I shall do my very best to justify your praise.

Best regards,

ACCEPTING A JOB OFFER

Dear (name of person making offer):

I have received your letter of (date) offering me the position of (title) and the accompanying contract. I am pleased to accept, in accordance with the provisions stipulated in the contract, which I have signed and enclosed.

As we discussed at the interview, I will arrive in (city) on (date) and will report directly to your office on (date) at (time).

I appreciate your encouragement throughout the application process and look forward to the opportunity to work with you. I will do my very best to justify your confidence.

Sincerely,

DECLINING A JOB OFFER

Dear (name of person making offer):

I have received your kind letter of (date) offering me the position of (title) with your (company/business/firm).

When I did not hear from you after my interview, I continued to explore opportunities with other (companies/businesses/firms) in the area. I recently accepted another position; therefore, I must decline your offer.

(Company whose offer you are declining) enjoys an excellent reputation, and I am certain you will have no difficulty filling this position.

I appreciate your confidence and thank you for this opportunity.

Sincerely,

REQUESTING A SALARY ADJUSTMENT

Dear (name of department head or supervisor):

On (date) I will complete (length of employment) with (company). Since I joined the (company/firm), I have been attending (school/college) to obtain certification in (vocation/profession). I have just completed my studies and am attaching a copy of (diploma/certification) to be included in my personnel file.

Based upon this accomplishment, and the excellent departmental reviews I have acquired, I respectfully request an interim review of my qualifications and a salary adjustment to reflect my contribution and value to the company.

Thank you for your consideration.

Respectfully,

REQUESTING LEAVE OF ABSENCE

Dear (**name of department head or supervisor**):

I am requesting a leave of absence of (**length of time**) due to (**family emergency/health reasons/to attend school**), which (**has occurred/or will occur or begin**) on (**date**).

I am enclosing supporting documents (**physician's statement/information on school**) for your review and consideration.

My absence will commence on (**date**), with an anticipated return date of (**date you expect to resume your duties/position**).

I appreciate your prompt consideration of and response to this request.

Sincerely,

NOTE: A copy of this letter should be sent to the director of Human Resources/Personnel Department.

ADDING DEPENDENT TO GROUP INSURANCE

Dear (**name of employee benefits administrator**):

I am planning to be married on (**date**) and would like to add my (**husband/wife**), (**name as it will appear on the enrollment form**), to my group medical insurance policy. Please forward the necessary forms to my attention at the (**area**) (**branch/division**) office.

In the interim, you are authorized to take whatever payroll deductions are necessary to provide this coverage, effective (**date**).

Thank you for your assistance.

Sincerely,

NOTE: A copy of this letter should be sent to the Payroll Department. Also, below the signature line include your title/position/department and if applicable, employee number and branch office number and location.

CANCELLATION OF DEPENDENT MEDICAL COVERAGE

Dear (**name of employee benefits administrator**):

Please be advised that I wish to discontinue dependent medical coverage for (**name of spouse as shown on record**) and applicable payroll deductions, effective (**date**).

Our marriage will officially terminate on that date, and (**he/she**) will no longer be entitled to benefits under this plan.

Please forward the necessary forms to effect this change to my attention at the (**area**) branch office.

Thank you for your assistance.

Sincerely,

NOTE: Copies of this letter should be sent to the Payroll Department, your former spouse or his/her attorney, your attorney, and work official, if required. Also, below the signature line, include your title/position/department and, if applicable, employee number and branch office number and location.

CONTINUING BENEFITS AFTER RESIGNATION

Dear (**name of employee benefits administrator**):

Please be advised that I wish to continue my present medical coverage for myself and my dependents for a period of (**length of time**) following my resignation date of (**date**).

As required, I am submitting (**$ amount**) for the month of (**month**) and will forward this amount each month on (**date**).

Thank you for your assistance.

Sincerely,

NOTE: A copy should be sent to the insurance carrier. Also, below the signature line include your title/position/department and, if applicable, employee number and branch office location.

PROTESTING REDUCTION OF COMPANY-PAID BENEFITS

Dear (**name of CEO, board chairman, or committee chairperson**):

We, the employees of (**area/branch**), wish to address your decision to (**discontinue/reduce**) (**company/employee**) benefits, effective (**date**). The (**reduction/loss**) of (**medical coverage/retirement plans**) will create hardship for all employees. For some, finding an affordable alternative will be difficult, and, for others, impossible.

According to the (**year**) financial report, issued in (**month**), (**name of company**) boasted a profit margin of (**. . . %**), heretofore unprecedented in the company's (**number of years**) history. We fail to understand why, when the company's financial strength is the greatest it has ever been, you have determined you can no longer afford to invest in the well-being of the work force whose efforts have generated this profit.

This directive undermines the very foundation and principles that have sustained the company through more difficult times—the loyalty of the work force. Should you elect to proceed with this unpopular plan, the loss in terms of diminished employee morale, increased turnover, absenteeism, and incentive to give 100% effort may prove to far outweigh the anticipated financial return this cut is expected to produce.

We therefore urge you to reconsider this decision and continue the benefits that prompted the majority of your employees to join (**name of company**) rather than your competitors.

Respectfully,

(**GROUP/ORGANIZATION/DEPARTMENT**)

(**Signatures**)

REQUESTING A DEPARTMENTAL TRANSFER

Dear (**name of personnel director, branch manager, or department head**):

I have just learned that the position of (**title**) has become available at the (**area/branch**) location. I would like to present my qualifications as a possible candidate to fill this vacancy.

I am currently employed as (**title**) in the (**area/branch**) office, a position I have held since (**date of employment**). Prior to joining (**company**), I was employed by (**previous employer**) as (**title**). My combined experience has afforded me the opportunity to learn all phases of (**type of work**).

I am particularly interested in the (**area/branch**) location because (**state reasons why such a transfer would be advantageous to you**).

My supervisor, (**name**), is aware of this request and has kindly offered to provide a recommendation on my behalf. If you would be interested in discussing the matter personally, I may be reached at (**telephone number**).

Thank you for your consideration.

Respectfully,

NOTE: Copies should be sent to your immediate supervisor and the director of Human Resources/Personnel Department. Also, below the signature line include your title/position/department and, if applicable, employee number and branch office location. Enclose a copy of your current resume.

REQUESTING A TRANSFER—RELOCATION

Dear (name of Corporate Director of Human Resources/Personnel Department):

I am currently employed as a (title/position/department) with the company in the (area), a position I have held for (length of employment).

Just recently I learned (spouse's offer of better job in another location/illness of family member/other), a situation that necessitates our moving to (city and state).

I have discussed the situation with (supervisor/administrator) and expressed my desire to continue employment with the company if there is a comparable opening in our (city/state) (branch/division).

(Supervisor/administrator) will be contacting you within a few days to confirm my request for transfer and offer (his/her) personal recommendations. If necessary, the Personnel Department will forward my employment records to determine if I might qualify for an alternate position.

I greatly appreciate your efforts to find a place for me in (name of city).

Sincerely,

NOTE: Copies should be sent to your supervisor/administrator and the director of your local Human Resource/Personnel Department. Also, below the signature line include your title/position/department, and if applicable, employee number and branch office location.

REBUTTAL TO WRONGFUL TERMINATION OF EMPLOYMENT

Dear (name of CEO or grievance committee chairperson):

On (date) I was informed by (name) that, effective (date/immediately), my employment was to be terminated. The reasons given were (state nature of grievance or alleged wrong doing). At that time, (name) asked for my voluntary resignation, which I declined to give.

Because of the potential damage to my (personal character/professional reputation) and future employment opportunities, I am requesting a meeting with you (and the other members of the board/grievance committee) to present my defense against these charges.

My employment reviews and productivity records clearly refute these allegations, and I am forced to conclude that the decision to terminate my employment is the result of deliberate misrepresentation.

Should I be denied the opportunity to challenge (**name**)'s irresponsible claims against me, I shall have no alternative but to pursue other options to safeguard my personal interests.

I await your response.

Respectfully,

NOTE: Copies should be sent to your attorney and to the Department of Labor.

REQUEST FOR INTERVENTION—DEPARTMENT OF LABOR

Gentlemen:

On (**date**) I was terminated without prior notice as (**title/position**) in the (**department**) of the (**name of company**), (**address**).

The reasons cited for this action were alleged instances of (**habitual tardiness/insubordination/violations of company policies/breach of confidentiality/security violations/ suspected theft/other**).

I have been employed by this company since (**date of employment**) and have compiled an excellent review and productivity rating for (**length of employment**). I am enclosing copies of my personal merit reviews, which will attest to this fact.

The allegations presented against me were unfounded, and on (**date**) I contacted (**name**) to ask for an opportunity to refute them before the (**grievance committee/board/other**). I have just learned that the request has been denied, with no explanation offered.

I believe the situation, left unchallenged, maligns my personal integrity and could jeopardize future employment possibilities. I therefore have no other options available than to ask for your intervention to help resolve this matter.

Please advise what you require to initiate an inquiry into this matter and be assured of my complete cooperation. I may be reached at the address above or by telephone at (**number**).

Thank you for your assistance.

Sincerely,

NOTE: This letter should be addressed to the Employment Security Division, nearest U.S. Department of Labor Office.

RIGHT TO KNOW—ENVIRONMENTAL HAZARD

Gentlemen (Occupational Safety and Health Administration office nearest you):

On (date), after (number) (months/years) with the (name of company), ill health forced me to resign from my job as (position). I first developed symptoms of (nature of illness) in (month/year), which became increasingly more severe as time passed.

My doctor, (name), conducted extensive tests to determine the origin of my illness and concluded it was directly related to my work environment. At (his/her) suggestion, I took a temporary leave of absence in (month/year), and the symptoms lessened in severity and frequency.

The company has since refused to respond to (my/my doctor's) request for an (inventory/disclosure) of the (chemicals/materials/procedures) that were used at the time preceding my illness. This is a direct violation of the federal Right to Know Act.

I request your help in persuading (company) to make this information available to determine if a potentially hazardous situation existed at that time and if it continues to exist for other employees today.

Sincerely,

NOTE: *This letter should be sent to the nearest Occupational Safety and Health Administration office. See "Information please . . ." in the appendix.*

DISCRIMINATORY PRACTICES

Dear (name of CEO, selection committee chairperson, or employee advisory council):

We are particularly dismayed at the board's recent decision to promote (name) to the position of (title).

While we do not dispute (his/her) enthusiasm for the task, there are others who are equally, if not more, qualified, most of whom have been with the company far longer than (name of person selected). This raises the question as to why (he/she) was selected; the obvious reason, it would appear, is that (he/she) is a (man/woman) and the company does not appear to welcome (men/women) to the board regardless of their abilities and dedication to their (vocation/profession).

Such obvious disregard for the accomplishments of very vital elements of your work force seriously diminishes their faith in the company and does little to support your alleged adherence to nondiscriminatory practices.

We urge you to reconsider this appointment and expand the field of candidates to include a fair representation of all eligible employees. This would do much to reestablish their faith and goodwill and would exemplify your promise to grant fair and equal opportunity to everyone.

Respectfully,

(GROUP/ORGANIZATION/DEPARTMENT)
(Signatures)

CC: (other board members)

SEXUAL HARASSMENT

Confidential

Dear **(name of department head or personnel director):**

On **(date)** I was approached by **(name)** who made reference to my interest in the managerial position in the **(department)**. **(Name)** proceeded to offer **(his/her)** support in helping me obtain this position in exchange for favors of a very personal nature. I was, of course, shocked and immediately terminated the discussion. I subsequently learned I was not the sole target of **(name)**'s inappropriate behavior. Other employees claim to have experienced similar problems with this individual.

This incident has seriously impaired my ability to continue working alongside **(name)**, and I ask that the Grievance Committee be convened immediately to address this matter.

I respectfully ask that another place be found for me or that **(name)** be moved to another **(area/department)** where it will be difficult for **(him/her)** to engage in such demeaning practices.

Thank you for your prompt resolution of this matter.

Sincerely,

NOTE: The word "Confidential" should also appear on the envelope in which this letter is sent.

RESIGNATION

Dear (**name of department head or supervisor**):

Please accept this letter as official notification of my intent to resign my position as (**title**), effective (**date**).

My decision is based upon personal considerations and is not intended to reflect adversely upon this organization.

I have enjoyed my (**length of time**) tenure with (**company**) and the opportunity to work with such an outstanding group of (**people/professionals**). I sincerely wish everyone at (**company**) well in their future endeavors.

Sincerely,

NOTE: A copy should be sent to the director of Human Resources/Personnel Department. Also, below the signature line include your title/position/department and, if applicable, employee number and branch office number and location.

Chapter 6

SELF-EMPLOYMENT

Who has not, at some point in time, dreamed of owning his or her own business, challenging the free enterprise system armed only with one's ambition, talents, and a fierce determination to succeed? Many who have pursued the dream and survived the uncertainty of those first months or years of obscurity admit they never worked as hard, endured longer hours, or experienced such stress as that generated by customer demands, employee needs, manufacturers' and suppliers' delays, and regulatory agencies' requirements. Yet most would do it all over again.

Initial preparation is obviously the key to success. Seeking out agencies and organizations equipped to provide invaluable advice should be the first priority. Sufficient operating capital to weather the first few months, a thorough working knowledge of your product or service, practical work experience in your chosen field, and a strong determination to make it work for you will count greatly toward your ultimate success.

Once you are established, you will quickly discover that written communication to customers, employees, vendors, manufacturers, tax collectors, insurance companies, regulatory agencies, and financial institutions, to name a few, is a never-ending process. How effectively you relate to those you depend upon to guarantee the continued success of your venture cannot be discounted.*

ANNOUNCING A GRAND OPENING

Dear area (**artists, craftsmen, sportsmen, students, other**):

We are proud to announce the Grand Opening of (**company**), located at (**address**).

We feature the most extensive selection of (**state products**) supplies in the entire (**geographic area**), with many name brands priced below wholesale.

Come and be a part of this exciting event on (**day/date**). Doors open at (**time**) until (**time**). Fun, prizes, and a tremendous selection of those hard-to-find items!

Bring in the special discount coupon below for an extra (%) discount on your purchases.

See you at (**company**), (**day/date**)!

---

* Listings of federal, national, and state offices of banking authorities, Better Business Bureaus, consumer protection offices, the Federal Trade Commission, insurance regulators, the Internal Revenue Service, the Occupational Safety and Health Administration, and the Small Business Administration can be found in the appendix under "Information Please . . .".

ADVERTISING—DIRECT MAIL: COVER LETTER ACCOMPANYING CATALOG

Dear (**school alumni, club member, sportsmen, other**):

(**Company**) is proud to offer a unique selection of personalized items and giftware featuring your (**school/club/organization's**) (**mascot/emblem/logo**). Designed especially for distribution through (**company**), this outstanding collection is guaranteed to please you and the many friends on your gift list.

Each item is crafted of the finest (**materials**) available and carries a (**lifetime/limited**) guarantee. If you are not completely satisfied, return it for a full refund.

Hurry! Don't miss out on this limited offer. Simply complete the attached order blank, and mail today!

Sincerely,

REQUESTING MANUFACTURER'S/SUPPLIER'S QUOTE

Dear (**name of distributor or manufacturer's representative**):

I am the owner of a small (**type**) business in (**city/state**) with several commercial accounts, primarily (**customers**). I am looking for a dependable (**product**) to (**purpose**).

(**Name of product**) has been recommended as the best of its kind for this type of application. (**I/we**) expect to (**use/order**) about (**amount/frequency**) per (**week/month**).

I am specifically interested in your recommendations as to proper usage and restrictions that may apply. It would also be very helpful to know the approximate delivery time from receipt of an order and your requirements for establishing an open account.

Thank you for your prompt response to my inquiry.

Sincerely,

PROVIDING QUOTES FOR PRODUCTS OR SERVICES

Dear (**name of person requesting information**):

Thank you for your (**letter/telephone call**) of (**date**), requesting information about (**service/product**). Enclosed is a brochure listing base prices for all (**services/models**).

We can provide (**service/product**) at a discount of (**$ amount**) for orders of (**amount**) or more, in a single order, plus a (**$ amount**) shipping and handling charge. We ship within (**time**) from receipt of an order by (**method of transportation**). We guarantee delivery within (**number**) days from receipt of your order.

Credit accounts are offered after we have received three prepaid orders from a customer. Our accounting department will be pleased to establish an account in the name of (**company/individual**) upon receipt of your third order.

We are confident that you will find our prices competitive and our service outstanding. If you have any questions, please contact us again at our toll-free number, (**number**), or by letter at the address shown (**above/below**). We will be happy to assist you.

Again, thank you for your interest in (**service/product**).

Sincerely,

REQUESTING PAYMENT

Dear (**name of customer**):

This letter represents our (**number**) attempt to contact you personally regarding the overdue balance on your account. We cannot understand why you have failed to respond to our inquiries.

We value all of our customers and realize delinquencies do occur from time to time. If you are experiencing problems, please contact our accounting department so that arrangements can be made to satisfy this obligation.

If we do not hear from you by (**date**), we will close the account and deny future credit until payment in full, including applicable late charges, has been made. Should this occur, it is our policy to ship all subsequent orders on a C.O.D. basis, and then only if there is no outstanding balance on the account.

We urge you to give this matter your prompt attention.

Sincerely,

RESPONDING TO A REFUND REQUEST

Dear (**name of customer**):

We were very sorry to learn you were dissatisfied with the (**item**) shipped to you on (**date**). We have examined the items you returned, and while we can find no evidence of the flaws you mentioned, we will be happy to issue a refund in the amount of (**$ amount**) upon receipt of the remaining (**item**), which you failed to include in the returned shipment.

Sincerely,

NOTIFICATION OF BACK ORDER

Dear (**name of customer**):

Thank you for your recent order for (**item**). Due to unexpected demand, our stock has been temporarily depleted. We are, however, expecting a shipment within (**number**) days.

We anticipate you should receive the (**item**) on or about (**date**). We apologize for the inconvenience, and assure you that your order will be filled before any others are accepted.

Thank you for your patience.

Sincerely,

RESPONDING TO CUSTOMER COMPLAINT

Dear (**name of customer**):

Thank you for your (**letter/telephone call**) of (**date**), calling our attention to the problem you experienced with the (**cleaning/repair**) work done at (**location**) by one of our (**workers/crews**).

We take pride in our work, and we are particularly distressed when a customer feels we have failed to provide the services promised in our agreement.

I have personally dispatched one of our managers, (**name**), to investigate this matter, and I am awaiting (**his/her**) report. You may be assured we will do whatever is necessary to correct this situation, based upon (**his/her**) findings and recommendations.

Again, thank you for your prompt notification. I will be back in touch with you as soon as I have had an opportunity to discuss this matter with (**Mr./Ms.**) (**name of manager**).

Cordially,

MOVING TO NEW LOCATION

Dear friends of (**business/school/other**):

We are pleased to announce the opening of our new facility located at (**address**).

You are cordially invited to a special open house on (**day/date**) beginning at (**time**) to come and view our new home. (**Parents/teachers/staff/others**) will be on hand to answer any questions you may have. Our (**business manager/secretary/other**) will be available to explain enrollment options and accept applications for the coming year.

For those who have come to rely upon our high standards of quality care for (**children/elderly/handicapped**), we pledge the same dedication to service. For others whose (**children/relatives/other**) are coming to (**business/school/other**) for the first time, we are confident that you will be delighted with the facility and the programs we offer.

We look forward to seeing you (**date**).

Sincerely,

Chapter 7

ENVIRONMENT

Requesting Repair of Public Thoroughfare
Supporting Bond Issue for Public Improvements
Protesting Environmental Pollution (Noise, Chemicals)
Protesting Airport Hazard Related to Housing
Notification of Suspected Chemical Contamination
Protesting Pollution of Public Facilities

Environmental Issues have now become the topic of widespread public concern. What was once only the business of specific environmental groups and lobbyists is now the affair of the average citizen. People have realized that they can and do have an impact on their environment and that they can put pressure on government agencies and privately owned businesses to take action to remedy detrimental or hazardous situations.

The letters in this chapter focus on local, neighborhood issues, such as pollution resulting from noise and garbage, and are designed so that they can be easily adapted to other situations that may arise. Most of the letters should be directed to the appropriate city, county, state, or federal department or local business owner. One letter needs to be directed to the Federal Aviation Administration.*

REQUESTING REPAIR OF PUBLIC THOROUGHFARE

Dear (**name of commissioner of local street or highway department**):

I am writing to request that you repair the (**pothole/broken curb/other**) at the (**street intersection or address**). The (**pothole/broken curb/other**) is a hazard to (**drivers/bicyclers/pedestrians/other**).

If you need additional information, please call me at (**your telephone number**).

I would appreciate your prompt attention to this matter. Thank you.

Sincerely,

SUPPORTING BOND ISSUE FOR PUBLIC IMPROVEMENTS

Dear (**name of city or county commissioner**):

I am writing in support of the bond issue for (**new schools/sewage treatment plant/ road improvements/other**). I believe that the (**county's or city's**) plan to (**relieve overcrowding in the schools/improve methods of waste disposal/make our roads more safe/other**) is an excellent one, and I will give this plan my vote and my wholehearted support.

Please let me know if I can do anything to help get this bond issue passed.

Sincerely,

---

* The address for the FAA is listed in "Information Please . . ." under U.S. Government Offices in the appendix. Other useful addresses may be found under Environmental Protection Agency, also in the appendix.

PROTESTING ENVIRONMENTAL POLLUTION
(NOISE, CHEMICALS)

Dear (name of commissioner of Department of Environmental Regulation):

(Describe type of pollution, location, and time(s) when pollution occurred, and why offensive or dangerous, e.g., noise pollution from radios in park abutting my property prevents me from opening my windows on weekends.)

I would appreciate it if you would ask the appropriate officials to monitor this situation and take action to prevent further occurrences so that I and other people in the area are no longer (**disturbed/endangered**).

Please let me know what actions you have taken. Thank you for your cooperation in this matter.

Sincerely,

PROTESTING AIRPORT HAZARD RELATED TO HOUSING

Dear (**name of administrator of Federal Aviation Administration**):

I live at (**your address**), which is near the (**name of airport**) Airport. The takeoff and landing flight pattern for planes takes them right over my house. Knowing that takeoffs and landings are the most dangerous part of flying, I am worried about a plane crashing into my house. Aside from that worry, the noise is, of course, extremely loud and often disruptive to our home life.

I will appreciate your investigating the possibility of changing the flight pattern so that planes circle on the other side of the airport where the land uses are much more compatible with the aircraft.

Thank you for your consideration of my request.

Sincerely,

NOTIFICATION OF SUSPECTED CHEMICAL
CONTAMINATION

Dear (**name of owner of business**):

I frequently (**drive past/patronize**) your (**gas station/restaurant/other**). The last time I (**drove by/was there**), I noticed one of your employees (**emptying an oil change pan on the ground/leaving garbage in uncovered containers/other**). If this is a regular practice at your business, it is not only polluting the environment but also a potential health hazard. I am concerned that this is happening without your knowledge and thought you would want to be aware of it. Your business is otherwise a credit to the neighborhood, and I would not want you or your employees to get in trouble for this potentially hazardous practice.

Thank you for your attention.

Sincerely,

PROTESTING POLLUTION OF PUBLIC FACILITIES

Dear (**name of Parks Department Commissioner**):

I (**live near/frequently visit**) (**name of facility**) located at (**address**). Recently, I have noticed that the (**basketball court/beach/playground**) is looking more like a dump than a recreational facility. People are not only carelessly discarding their picnic supplies **all** over the grounds, but they are also using the (**type of facility**) to dispose of household trash. If this situation continues, the (**type of facility**) will become an eyesore instead of a beautiful place for people to come and enjoy (**purpose of the facility**).

Please do whatever is necessary to see to it that this facility's rules are enforced.

Thank you.

Sincerely,

Chapter 8

FINANCE

Financial institutions in the 1990s are interested in cordial customer relations and will work with you to respond to your requests or correct any misunderstanding. Always give your bank or loan company officer all the information he or she needs in order to expedite a response to your request. Account numbers or loan numbers are particularly critical; most financial institutions maintain their records under your number rather than your name.

Although many of the situations covered in this chapter could be addressed by telephone or in person, letters are recommended because they provide a permanent, dated record of your request or concern. It is easier to follow up, when necessary, if you (and your recipient) have a written record to which to refer.*

The last four letters in this chapter are related to personal loans and are, therefore, more informal in nature. In these four letters, it is not customary to have an inside address; however, the date should always be included.

OPENING AN ACCOUNT BY MAIL

Dear (**name of branch manager**):

Within the next month, I will be moving to (**name of new town**) and would like to open a checking account at your bank. I have enclosed a check made out to your bank for (**$ amount**) to be deposited in my new account. The account will be in my name only.

My current address is indicated above. My new address, effective (**date you are moving**), is (**complete new address**). My Social Security number is (**Social Security number**). My birth date is (**birth date**).

If you need additional information, please let me know. You may call me collect at home, (**number**), or at work, (**number**).

Thank you for your assistance.

Sincerely,

CLOSING AN ACCOUNT BY MAIL

Dear (**name of branch manager**):

Last month I moved from (**name of former town**) to (**name of new town**). Since I am no longer living in (**name of old town**), I would appreciate your closing my account at your

---

* Consult the banking authorities listings in "Information Please . . ." for the addresses of state-level banking authorities if you do not receive the response you need from your personal financial institution.

bank. My account number is (number). According to my last statement, all the checks I wrote have cleared, and my balance is ($ amount). Please send me a cashier's check for that amount.

Thank you for your assistance.

Sincerely,

DISPUTING SERVICE CHARGES

Dear (name of branch manager):

On (date that you opened the account), I opened a (type of account) account (account number) at your branch. At that time, I was told that if I kept my balance above ($ amount), there would be no service charge on my account.

I just received my first statement, dated (date), which includes a service charge of ($ amount). I do not understand the reason for this charge since the statement clearly indicates that my balance never went below ($ amount).

I would appreciate your crediting my account in the amount of ($ amount of service charge) as well as the accrued interest on this amount. Please notify me as to the date when my account is credited. If there is a reason for the charge that I am not aware of, please call me at (number).

Thank you for your prompt attention to this matter.

Sincerely,

FAILURE TO CREDIT DEPOSIT

Dear (name of branch manager):

I have just received my (date) statement for my (type of) account, (number). I noted that there is a ($ amount) deposit that has not been credited to my account. The deposit was made on (date).

Please check your records and correct this error. I have enclosed a copy of my deposit receipt. Please notify me as soon as this deposit has been credited to my account.

Thank you for your prompt attention to this matter.

Sincerely,

DISPUTING INSUFFICIENT FUNDS NOTIFICATION

Dear (**name of branch manager**):

I have just received your notification that check (**number**) was not honored by your bank due to insufficient funds in my account (**number**), and that you have charged my account (**$ amount**).

According to my records, there was more than enough money in my account to cover that check. Based on my last statement and the checks I have written since then, I have (**$ amount**) remaining in my account after deducting check (**number of bounced check**). I have not written any additional checks since that time.

Please have your Collections Department contact me immediately regarding this problem. If I have made an error in my computations, I need to know so I can correct it. On the other hand, if the error is yours, I would appreciate your correcting it promptly. Please also reimburse my account for any service charges that I have incurred both from your bank and from the payee.

You may call me at (**number**). Thank you for your attention to this matter.

Sincerely,

COVER LETTER ACCOMPANYING LOAN PROPOSAL

Dear (**name of branch manager/loan officer**):

Enclosed please find a complete (**type of loan**) application. As we discussed, I am planning to (**buy a car/purchase a home/attend college/other**). I believe that the application contains all the information you will need to process my request.

If you need additional information, please call me at (**number**).

Thank you for your prompt attention to this matter.

Sincerely,

REQUESTING EXPLANATION FOR DENIAL OF LOAN REQUEST

Dear (**name of branch manager/loan officer**):

On (**date**), I submitted my application for a (**student/home/auto/other**) loan. I have just received notification from you that my loan request has been denied. The letter does not state the reason for the denial.

Please contact me at your earliest convenience to let me know why my application has been denied. I would also appreciate the opportunity to discuss this matter with you in person. My phone number is (**number**).

Thank you for your attention to this matter.

Sincerely,

REQUESTING DEFERRED PAYMENT ON LOAN

Dear (**name of branch manager/loan officer**):

Currently, I have a (**home improvement/business/personal/other**) loan from your bank. The loan number is: (**number**). Payments are due on the first of each month. Due to unusual (**medical/auto repair/other**) expenses, I am experiencing financial problems that will make it difficult, if not impossible, for me to make my (**month of payment that is to be deferred**) payment on time. I am, therefore, requesting that my (**month**) payment be deferred to (**date that you will make the payment**). As your records will show, I have made all previous loan payments on time.

Thank you for your attention to this matter. I would appreciate a prompt response to my request.

Sincerely,

REQUESTING ADJUSTMENT OF PAYMENT DUE DATE

Dear (**name of branch manager/loan officer**):

On (**date of loan agreement**), I completed the arrangements for a (**mortgage/home equity/student/other**) loan with your bank. My loan number is (**number**). At that time, it was determined that payments on the loan would be due on the (**day**) of each month for the duration of the loan.

Since most of my bills are due on or around the (**date**) of the month, it would be helpful to me if the loan payment due date could be changed to the (**date desired**) of each month. Please let me know as soon as possible if this arrangement would be an acceptable alternative.

Thank you for your attention to this matter.

Sincerely,

NOTICE OF INTENT TO CASH CERTIFICATE OF DEPOSIT

Dear (**name of branch manager**):

Please accept this letter as my notification of intent to cash my certificate of deposit in the amount of (**$ amount**). The CD is in my name only. I will be cashing it on (**date**).

If you need additional information, or if you need to contact me, please call me at (**number**).

Thank you for your assistance.

Sincerely,

REQUESTING CURRENT STATEMENT OF INVESTMENT ACCOUNT

Dear (**name of branch manager**):

I have a (**type of investment**) account at your bank. My account number is (**number**). Please send a current statement of the amount in that account to me at the above address.

Thank you for your assistance.

Sincerely,

NOTIFICATION OF LOST SAFE DEPOSIT BOX KEY

Dear (**name of branch manager**):

I am writing to inform you that I have lost my safe deposit box key. The box is in my name, as indicated in the signature on this letter, and the number is (**number**).

Please let me know the cost of changing the lock and obtaining a new key. Thank you.

Sincerely,

REQUEST TO WITHHOLD NAME AND ADDRESS

Dear (**name of compliance officer**):

I am writing in response to your notice about releasing my name and address to other organizations. In that notice, you indicated that you sometimes release names and addresses of customers to organizations that would provide them with information about products and services of interest. I consider this to be a violation of my privacy and request that you do not release my name or address to these organizations.

My name and address, as they appear on my account, are

(Name on account)
(Address on account)
(City, state, zip code).

My account number is **(number)**.

Thank you for honoring my request.

Sincerely,

REQUESTING PERSONAL LOAN FROM A FRIEND

Dear **(name)**:

I am writing because I know you will respond candidly to my request. Due to some recent, unanticipated **(medical/auto/other)** expenses, I am experiencing severe financial problems. Would it be possible for you to lend me some money? I think that **($ amount)** would enable me to cover my current bills.

I do not know what your situation is at this time, and I do not want to put you in any kind of financial bind. Please do not hesitate to tell me if you are unable to help me out. I will certainly understand if that is the case. I treasure our friendship and do not want to put a strain on our relationship.

If you are able to lend me the money, I would truly appreciate it. I will be able to start paying you back in **(month)**. Would **($ amount)** a month be acceptable to you?

Thank you for considering my request. I look forward to hearing from you soon.

As always, my best to you and your family.

Love,

GRANTING PERSONAL LOAN TO A FRIEND

Dear **(name)**:

I received your letter today and wanted to respond immediately. I will be happy to lend you the money you requested and have enclosed a check for **($ amount)**. I know what it's like to be faced with unanticipated expenses and what a strain that can put on your budget. You have been there for me in the past, and I am glad I can help you out now. I know it wasn't easy for you to ask me for money, and I appreciate your trusting our relationship enough to do so. After all, what are friends for?!

If you are able to start paying me back in (**month**), that would be great. However, if that is not possible, we can certainly work out other arrangements.

I would write a longer letter, sharing our news with you, but I want to get this letter in the mail so you will have the check as soon as possible.

Love,

DECLINING A REQUEST FOR A PERSONAL LOAN

Dear (**name**):

I received your letter today asking me for a personal loan. I truly wish I could help you out, but I am operating within a tight budget right now and simply do not have any money to spare. Unfortunately, times have been hard for me too.

I am really sorry to have to say "no" to you and trust that this will not have an adverse affect on our relationship. You know how much I value our friendship.

Please write soon and let me know how things are going.

Love,

REQUESTING REPAYMENT OF A PERSONAL LOAN

Dear (**name**):

A few months ago, you wrote me asking for a (**$ amount**) loan. I was happy to help and promptly sent you a check. You said in your letter that you would start paying me back in (**month**). It is now (**month**) and I have not heard from you.

I am concerned that you have either forgotten about repaying me or that you are still experiencing financial difficulties. Please write soon and let me know what is happening.

I could really use the money right now and hope you can send a check along with your letter.

I am looking forward to hearing from you.

Sincerely,

Chapter 9

GOVERNMENT

The U.S. Constitution provides for government "of, by, and for the people." If you are going to be involved in your government, then you must write letters. For most of you, it may not be possible for you to be involved more directly. Therefore, knowing, for example, how to state your position on an issue, bill, or policy is critical. The printed word is more powerful than you may realize, and if you can write clear, concise, potent letters, you have a good chance of being able to affect government policy and programs. The letters in this chapter are designed to help you do just that.*

LETTER TO THE PRESIDENT SUPPORTING
POSITION ON ISSUE

Dear Mr. President:

I followed with interest the newspaper and magazine reports on your recent **(briefly describe activity or position of interest, e.g., education summit)**. I applaud your plea for **(briefly describe what president has asked for; e.g., "radical reform" in the public schools)**. I hope you will provide the leadership we need in bringing about specific reforms in **(briefly describe what you hope will happen next, e.g., teacher education, special programs that prevent dropouts, and innovative reading and writing strategies)**.

I would be happy to serve on a national or state commission with the mandate of **(briefly indicate how you would like to be involved; e.g., developing dropout prevention programs)**.

Thank you for your attention to my concerns.

Sincerely,

---

* For the addresses needed for the various letters in this chapter, consult "Information Please . . . ," U.S. Government Offices, in the appendix. Also check the Table of Contents for "Information Please . . ." for other agencies related to your concerns.

LETTER TO CONGRESSPERSON OPPOSING BILL

Dear (Senator or Mr./Ms. for representative) (name):

I wish to register my strong disapproval of Bill (number or title) that (briefly describe content of bill, e.g., censors the arts by eliminating government support). I believe that (state your reason(s) for opposition to the bill; e.g., government censoring of the creative process in any form is unconstitutional).

I encourage you to vote against this bill. Thank you for your consideration of my views.

Sincerely,

LETTER TO CABINET MEMBER SUPPORTING STAND

Dear (Mr./Madam Secretary):

I am writing to urge you to maintain your stand on (briefly describe the position that you support; e.g., limiting the dumping of Japanese microchips into the American market). I believe that (state your reasons for supporting his/her position; e.g., the invasion of foreign items into our economy is detrimental to our capitalistic system).

Thank you for your attention to my concerns.

Sincerely,

LETTER TO FOREIGN DIGNITARY STATING DISAPPROVAL OF POLICY

Dear (Mr./Madam Ambassador):

I am aware that your country's (briefly describe policy that you disapprove; e.g., apartheid) policy (state why you believe the policy is bad; e.g., severely strains diplomatic relations between the United States and South Africa). As an American citizen who is concerned about global cooperation, I urge you to use whatever power you possess to convince your government to abolish this policy.

Thank you for your consideration of my views.

Sincerely,

LETTER TO GOVERNOR SUPPORTING STAND

Dear Governor (**name**):

As governor of our state, you have considerable power when it comes to (**area of concern; e.g., education**). I want to applaud your stand on (**briefly describe the specific policy; e.g., the need for strong support of public schools at the state level**). Your recommendation to the state legislature that they (**describe specific action recommended; e.g., vote to increase the education budget for the coming year**) is commendable. I can only hope that they follow through with appropriate legislation. If there is anything I can do to support this cause, please let me know.

Once again, thank you for believing that (**area of concern**) should be a major legislative concern.

Sincerely,

LETTER TO MAYOR REQUESTING COMMITTEE APPOINTMENT

Dear Mayor (**name**):

I am a long-time resident of (**city/town**) and I have always been active in (**city/town**) affairs. I am particularly concerned about (**area of concern; e.g., zoning**) issues and am requesting that you appoint me to the (**area of concern; e.g., zoning**) committee. My special qualifications are (**list your qualifications; e.g., knowledge of desires of community residents**).

Thank you for your consideration of my request.

Sincerely,

LETTER TO COMMISSIONER STATING POSITION ON ISSUE

Dear Mr./Ms. (**name**):

I am writing to urge you to vote (**for/against**) (**briefly describe your area of concern; e.g., the budget cuts**) currently proposed. (**List reasons you believe this stand is correct; e.g., lower/higher taxes, better/poorer schools, services, etc./other**).

Thank you for your attention to my views.

Sincerely,

LETTER TO COUNCIL MEMBER REQUESTING ACTION

Dear (name):

I am concerned about (briefly describe your area of concern; e.g., the fact that the up-keep of our city parks is not what it should be). The last time [describe incident that caused you to write; e.g., I was at (name of park) on a picnic with my family, and was appalled by the amount of litter]. [State any other pertinent information; e.g., I have discovered that only (number) maintenance people have the job of keeping our parks clean. (Number) people is definitely not enough to maintain all of our city's parks.]

I am hereby requesting that you make this appalling situation known to the other council members with a recommendation for appropriate action.

Thank you for your consideration of my request.

Sincerely,

LETTER TO COMMITTEE CHAIRPERSON PROTESTING PROPOSED ACTION

Dear (name):

I am writing to protest the proposed [briefly describe the potential situation of concern; e.g., rezoning of the property at (address of property). The proposed rezoning calls for it to be changed from residential to commercial] . This proposal is clearly not in the interest of (explain why you believe the proposed action will not be beneficial; e.g., the residents of the adjacent area who all live in single-family homes).

I hope I can count on you to convince the other members of your committee that this proposal is undesirable.

Thank you for your consideration of my views.

Sincerely,

DEPARTMENT OF AGRICULTURE OPPOSING REDUCTION OF FARM SUBSIDIES

Dear (Mr./Madam Secretary):

I am writing in opposition to the proposed reduction of subsidies for (milk/ wheat/ soybeans/other). This action will cause a hardship for (identify whom or what will be hurt by the proposal; e.g., dairy farmers, Midwest wheat cooperative, U.S. ability to compete in world markets due to increased farm failures).

I am respectfully requesting that you oppose this action.

Thank you for your attention to my concerns.

Sincerely,

DEPARTMENT OF COMMERCE CONCERNING PATENT APPLICATION

Dear (Mr./Madam Secretary):

I have invented a device that (**briefly describe your invention; e.g., prevents accidental scalding in showers**). I believe that my invention needs to be patented so I can be protected while I determine the feasibility of manufacturing and marketing this device.

Please send me the necessary patent application forms.

Thank you.

Sincerely,

DEPARTMENT OF DEFENSE OPPOSING CLOSING OF MILITARY BASE

Dear (Mr./Madam Secretary):

I understand that the Defense Department is planning to close the (**name of base**) near (**city/town/county and state**). I am hoping to convince you to reconsider this plan and keep the base open.

The base is vital to the economy of (**city/town/county**). A large number of our townspeople either work at the base or in support services to the base. The closing of the base would leave these people without jobs and with limited alternatives for other employment.

I encourage you to use your power to keep the (**name of base**) open. I have enclosed a petition signed by (**number**) people who are dependent on this base for their livelihood.

Thank you for your attention to my concerns.

Sincerely,

DEPARTMENT OF ENERGY REQUESTING ENERGY CONSERVATION INFORMATION

Dear (Mr./Madam Secretary):

I am building a new home and want to make it as energy efficient as possible.

Please send me any information you have on home energy conservation, or, if there is a local office that distributes this kind of information, please send me the address.

Thank you.

Sincerely,

DEPARTMENT OF HEALTH AND HUMAN SERVICES REQUESTING INFORMATION ABOUT AVAILABLE SERVICES

Dear (Mr./Madam Secretary):

I am writing to request information about government services available to (**the deaf/ aphasics/pregnant teenagers/other**) in (**city/town/county and state**).

Please direct me to one of your regional offices or send me the appropriate information.

Thank you for your attention to my concerns.

Sincerely,

DEPARTMENT OF HOUSING AND URBAN DEVELOPMENT REQUESTING MODERNIZING OF PUBLIC HOUSING

Dear (Mr./Madam Secretary):

I live in a public housing project in (**city/town/county and state**). I have recently learned that your department allots funds for modernization of these projects. Since our project was built in (**year**) and has not been modernized since that time, it is desperately in need of improvements.

Please send me the information I need to apply for modernization funds.

Thank you for your assistance.

Sincerely,

DEPARTMENT OF THE INTERIOR OPPOSING
OIL DRILLING IN NATIONAL PARKS

Dear (**Mr./Madam Secretary**):

I understand that your department is considering oil drilling in some of our national parks. I strongly disapprove of such an action. Our national parks are one of our most valuable natural resources. Drilling for oil would not only destroy the delicate balance of nature that exists in these parks but also would mar their natural beauty. I realize that our country needs to increase our oil reserves, but, surely, there are other less sensitive areas that can be explored.

I strongly encourage you to explore other alternatives for oil drilling sites.

Thank you for your attention to my concerns.

Sincerely,

DEPARTMENT OF JUSTICE SUPPORTING
PROSECUTION

Dear (**Mr./Madam Attorney General**):

I am hereby requesting that you use your personnel to investigate and vigorously prosecute those responsible for (**nature of suspected crime; e.g., causing the collapse of Hometown Savings and Loan**). I believe that the guilty parties have violated not only the banking and fraud laws of this country, but have also put our entire economy at risk by their despicable behavior.

As a (**state nature of your experience; e.g., depositor, investor**), I may be able to assist in your investigation. Please let me know what information you need in order to begin an inquiry.

Thank you for your attention and interest. I look forward to hearing from you or someone in your department soon.

Sincerely,

DEPARTMENT OF LABOR REQUESTING LABOR LAW INFORMATION

Dear (Mr./Madam Secretary):

I need some information about (area of concern; e.g., child labor laws). One of the businesses in my area is (briefly describe nature of the suspected violation; e.g., employing children under the age of 14 as waiters and waitresses), and I need to know whether or not that is legal.

Please send me the information requested at your earliest convenience.

Thank you.

Sincerely,

DEPARTMENT OF STATE SUPPORTING ACTION OR POLICY

Dear (Mr./Madam Secretary):

I want to go on record as being in favor of (action or proposal of concern, e.g., military intervention to protect the lives of American citizens abroad). (Briefly describe the reasons for your support, e.g., terrorism affecting the lives of American citizens in foreign countries is on the rise). (Briefly describe the result that you foresee from the proposed action or proposal; e.g., terrorism must be stopped, and it seems that nothing short of military force will do the job).

Please use your influence to encourage (continuation/implementation) of this course so that our country's objectives will be met.

I know you must be as concerned about this problem as I am, and hope you will do everything in your power to (repeat expected result of action or proposal, e.g., show terrorists that we will not tolerate their activities).

Thank you.

Sincerely,

DEPARTMENT OF TRANSPORTATION
SUGGESTING ACTION

Dear (**Mr./Madam Secretary**):

I want to encourage your department to consider (**type of project or alternative, e.g., mass transit alternatives to building new highways**). I believe that (**project/alternative**) would (**briefly describe expected benefits of project or alternative, e.g., mass transit would not only result in the conservation of energy but would help to preserve the natural beauty of our country**). Our (**highways/airports/seaports**) are clogged with traffic and the resultant pollution. I believe that the people of this country would appreciate and deserve a modern, efficient transportation system.

Thank you for your consideration of my beliefs and concerns.

Sincerely,

DEPARTMENT OF THE TREASURY REQUESTING
CURRENCY INFORMATION

Dear (**Mr./Madam Secretary**):

I am a coin collector and am interested in receiving an updated list of available (**currency of interest, e.g., commemorative coins**).

Please send me this list at your earliest convenience.

Thank you.

Sincerely,

Chapter 10

HEALTH CARE

Authorizing Release of Medical Records
Letter of Appreciation
Research Organizations and Associations
Disputing Charges on a Medical Bill
Requesting Payment Arrangements
Account in Collections
Refusal to Accept Insurance
Terminating Medical Services
Terminating Facility Services
Emergency Medical Care Authorization

All other considerations tend to pale alongside the urgency to secure competent and affordable attention for ourselves or loved ones when it pertains to physical or emotional well-being.

Reports of escalating costs, personnel shortages throughout the health care industry, reductions in hospital services, and, occasionally, headlines denouncing unscrupulous practices by some health care professionals, add to our stress. Yet it is unlikely that any other collective group imposes more stringent and demanding guidelines upon itself than those who render medical services to the American public. Constant monitoring by governmental agencies, state regulatory commissions, internal quality assurance committees, and utilization review committees all focus on providing the best possible care available.

Those seeking professional health-related services may request information from their state departments of health and human services regarding facilities they are considering, state departments of professional regulations for questions pertaining to "licensure" and credentials, or local physicians' or care givers' referral agencies for the names of individuals qualified to render specific health care services.*

AUTHORIZING RELEASE OF MEDICAL RECORDS

Dear Dr. (**name of physician, therapist, or head of facility**):

Please accept this authorization to release my medical file to Dr. (**other physician**) so that (**he/she**) may review my previous medical history.

In compliance with the requirements of my insurance carrier, a second opinion must be obtained before (**insurance company**) will approve (**nature of treatment**).

Dr. (**other physician**) has agreed to forgo (**specific procedures/testing**), providing the results of your recent findings can be made available for (**his/her**) review.

Please make this information available to (**him/her**) as soon as possible.

Thank you for your cooperation in this matter.

Sincerely,

Note: Copies of this letter should be sent to the other physician and your insurance company.

---

* See "Information Please . . ." in the appendix for listings of state departments of health and human services and health-related organizations.

LETTER OF APPRECIATION

Dear (name of administrator, physician, director of nursing or facility):

Our family would like to express our heartfelt thanks and appreciation for the excellent care given to (relationship), (name), prior to (his/her) recent demise at (facility).

Your honesty enabled each of us to accept the painful realization (his/her) illness was terminal, while at the same time, we were comforted by the efforts of your staff to do everything possible to ease (his/her) suffering.

Long after the pain of our loss has diminished, your many kindnesses will be remembered.

Respectfully,

RESEARCH ORGANIZATIONS AND ASSOCIATIONS

Dear (name of director, national health organization, or related associations):

I was recently diagnosed with (disease/disability). Since that time I have attempted to learn as much as possible about this condition, specifically (state nature of inquiry).

I understand there are (printed materials/audiovisual aids) available through your organization to help victims of (disease/disability) understand the nature of their (disability/handicap) and how to deal effectively with the problem.

I would appreciate any information you can provide regarding (treatment/ rehabilitation/control/cure) of this condition.

Thank you for your prompt response to my inquiry.

Sincerely,

DISPUTING CHARGES ON A MEDICAL BILL

Dear (name of patient accounts manager):

I have just received a statement from your office in the amount of ($ amount), for (service/treatment/test/medication).

I did see Dr. (name) on (date); however, the (treatment/procedure/medication) reflected on the statement was not (performed/administered to me).

Please review my record for the correct charges and issue a revised statement.

Thank you for your prompt attention to this matter.

Sincerely,

REQUESTING PAYMENT ARRANGEMENTS

Dear (name of patient accounts manager):

I have received your (letter/statement) indicating a balance of ($ amount), which my insurance has declined to cover.

This far exceeds what we are able to pay in a lump sum. We do, however, intend to satisfy this obligation and feel we could reasonably manage a monthly payment of ($ amount).

We would like to arrange to make monthly payments of ($ amount) until this balance is paid.

Please contact me if this is satisfactory, or if you have questions. I can be reached at (telephone number) or by letter at the address above.

Thank you for your assistance.

Sincerely,

Note: If you were not the patient, state your relationship below the signature line.

ACCOUNT IN COLLECTIONS

Dear (name of administrator or patient accounts manager):

At the time I was admitted to (facility) on (date), I explained to (name) that I was covered under a group medical plan through my employer, (company), and understood I was responsible for any charges not covered under this plan. (Length of time) following my release on (date), I received a bill for the full amount of my care at your facility.

I have made numerous attempts to contact (name) in your accounting department regarding this matter. Each time I was told (he/she) was unavailable, but would return my telephone call. After (number of attempts) to speak with (him/her) by telephone I finally wrote the attached letter asking (**him/her**) to respond, explaining I intended to satisfy the obligation in question.

I never heard from (**name**); however, I did receive the attached notice from (**name of collection agency**), informing me the account had been turned over to them and demanding "PAYMENT IN FULL, AT ONCE."

I am very distressed at the way this situation has been handled by your facility, and even more so by the implied threats made by (**collection agency**), which, under the circumstances, are totally unwarranted.

I would appreciate intervention from someone at your facility who has the authority to retrieve this account from collections and work with me to resolve this situation to our mutual benefit.

Sincerely,

REFUSAL TO ACCEPT INSURANCE

Dear (**name of physician, care giver, or facility**):

On (**date**) I telephoned your office for an appointment and was informed you are no longer filing insurance claims on behalf of your patients. Have you considered the potential hardships this will create for those of us who are on fixed incomes and must rely upon our insurance companies to satisfy these obligations directly to the (**physician/facility**)?

Many of us are not financially able to pay these charges as they occur and then wait for weeks or months to receive reimbursement. This, of course, is secondary to the primary concern. Unless we are prepared to meet these costs, we are in danger of delaying medical care and face the very real possibility that our condition will become more serious.

If you insist upon adhering to this policy, I will have no choice but to find an alternate source of care. I can no longer afford you!

Sincerely,

TERMINATING MEDICAL SERVICES

Dear (**name of physician or care giver**):

Since (**date**) (**I/my relative/ward**) (**have/has**) been (**under your care/the care of your facility**). During the past (**days/weeks/months**), (**my/his/her**) condition has continued to deteriorate, which has caused me increasing alarm.

I have attempted to contact you (**number of times/dates**) by (**letter/phone call/both**) with regard to this situation. To date, I have received no response from you. Therefore, I have arranged to (**leave this facility/remove patient from the facility/secure the services of another physician/care giver**), and effective (**immediately/date**), your services will no longer be required.

Please forward a copy of (**my/other person's**) records directly to (**name and address of other physician or facility**).

Your cooperation is appreciated.

Sincerely,

TERMINATING FACILITY SERVICES

Dear (**name of administrator**):

On (**date**), at (**time**) I was contacted by (**name**), (**position**), at your facility, informing me (**relative/ward**) had (**nature of incident**) and was being transported to (**other facility**). (**Tests/attending physician**) indicated (**nature and degree of injuries**).

It was later determined the accident had occurred as a result of (**reason**), which is clearly against your own policy, and constitutes an act of negligence.

I have decided not to permit (**relative/ward**) to be returned to (**facility**) and have instructed (**my/our**) attorney to ensure that all bills related to this matter are forwarded directly to you for payment.

Sincerely,

Note: A copy of this letter should be sent to your attorney.

EMERGENCY MEDICAL CARE AUTHORIZATION

Attention: (**health care facility, attending physician**)

In the event emergency medical care services or procedures are required for (**myself**) (**my son/daughter/other**) during my absence, I, (**name**), do hereby appoint (**my/his/her**) (**relationship to you or son/daughter/other**), (**name of individual**), of (**address**), to obtain and/or authorize whatever care may be deemed appropriate. This authorization will not commence before (**date**) nor extend beyond (**date**) and is relevant to *Emergency Care Only*.

In witness whereof I have hereunto set my hand this_____day of

_____, 19_____.

_____

(SIGNATURE)

Subscribed and sworn to before me this_____

day of _____, 19_____.

_____

Notary Public in and for

_____County, State of_____

(SEAL)

- -

My commission expires_____

Copies (5): **Health care facility**
        Attending physician
        Appointee
        Emergency transport service
        Personal copy

Chapter 11

HOBBIES AND SPECIAL INTERESTS

Seeking Information on a New Product
Ordering Special Equipment
Applying for Association Membership
Requesting Registration Form—Trade Show or Convention
Reserving Space in a Trade Show
Registering Complaint with Convention Committee

A stroll through a museum, arts and crafts show, a sidewalk gallery, or a county fair pavillion offers but a hint of the creativity of individuals whose special interests have earned them a notable place in American contemporary culture.

Valued for simple beauty or exquisite detail, each personal expression of the artisan's skill is testament to his or her dedication and determination and offers a glimpse into the artist within.

The letters featured in this chapter focus on ways to inquire about, and obtain, special equipment, to apply for membership in associations of your peers, and, if you have suddenly found your work in demand, to arrange to exhibit it at a trade show or exhibition.

SEEKING INFORMATION ON A NEW PRODUCT

Dear (**name of marketing or sales representative**):

I would like additional information about your (**product and model number**), which is advertised in the (**month/season**) issue of (**publication**).

I have a (**similar product**) in my (**home/studio/classroom**), which I use for personal projects as well as the classes I teach. I am looking for a more cost-efficient item, and your (**product**) appears to be exactly what I am seeking.

I am specifically interested in its (**specifications/production capacity**). My price range, depending upon specifications and performance, is approximately (**$ amount**).

I would also be interested in talking with one of your local representatives as well as someone in the area who has purchased this particular model.

Thank you for your attention and prompt response to my inquiry.

Sincerely,

ORDERING SPECIAL EQUIPMENT

Dear (**name of responding sales representative**):

Thank you for responding so quickly to my inquiry about the (**product and model number**) and for offering the name of a reference familiar with this product.

I am satisfied the (**product**) will be quite satisfactory for my needs, and I am enclosing a certified check (**or other requested method of payment**) in the amount of (**$ amount**) to cover the full cost of the (**product**) and the shipping charges.

As I indicated to you in our telephone conversation, the (**product**) is to be shipped directly to (**address**).

Please send me a written confirmation of this order including the anticipated delivery date.

Thank you for your prompt handling of this order.

Sincerely,

APPLYING FOR ASSOCIATION MEMBERSHIP

Dear (**name of membership chairperson or secretary**):

I would appreciate receiving a membership application to the (**name of association**).

As (**title/collector**) of (**business or items**) for the past (**number**) years, my experience and qualifications meet the criteria for membership in this organization.

I have enclosed, for your consideration, a current resume of my (**career/work**) in the field of (**interest**) and a listing of other related clubs and organizations in which I am a member in good standing. Please feel free to contact any personal or professional references I have included.

If you have any questions or require additional information, I can be contacted at the address shown above or by telephone at (**number**).

Thank you for your prompt attention to this request.

Sincerely,

REQUESTING REGISTRATION FORM—TRADE SHOW OR CONVENTION

Dear (**name of trade show or convention organizer**):

I would appreciate any information you can provide about the (**trade show/ convention**) that is scheduled to be held in (**location**) in (**month**).

Specifically, I would like a copy of the guidelines and requirements for vendors; what facilities are available; any limitations on space or volume of products that may be displayed; size, location, and cost of booth/spaces; registration fees; and arrangements for overnight accommodations for out-of-town participants.

Thank you for your prompt response. I look forward to reviewing the information and possibly participating in this event.

Sincerely,

RESERVING SPACE IN TRADE SHOW

Dear (**name of show chairperson or function coordinator**):

Enclosed please find my completed application and check in the amount of (**$ amount**) to cover the cost of registration for the (**event**) in (**location**) on (**date(s)**).

I am scheduled to arrive in (**location**), (**day/date**), and will be prepared to set up my display upon arrival. Also enclosed is a complete inventory showing the items to be displayed, the wholesale value of each item, and a copy of personal liability insurance coverage, which you require.

I estimate I will need a space approximately (**specifications**), with (**additional display equipment**). My location preference is (**state where you wish to be for most advantageous exposure to visitors and customers**).

If you require additional information, please contact me by telephone at (**number**).

Thank you for your assistance. I look forward to receiving your confirmation and participating in this event.

Sincerely,

REGISTERING COMPLAINT WITH CONVENTION COMMITTEE

Dear (**name of show chairperson**):

I would like to make you aware of several problems I encountered at the (**specific event**) in (**location**) in (**month**).

Prior to arriving at the convention site, I received a written confirmation from your committee clearly stating my display area was (**location and number**), a (**specifications**) booth, located in (**aisle/area and number**), near (**point of reference**). When I arrived I found, instead, the space had also been assigned to (**name of individual**) from (**area**). Since (**he/she/they**) had arrived earlier, (**he/she/they**) were permitted to retain this space, and I was hurriedly assigned (**area/space and number**), (**location**), which was considerably smaller and located (**point of reference**).

As a result of this mix-up, my exposure was greatly reduced, and my potential sales suffered.

I am requesting a full investigation into this matter and feel an amount equal to the estimated loss of sales, which I calculate to be (**$ amount**), should be refunded to me.

I am aware problems will occur in an undertaking of this magnitude; however, without assurance that such an incident will not occur again, I do not feel it will be to my advantage to participate in the next event.

Sincerely,
Note: A copy of this letter should be sent to the president of the sponsoring organization.

Chapter 12

INSURANCE

Insurance is based upon the concept of shared risk, or several individuals contributing against the possibility that statistically fewer will actually sustain a loss. Practically everyone has had some experience with insurance either through homeowner policies, automobile policies, credit life, health and life insurance, special policies for luxury items, and liability coverage, to name a few. In some instances, such as a homeowner's policy attached to a mortgage, or auto insurance to driving privileges, obtaining insurance is not a matter of personal choice but a requirement.

Consumers should carefully assess how much coverage they actually need. Statistics often reveal most of us are either over or under insured. Discuss your needs with your agent or insurance company representative. Be sure you understand exactly what protection you have, or intend to purchase. Do not ignore the small print in the contract. It's there for a reason. If you are not satisfied with the explanation, take your policy or proposal to another agent or company for comparison of services and costs.

If you have problems with a disputed settlement or denial of a legitimate claim, attempt to first resolve it with the company. If you question the handling of a claim, or the reputation of a particular company, or wish to inquire about claims satisfaction ratings, contact your state insurance commission to obtain the facts.*

INQUIRY: INSURANCE COMPANY RATING

Dear (**name of commissioner, state department of insurance—consumer division**):

Recently I (**received a letter/direct mail advertisement/call from a representative**) from (**name of insurance company**) regarding (**auto/homeowner/health/life**) coverage. An offering of (**amount/type of coverage**) for an annual premium of (**$ amount**) seems reasonable indeed; however, being unfamiliar with this particular company, I would like more information before submitting an application for this policy.

Specifically, I would like to know if they are licensed to operate in the state of (**your state**), if there is any information available regarding their claims service, how they are rated by the industry, their financial stability, and if any complaints have been filed with your department that would indicate misrepresentation of the services outlined in the attached copy of their (**letter/brochure/recorded statements of representative**).

Any assistance you may be able to provide will be greatly appreciated.

Sincerely,

---

* A listing of addresses and telephone numbers of state departments of insurance is featured in the appendix, under "Information Please . . ."

CONVERSION OF GROUP COVERAGE
TO INDIVIDUAL POLICY

Dear (name of insurance company regional service center representative):

I am currently employed by (name of employer) and participate in their term life group coverage (policy number). I will be leaving this company on (date), and I am considering exercising my option to convert my group coverage to an individual policy within (number of days) of my termination date.

I would appreciate it if you would provide me with an explanation of benefits available under the conversion provision, enrollment procedures, monthly premium for ($ amount) of coverage, and the necessary forms needed to initiate this conversion.

I am (number) years of age, (married/single/separated/divorced), with (no/number of) dependents. My duties in my new position consist of (state whether or not you will perform basically the same duties as before or if the new position will present a greater or lesser insurable risk).

Thank you for your assistance.

Sincerely,

CHANGING BENEFICIARY

Dear (name of agent, broker, or insurance company representative):

Effective (date you wish change to occur), I wish to change the (beneficiary/beneficiaries) on my (term/whole) life insurance policy, (policy number), from (relationship and name(s) of individual(s)/organization) to (relationship and name(s) of individual(s)/organization). No other changes are required. The amount and disbursement provisions will remain the same.

Please forward whatever forms are necessary to implement this change as soon as possible.

Thank you for your immediate attention to this matter.

Sincerely,

CLAIMING LIFE INSURANCE BENEFITS

Dear (**name of insurance company claims division representative**):

This letter is to advise you of the death of your policyholder, (**name of deceased**), in (**location**) on (**date**). As (**his/her**) named beneficiary, I am requesting settlement of this policy, (**number**), in the amount of (**$ amount**), according to the disbursement provisions contained in the contract.

Attached is the required Certificate of Death. If you have any questions, or require forms to be signed, please contact me at the above address or by telephone at (**number**).

Thank you for your assistance.

Sincerely,

REQUESTING REDUCTION OF PREMIUM (HEALTH)

Dear (**name of agent, broker, or insurance company premium rating division**):

Based upon (**a recent physical/follow-up visit to physician/other**) and verification by Dr. (**name**), whose letter is attached, I would like to request a reevaluation of the risk factors on which my original policy premium was based.

Dr. (**name**)'s letter attests that I no longer (**smoke/am excessively overweight/suffer from a particular ailment/other**), which was a consideration at the time this policy, (**number**), was initially issued. Since the condition no longer exists, I believe I may qualify for a premium reduction.

I appreciate your assistance.

Sincerely,

AUTO INSURANCE DISCOUNTS

Dear (**agent, broker, or insurance company premium rating division**):

I recently arranged for my (**age**) (**son/daughter/other**), (**name**), to be added to my automobile policy, (**number**). I have just received the premium notice in the amount of (**$ amount**), which appears to be excessive considering (**his/her**) limited use of this automobile.

(Name of son/daughter/other) is an honor roll student at (name of school), has taken a state-approved safe driving course (at his/her school or through private instruction), and will be restricted to limited travel to and from school, which is (distance) from home.

I respectfully request that you reevaluate the potential risk based upon these facts and advise if discounts are appropriate in this situation.

Thank you for your prompt attention to this request.

Sincerely,

DISPUTED SETTLEMENT

Dear (name of insurance claims representative or adjuster):

Pursuant to (your notification/our telephone conversation) on (date) regarding (policy and claim numbers), this is to advise that I find the settlement offered for (loss/damage to/replacement of) (item) to be unacceptable.

I am enclosing an (appraisal for an identical item of comparable age and condition/ original appraisal of item in question/bill of sale for original item/other) that shows the value to be ($ amount) in (month/year of purchase). Obviously, such items do not decrease in value, but are worth more now than when originally purchased. Its replacement value today would be approximately ($ amount), ($ amount) greater than your assessment.

I respectfully request that you reevaluate this situation to arrive at a more appropriate figure.

Sincerely,

CANCELLATION OF POLICY (BY INSURED)

Dear (name of agent, broker, or insurance company customer service representative):

On (date) I signed an application for a (health/life/auto/homeowner/other) policy and issued a personal check to cover the initial premium in the amount of ($ amount).

I have since had an opportunity to (examine the application more thoroughly/compare coverage and cost with other companies/been advised of your problems with claim settlements/other reasons) and feel this policy would not be as beneficial as I had originally thought. Therefore, I am requesting that you take steps to see that this policy is not issued and arrange to have my initial payment refunded in full.

Thank you for your prompt attention and response to this request.

Sincerely,

UNEXPECTED TERMINATION OF POLICY (BY COMPANY)

Dear (name of commissioner, state department of insurance—consumer division):

For the past (number) years I have carried (auto/homeowner/health/other) insurance with (name of company). With the exception of a minor accident and a claim in the amount of ($ amount) on (date), I have no claims history with this company. On (date), (length of time after claim was paid), I unexpectedly received the attached notice of cancellation.

I have always paid my premiums in a timely manner and can think of no reason why they would terminate my coverage other than the recent claim I submitted in (month/year). Considering the total amount of premiums I have paid to date, ($ amount), cancellation due to a ($ amount) claim is unwarranted.

Unless (name of company) can be persuaded to reverse their decision, I will be forced to secure coverage through another company. I am very displeased with the way this matter has been handled, and I would appreciate any assistance you may provide in determining why (name of company) has taken this action.

If necessary, please do not hesitate to contact me at the above address or by telephone at (number).

Sincerely,

Chapter 13

MEDIA

The media—newspapers, magazines, and television—have a powerful impact on the everyday lives of Americans. We often forget that we, the people, can have an impact on the media! It works both ways. The letters in this chapter will assist you in making that impact when you want your opinions and feelings known and acted upon.*

PUBLIC SERVICE ANNOUNCEMENT

Dear (**name**):

I am the (**secretary/president/other**) of the (**Tampa Historical Society/other**). We will be having a (**rummage sale/concert/other**) to raise money for (**a new wing/whale research/ other**). (**Briefly describe the public benefit of the event**). The (**rummage sale/concert/ other**) will take place on (**date(s) of event**) from (**time(s) when event will be held**). The (**rummage sale/concert/other**) will be open to the public. (**Add any other pertinent information: dropoff point for sale items/ticket cost and purchase place/other**).

I would appreciate it if you would announce the (**rummage sale/concert/other**) on (**name of television or radio station**) during your (**noon/6:00 P.M./other**) news broadcast.

If you need additional information, please call the (**Tampa Historical Society/other**) at (**number of organization**).

Thank you for your help.

Sincerely,

COMPLAINT: DELIVERY OF NEWSPAPER

Dear (**name**):

I have had a subscription to your newspaper for the past (**number**) years. Until recently, there has been no problem with delivery. However, for the past few weeks, delivery has been erratic. I did not receive a paper on (**list dates**).

Please credit my account, (**account number**), for the days when the paper was not delivered. I am also requesting that you straighten out this situation with the carrier who delivers my papers. If you need to contact me, I can be reached at (**number**).

Thank you for your prompt attention to this matter.

Sincerely,

---

* See the Broadcast Networks section of "Information Please . . ." in the appendix for the addresses and phone numbers of major networks.

LETTER TO THE EDITOR

Dear (name of editor):

I am writing in response to your recent article, "(title of article)." I am appalled by the current situation in the (public schools/shopping mall/other) and applaud your bringing it to the attention of the public. Your staff writer, (name), did an excellent job of researching the article and digging up information about the causes of the (overcrowded classrooms/vandalism/other).

My only concern about the article is that it did not point to a possible solution to the problem. I hope (name of writer) will be doing some follow-up articles indicating what can be done and how individual citizens can help.

Sincerely,

REQUEST FOR ASSISTANCE—CONSUMER ACTION REPORTER

Dear (name of consumer action reporter):

(Describe your problem, including the steps that you have already taken and the outcome of your actions. If applicable, enclose copies of any letters you have written or received. Be sure to include how the present outcome is unsatisfactory and that you do not know where else to turn.)

Sample: I live in an apartment complex at 439 West 125th Street. The complex is owned and managed by the (your community) Housing Authority. During the winter, the front entrance to the building often is covered with ice. Despite repeated requests, the Housing Authority refuses to send someone either to clear away the ice or spread sand over it. Recently, one of our older tenants slipped on the ice, broke her hip, and is currently hospitalized. The Tenants' Association has used every legal means available to put pressure on the Housing Authority. The people we have talked to at the Authority have promised to remedy the situation; however, as of this date, nothing has been done.

I am respectfully requesting that you look into this situation and interview some of the people involved on your news program. You are my last hope. You may telephone me at (number).

Thank you.

Sincerely,

CLASSIFIED ADVERTISING—ITEM FOR SALE

Dear (**name of advertising manager**):

Please place the following advertisement in your Classified section under the heading (**Pets/Furniture/other**):

(**Carefully write your advertisement exactly as you want it to appear including your address or telephone number.**)

Sample: BEDROOM SET—5 Piece including desk and bookcase.
                     $300. Call after 6:00 P.M.—987-3452.

I understand that the ad will run for (**number**) days, at a cost of (**$ amount**). I have enclosed a (**check/money order**) for that amount made out to the (**name of publication**). If you need additional information, contact me at (**telephone number**).

Thank you.

Sincerely,

PROFESSIONAL ANNOUNCEMENT

Dear (**name of sales representative**):

As we discussed over the phone, I am requesting that you place the announcement below in the (**particular section, if applicable**) section of your newspaper. I understand that the announcement will run for (**number**) days, beginning on (**date**), and that you will notify me of the cost. In addition, you will send me a copy of the announcement to proof before you run it. The announcement is as follows:

(**Your announcement, exactly as you want it to appear.**)

Sample: John Q. Counselor, Ph.D.
                     Counseling for Individuals, Couples, and Families
                     Specialist in Hypnosis and Treatment of Phobias
                     987 Fuscia Boulevard
                     Any Town, NE 45698
                     Day and evening appointments available
                     786-4231

Please call me at (**number**) if you think the announcement should be changed in any way.

Thank you for your assistance.

Sincerely,

OBJECTING TO CANCELLATION OF PROGRAM

Dear (name of president of network):

I recently found out that you are planning to cancel "(name of program)," a program that is aired in my section of the country on (day(s)) at (time). I strongly object to your canceling this wonderful program.

It is the one show that we, as a family, watch every week. For me, it provides perfect "prime-time" entertainment for all ages. As a parent, I particularly appreciate the way in which "(name of program)" deals with sensitive issues. There are too many programs these days that portray (objectional features of other shows). "(name of program)" confronts these issues within the framework of constructive decision making, which, for me, is the only appropriate framework. Moreover, the script is always well written and the acting is excellent.

I am urging you to reconsider canceling this program. We need more like it.

Sincerely,

OBJECTING TO PROGRAM CONTENT

Dear (name of president of network):

I recently watched "(name of program)" and was shocked and disturbed by its content. I am particularly upset by the way in which the characters in the program portray (sexual relationships/drug involvement/other). Their portrayal is irresponsible at best, and morally degrading at worst. Moreover, in my area, the program is aired during "prime-time" hours when young children might be exposed to its offensive content.

I strongly object to the content of "(name of program)" and respectfully request that you cancel the program, or, at the very least, air it at a later hour.

Thank you for your consideration of my request.

Sincerely,

COMPLAINT TO SPONSOR

Dear (**name of president of sponsoring company**):

I was shocked to discover that your company is one of the sponsors of the television program, "(**name of program**)."

Frankly, I was surprised that a reputable company like yours would associate itself with such a disreputable program. The program makes a farce out of (**marriage/family life/ other**), and I find its content blatantly offensive. Moreover, "(**name of program**)" is aired during "prime time," when young children might be watching it.

I strongly urge you to cancel your sponsorship of this program and to encourage the other sponsors to do the same. Perhaps if you do this, the network will cancel "(**name of program**)" or alter its content.

Thank you for your attention to this matter.

Sincerely,

SUPPORTING AN ISSUE

Dear (**name of president of station**):

I want to applaud you for your station's stand on the (**briefly describe the issue that you support**) issue. I agree that (**briefly describe why you agree with the station's stand**), and I am delighted that your opinion on this critical issue is similar to mine. In addition, I was impressed by your representative's clear and reasonable statement of your station's stance.

If more stations like yours would take a stand on the important issues of our time, it would help to inform the people, and thereby assist them in forming their own opinions.

Thank you for your courage.

Sincerely,

Chapter 14

MEDICARE

Medicare is a federal health insurance program under the direction of the U.S. Department of Health and Human Services and is administered by the Health Care Financing Administration. It is designed to provide coverage for qualified individuals 65 years of age or older and other specific disabled persons.

Part A, the premium-free provision, covers the cost of inpatient hospital care, some skilled nursing facilities inpatient care, home health care, and hospice care. Part B, which covers physicians' services, outpatient services, durable medical equipment, other services and supplies not covered under Part A, is an elective option requiring an application for coverage, and a premium.

To determine if you are eligible for coverage, and to obtain information on the full range of Medicare benefits, you should contact your nearest Social Security Administration Office.*

ELIGIBILITY: STATEMENT OF EARNINGS

Dear (**name of commissioner**):

In (**month/year**) I will become 65 years of age. Three months prior to this date I intend to apply for Social Security and Medicare. In order to verify my eligibility for these benefits I would like to obtain a copy of earnings that have been attributed to me since I entered the work force in (**month/year**).

My Social Security number is (**number assigned**), and my legal name is (**give full name, including maiden name if applicable**). Prior to my (**marriage/divorce/other**) in (**year**), my name was (**other name under which earnings may have been recorded**).

Thank you for your assistance.

Sincerely,

NOTE: This letter should be addressed to the nearest Social Security regional service center.

---

* Listings of national and regional Social Security Administration offices, designated state Medicare Carriers, and state Medicare Peer Review Organizations can be found in the appendix, under "Information Please . . .".

REQUESTING LIST OF PARTICIPATING PHYSICIANS

Dear (**name of Medicare carrier representative**):

I recently retired and am now enrolled as a recipient of Medicare, Parts A & B. As this is now my primary source of medical insurance coverage, I would like to obtain a list of physicians in the (**location**) area who accept Medicare assignment for the services they render. I understand this information is available free of charge upon request.

Thank you for your prompt response to this request.

Sincerely,

INCORRECT BILLING: ASSIGNMENT OF BENEFITS

Dear (**name of physician or supplier**):

I have just received the enclosed statement from your (**office/store**) for (**procedure/ product**), (**performed/purchased**) on (**date**).

While I appreciate your willingness to accept Medicare assignment in the amount of (**$ amount**) as full payment in lieu of (**$ amount**) that you normally charge for this (**procedure/product**), it appears you have neglected to advise your (**billing service/ accounting department**) of this arrangement. The unpaid balance of (**$ amount**) shown on the statement is actually the difference in the Medicare approved (**charges/cost**) and the (**fee/amount**) you usually (**require/charge**).

Please advise your (**billing service/accounting department**) of this error and send me a revised statement reflecting the correct Medicare approved amount and billing me only for the 20% co-payment Medicare does not cover.

Thank you for your prompt attention to this matter.

Sincerely,

HEALTH MAINTENANCE ORGANIZATION BENEFITS

Dear (**name of HMO manager**):

I am (**state your age**) and am enrolled in Medicare Part A and Part B. I am interested in comparing coverage available to Medicare beneficiaries through an HMO program. I would appreciate information about your program, benefits, membership guidelines, enrollment procedures, and the cost of monthly premiums.

I do not suffer from chronic kidney disease, and I am not a recipient of hospice care benefits.

Thank you for your attention to this inquiry.

Sincerely,

APPEAL TO MEDICARE PEER REVIEW ORGANIZATION

Dear (name of representative, state Medicare Peer Review Organization):

This letter represents an appeal of your decision of (date statement of denial was issued), denying approval for my (parent/ward/other), (name and Medicare insurance claim number), to be admitted as an inpatient to (name of facility) for the purpose of (state nature of proposed surgical procedure/testing/other).

Although this is generally considered to be a minor procedure that does not ordinarily require hospitalization, (his/her) previous medical history and (give details of present contributing factors) clearly indicate the possibility that serious complications could develop should this (procedure/test/other) be attempted on an outpatient basis.

I am enclosing a statement from Dr. (name of beneficiary's physician) that provides an overview of (beneficiary)'s previous medical history, and why (he/she) feels such precautionary measures are advisable in this situation.

I ask that you recognize the medical necessity for inpatient care and reverse your original decision to enable my (parent/ward/other) to receive the care (his/her) condition warrants.

I am also enclosing a statement signed by (name of beneficiary) authorizing me to initiate this appeal on (his/her) behalf.

Respectfully,

NOTE: Copies of this letter should be sent to beneficiary's physician and beneficiary.

COMPLAINT TO MEDICARE PEER REVIEW ORGANIZATION

Dear (name of director, state Medicare Peer Review Organization):

On (date) I was admitted to (name of facility) for (nature of procedure or illness). I was released on (date), which coincided precisely with the approved number of days Medicare guidelines prescribe for this (problem/condition).

As a result, my subsequent recovery was unduly stressful and prolonged. It is obvious more emphasis was placed upon financial considerations than on my condition at the time of discharge. Had I not been a Medicare recipient, it is likely I would not have been released prematurely and my recovery would have been uneventful.

I am attaching copies of supporting (**medical bills/other documentation**) that attest to the fact I required additional medical attention after my release.

I believe this matter warrants an inquiry by your organization. If you have any questions, or require additional information, please feel free to contact me at the address above or by telephone at (**number**).

Thank you for your interest in this matter.

Sincerely,

INQUIRY: SUPPLEMENTAL INSURANCE CLAIM DENIED

Dear (**name of insurance company claims representative**):

Several months ago I purchased a supplemental health insurance policy, (**number**), from (**name of company**). I was told by your (**agent/representative**) that this policy would take care of any expenses that Medicare did not cover, specifically (**detail services claimed to be covered**).

On (**date**) I required (**hospitalization/surgery/test/other**) for (**illness/suspected condition**), which resulted in charges of (**$ amount**). Medicare paid (**$ amount**), leaving an unpaid balance of (**$ amount**). I immediately filed a claim with your company, only to be informed that it had been denied. The reasons cited were (**state reasons why company rejected the claim**). This is contradictory to the information I was given at the time I purchased this policy.

I continue to receive bills from (**physician/facility/other**) for the amount you refuse to honor. According to (**physician/facility/other**), I am responsible for the additional expenses Medicare did not cover.

I feel the (**agent/representative/company**) misrepresented the benefits of this policy, and by way of a copy of this letter to the (**state**) Department of Insurance, Consumer Division, I am requesting an investigation of this matter to determine if (**company**) should be permitted to continue marketing a product which, in my situation, failed to measure up to its promises. I am enclosing for your review photocopies of the policy, the bills in question, and your statement of denial.

I would appreciate an immediate reevaluation of my claim. If you require additional information, please contact me at the address above or by telephone at (**number**).

Sincerely,

Chapter 15

REAL ESTATE

• MORTGAGE •
Terminating Agency Contract to Sell
Withdrawing Offer to Purchase
Requesting Information: Permit for Improvements
Change of Address to Mortgagor
Requesting Amortization Schedule of Payments
Requesting Payoff of Mortgage

• RENTAL •
Requesting Repairs to Property/Fixtures
Protesting Monthly Rent Increase
Complaint About Neighbors
Notification of Possible Theft by Employee
Notification of Inappropriate Behavior by Employee
Notice of Intent to Vacate
Terminating Lease
Requesting Security Deposit Refund

• INCOME PROPERTY •
Warning to Disruptive Tenants
Notification of Rent Increase
Warning Notice: Late Rent Payments
Reminder of "NO PETS" Clause
Responsibility for Actions of Guests
Notification of Sale of Property—New Landlord

Whether you own your own house, co-op, or condominium, rent an apartment, own income-producing property, or have a business interest in any of the above, you are involved in real estate. As a homeowner, you need to be able to communicate with your bank or loan company. As a renter, you need to be able to communicate with your landlord or management company. As an income property owner, you need to be able to communicate with your tenants. The letters in this chapter are designed to help you communicate effectively, with the best possibility of getting the results you desire.

MORTGAGE

TERMINATING AGENCY CONTRACT TO SELL

Dear (name of real estate agent or broker):

Please be advised that we are hereby terminating our contract with you to sell our (house, co-op or condominium) at (address).

We appreciate your efforts on our behalf; however, our plans have changed, and we have decided not to sell our (house, co-op, or condominium) at this time.

Sincerely,

WITHDRAWING OFFER TO PURCHASE

Dear (name of real estate agent or broker):

We are hereby withdrawing our offer of ($ amount) to purchase the property at (address). Since the current owner has not yet accepted or rejected our offer, we assume there will be no problem with this withdrawal.

Sincerely,

REQUESTING INFORMATION: PERMIT FOR IMPROVEMENTS

Dear (name of building inspector):

I am planning to build a (porch/deck/garage/other) on my property at (address). Please send me the forms that I will need to submit in order to obtain a permit for this construction.

Thank you.

Sincerely,

CHANGE OF ADDRESS TO MORTGAGOR

Dear (name of loan officer):

Please be advised that I have changed my permanent mailing address from (old address) to (new address), effective (date). Any correspondence from you after that date should be mailed to me at my new address. Please adjust your records accordingly. My loan number is (loan number).

Thank you.

Sincerely,

REQUESTING AMORTIZATION SCHEDULE OF PAYMENTS

Dear (name of loan officer):

I currently have a (home, co-op, or condominium) mortgage with your institution. My loan number is (loan number).

Please send me an amortization schedule of payments beginning with (date).

Thank you for your assistance.

Sincerely,

REQUESTING PAYOFF OF MORTGAGE

Dear (name of loan officer):

We currently have a mortgage on our (house, co-op, or condominium) with your (bank or company). Our loan number is (loan number). We are hereby requesting the payoff amount on our loan as of (date). We are hoping to pay off the loan at that time. If there will be a penalty for paying off the loan ahead of schedule, please let us know the amount.

Thank you.

Sincerely,

RENTAL

REQUESTING REPAIRS TO PROPERTY/FIXTURES

Dear (name of landlord/managing agent):

I live in apartment (number) in (name of community, if applicable) at (address).

The (stove/refrigerator/sink/other or part of appliance) has stopped working. Please send one of your maintenance workers to fix it as soon as possible. I am available (day(s) of week and time(s)).

Thank you for your attention to this matter.

Sincerely,

PROTESTING MONTHLY RENT INCREASE

Dear (name of landlord/managing agent):

You recently notified me that my monthly rent will be increased from ($ amount) per month to ($ amount) per month, effective (date).

Along with many other tenants, I strongly protest this increase. I understand that your management costs have gone up; however, my living costs have also gone up due to inflation. In addition, I would be more amenable to a rent increase if I were being provided with the services you agreed to in my lease. My apartment is overdue for (re-painting, recarpeting, installing new appliance/other); as of this date, you have neither performed nor contacted me to arrange a time for this service.

I respectfully request that you reconsider this increase until such time as you have fulfilled your obligations to me.

Sincerely,

COMPLAINT ABOUT NEIGHBORS

Dear (name of landlord/managing agent):

We live in apartment (number) in (name, if applicable, and address of apartment community). For the past few weeks, we have been having a problem with our neighbors in apartment (number). (Describe in detail the offensive behavior and how it

interferes with your use or enjoyment of your residence: noisy, late-night parties/
leaving garbage piled up in hallway/other). Repeated requests to stop (state the offensive behavior) have been to no avail. Conversations with other tenants in our building have revealed similar complaints.

Please contact the tenants of apartment (number) and ask that they be more considerate
of their neighbors. Perhaps if this request comes from you, they will be more likely to
comply.

Thank you.

Sincerely,

NOTIFICATION OF POSSIBLE THEFT BY EMPLOYEE

Dear (name of landlord/managing agent):

On (date), one of your maintenance workers (name if you know it) was in our apartment (number) at (name, if applicable and address of apartment community) to (reason person was in your apartment; e.g., fix an appliance/paint the living room/other).
After (he/she) left, I noticed that my (article) was missing. While (he/she) was here, the
(article) was (location of missing article). Although we have never had problems with
any of your maintenance people before, I have to consider the possibility that this person
took my (article) while (he/she) was in my apartment.

I would appreciate your following up on this matter with your employee immediately
and letting me know what you find out.

Thank you for your cooperation. I can be reached at (telephone number).

Sincerely,

NOTIFICATION OF INAPPROPRIATE BEHAVIOR
BY EMPLOYEE

Dear (name of landlord/managing agent):

On (date), one of your maintenance workers (name, if you know it) was in our apartment (number) at (name, if applicable, and address of apartment community) (reason
person was in your apartment; e.g., repairing kitchen fixture/replacing screen door/
other). While (he/she) was there, (he/she) (describe offensive behavior; e.g., made sug-
gestive comments/other).

I immediately asked (**him/her**) to leave my apartment, which (**he/she**) did. Although (**he/she**) apologized profusely, I thought you should know about this incident.

I would appreciate your discussing this incident with (**name/him/her**) and letting me know the results of your conversation. I can be reached at (**telephone number**).

Thank you for your cooperation.

Sincerely,

NOTICE OF INTENT TO VACATE

Dear (**name of landlord/managing agent**):

Please be advised that I will be vacating apartment (**number**) at (**name, if applicable, and address of apartment community**) on (**date**). Please pro-rate my rent accordingly and let me know how much I will owe you at that time.

If you need additional information, I can be reached at (**telephone number**).

Thank you.

Sincerely,

TERMINATING LEASE

Dear (**name of landlord/managing agent**):

Please be advised that I am terminating my lease on apartment (**number**) at (**name, if applicable, and address of apartment community**), effective (**date**). This letter fulfills the terms of the lease requiring (**number**) (**days/months**) notice of termination.

I have enjoyed living here and hope I can find as cooperative a landlord as you at my new residence.

I am assuming that, according to the stipulations of my lease, you will return my security deposit within (**number**) days of termination. I will let you know my new address as soon as I can. Thank you for your prompt responses to my requests.

Sincerely,

REQUESTING SECURITY DEPOSIT REFUND

Dear (**name of landlord/managing agent**):

For the past (**period of time**), until (**date of move**), I was a resident of (**name, if applicable, and address**). During those years, I always paid my rent on time and kept my (**apartment/house**) neat and clean. In addition, I found the management to be very cooperative and responsive when I needed their assistance.

However, since vacating my (**apartment/house**) at (**address**) and moving on (**date of move**), I have been unable to get the management to refund my security deposit of (**$ amount**). My lease states that security deposit refunds may be expected within (**number**) days of vacating the premises; it has now been (**number**) days! Repeated requests (**state number of letters and/or telephone calls**) have been to no avail. The (**apartment/ house**) was left in immaculate condition with all appliances and fixtures that were furnished intact.

I am requesting that you contact the (**appropriate manager**) immediately and instruct (**him/her**) to send my security deposit refund to me at the following address:

(**Your name**)
(**Post office box/street address**)
(**City, state, zip code**)

I deeply appreciate your efforts to expedite this claim.

Sincerely,

INCOME PROPERTY

WARNING TO DISRUPTIVE TENANTS

Dear (**name of tenant**):

I have received several phone calls and letters from your neighbors complaining about your (**noise, late night parties/loud arguments/other**). What you do in your own apartment is, of course, your private business; however, when your behavior becomes so disruptive that it disturbs other tenants, you must change that behavior or risk eviction and/or police involvement.

Consider this letter a warning: if I continue to receive complaints, I will have no choice but to serve you with an eviction notice.

Please be considerate of your neighbors, and alter your behavior accordingly.

Sincerely,

NOTIFICATION OF RENT INCREASE

Dear (name of tenant):

Due to increased costs, your monthly rent will be raised from its current amount of ($ amount) to ($ amount), effective (date). If you have any questions, please call me at (number).

Thank you for your cooperation.

Sincerely,

WARNING NOTICE: LATE RENT PAYMENTS

Dear (name of tenant):

For the past (number) months, your rent payment has been late, and (number of times payment was within "grace period," if any) times, your payment was within the (number of days) "grace period." However, for the past (most recent number) months, we received your payment (range of number, e.g. 10 to15) days late.

According to your lease, your rent is due on the (date, e.g., first, tenth) day of every month. Please contact me immediately at (telephone number) if you are having problems we need to discuss. If I do not hear from you within one week from the date of this letter, I will assume your problem is temporary, and I will expect to receive your rent on time from now on.

Thank you for your cooperation.

Sincerely,

REMINDER OF "NO PETS" CLAUSE

Dear (name of tenant):

When my maintenance worker was in your apartment last week (fixing your stove/ unclogging your toilet/other), (he/she) noticed (describe evidence of pet habitation: litter box/chew toy/other). The lease you signed clearly states that pets are not allowed in your apartment.

Please remove the (**cat/dog/other**) from your premises. I will be coming by within the next few days to check on your compliance with the terms of your lease.

Thank you for your cooperation.

Sincerely,

RESPONSIBILITY FOR ACTIONS OF GUESTS

Dear (**name of tenant**):

Thank you for letting me know that one of your house guests (**drove his car through the hedge/broke a window/other**) at the (**house/apartment**) you are renting from me at (**address**). I cannot comply with your request that I (**replace the hedge/replace the window/other**). Your lease clearly states that you are responsible for damage to the property, even if that damage is caused by someone who was your guest.

I suggest you ask your guest to (**pay for/replace the hedge/window/other**). Otherwise, you will have to repair the damage yourself.

I am sorry this incident occurred, but I have to hold you responsible for remedying the situation.

Thank you for your cooperation.

Sincerely,

NOTIFICATION OF SALE OF PROPERTY—NEW LANDLORD

Dear (**name of tenant**):

Please be advised that I have sold th (**house/condominium/other**) you are renting at (**address**) to (**name of purchaser**). Starting with your (**month**) rent payment, you should make your check payable to (**name**) and mail it to (**address**).

I hope you will be as good a tenant for (**name**) as you have been for me.

Thank you for your cooperation.

Sincerely,

Chapter 16

SENIOR SERVICES

*Requesting Membership Information—American Association
of Retired Persons*

Requesting Information—Administration on Aging
Requesting Information—National Institute on Aging
Job Opportunities: Senior Community Service Employment Program
Volunteer Opportunities: ACTION
Requesting Information—Local Services

Sociologists predict that there will continue to be an increase in the over-55 year old segment of the population. This means that social and medical services will have to be expanded to meet the growing needs of this group. Sometimes it is difficult to track down information about services on a local level. This chapter addresses that difficulty by providing a variety of letters to federal agencies that contribute financial support to local programs. You can obtain valuable information from these agencies that will help you identify local programs that meet your needs or those of older family members. Be sure to be clear and specific about the information you desire so that your recipient will be able to reply appropriately. Also included in this chapter are a letter to AARP and a letter to a local chamber of commerce.*

REQUESTING MEMBERSHIP INFORMATION— AMERICAN ASSOCIATION OF RETIRED PERSONS

Dear (name of executive director):

I am interested in joining AARP. I understand that you accept members who are 50 years of age and older whether or not they are retired.

Please send me an application form, information about the cost of membership, and a listing of the benefits I will receive when I am a member. My address is

> (Your name)
> (Your address)
> (City, state, zip code)

Thank you.

Sincerely,

REQUESTING INFORMATION—ADMINISTRATION ON AGING

Dear (name of commissioner):

I am a retired older American, aged (age), living in (town and state). I would like to know what social services are available in my area. I am particularly interested in information on (contract bridge clubs/swimming classes for arthritics/other). My address is

---

* See the Agencies on Aging section of "Information Please . . ." in the appendix for the addresses and phone numbers of many federal and state agencies.

(Your name)
(Your address)
(City, state, zip code)

Thank you for your attention to my concerns.

Sincerely,

REQUESTING INFORMATION— NATIONAL INSTITUTE ON AGING

Dear (name of director):

I am responsible for the care of my (mother/father/aunt/uncle/other) who is (age) years old. (He/she) is in remarkably good health for (his/her) age; however (he/she) is beginning to have (memory lapses/periods of confusion/other). These (lapses/confused periods/other) cause (him/her) a great deal of anxiety and frustration, and I want to help (him/her) as much as I can.

I understand that your institute does research in the area of (memory loss/confusion/senility/other) in older persons, and I am wondering if you could send me some information on this subject. My address is

(Your name)
(Your address)
(City, state, zip code)

I appreciate your attention to my concerns.

Sincerely,

JOB OPPORTUNITIES: SENIOR COMMUNITY SERVICE EMPLOYMENT PROGRAM

Dear (name of assistant secretary for employment and training):

I am a senior citizen, aged (age), living in (city and state). I am in excellent health and, before retirement, was employed as (your previous employment). I am interested in part-time employment that will not interfere with my Social Security payments.

I understand that your department subsidizes jobs through your Senior Community Service Employment Program. Please send me information about who to contact in my area about possible job opportunities. My address is

(Your name)
(Your address)
(City, state, zip code)

Thank you.

Sincerely,

VOLUNTEER OPPORTUNITIES: ACTION

Dear (name of assistant director of Older American Volunteer Programs):

I have worked and been involved in community service activities all of my life. I have recently retired and am living in (city and state). I would like to get involved in some kind of volunteer work, but I do not know what kind of opportunities are available in my area.

Please send me information about volunteer opportunities in this area. I am particularly interested in (tutoring/adopt-a-grandparent programs/other). My address is

(Your name)
(Your address)
(City, state, zip code).

Thank you.

Sincerely,

REQUESTING INFORMATION—LOCAL SERVICES

Dear (name of president of Chamber of Commerce):

I will be retiring and moving from (city and state) to (city and state) in (date). I am interested in finding out about the services provided there for senior citizens.

Please send me any information you have available. My present address is

(Your name)
(Your address)
(City, state, zip code)

Thank you.

Sincerely,

Chapter 17

SOCIAL EVENTS

Request for Volunteers
Confirming Reservations
Confirming Quotes from Vendors
Postponing an Event
Canceling Arrangements
Returning Gifts (Canceled Event)
Regrets to Invited Guests

Business-sponsored social functions differ from personal events in that they are usually conducted to promote or benefit a specific group, business, or cause. Being charged with the responsibility for such an event can test the fortitude of the most experienced coordinator. Budgetary constraints often mean contacting several vendors for the best price and services; reserving a special hall or room at your location of choice; contracting with musicians, caterers, and florists; arranging for guest speakers; obtaining accommodations for out of town guests, issuing invitations; overseeing seating arrangements; and following up on RSVPs that are not readily forthcoming.

Once this has been accomplished, there is the possibility an unforeseen circumstance may force a postponement or cancellation, at which time a reversal of the process begins. Reservations must be canceled, deposits reclaimed, and notifications sent to each invited guest informing them of the circumstances prompting the cancellation or postponement.

Successful events do not simply happen, but require precise coordination of people, skills, services, and budget. The letters featured in this chapter not only provide the means to assist you with the arrangements, but offer solutions when those unexpected problems do occur.

REQUEST FOR VOLUNTEERS

Dear (**organization**) members:

Our annual (**special event**) will be held on (**day/date**), just (**number weeks/months**) away, and we need volunteers to help make this the most memorable event ever.

Each of you did such an outstanding job last year! We are counting on you to lend your time and special talents again this year.

(**Designated person**) will be contacting each of you personally within the next few days to sign you up for the various committees. Please think about how you can best put your energy and talents to work.

Thank you for your enthusiasm and participation.

Sincerely,

CONFIRMING RESERVATIONS

Dear (**name of hotel/club/hall reservations or banquet manager**):

This letter and accompanying cashier's check, in the amount of (**$ amount**), will confirm our reservation for (**specific area/room**) on (**day/date, morning/afternoon/evening**).

As agreed in our discussion of (**date**), you will provide seating for (**number**) guests along with (**other special amenities/services**). All table seating will be positioned (**for optimum view/around dance floor/other**).

(**Caterer/florist/bartenders/band**) have been advised they will have access to the premises to begin setting up for the (**dinner/reception/dance/other**) by (**time**).

If you have any questions, or require additional information, please contact me immediately at (**telephone number**).

Thank you for your assistance.

Sincerely,

CONFIRMING QUOTES FROM VENDORS

Dear (**name of business marketing or sales representative**):

The (**sponsoring organization**) has reviewed the bids from several (**vendors/suppliers/merchants/other**) in the area, and I am pleased to inform you that your (**business/other**) has been selected to provide (**product/service**) for (**event**) on (**date**).

We will require (**state items listed in bid, with accompanying prices quoted, include specific colors, sizes, and number of each item**), to be (**placed/arranged/served**) at (**location**). (**Designated person**) will be at (**location**) to accept delivery of these items and present you with a check in the amount of (**$ amount**), as stipulated in your bid.

If you have any questions, or require more information, please contact me at (**telephone number**).

Sincerely,

POSTPONING AN EVENT

To all (**organization**) members:

The special meeting featuring (**special guest**), scheduled for (**day/date/time**), at (**location**), has been postponed until further notice.

An unexpected emergency has forced (**special guest**) to postpone all engagements for several weeks, and (**he/she**) has asked that we express (**his/her**) personal apologies and regrets to each of you.

As soon as an alternate date can be arranged, the meeting will be rescheduled, and all members notified.

We, and (**special guest**), appreciate your understanding.

Sincerely,

CANCELING ARRANGEMENTS

Dear (**name of hotel/club/hall reservations or banquet manager**):

Regretfully, I must cancel the arrangements for the (**event**), scheduled for (**day/date/time**) in (**specific area/room/other**).

You have been very helpful throughout the planning and final arrangements for this event, and we appreciate your efforts to make this a special affair.

We understand that cancellation within (**number days/weeks**) does require forfeiture of (%) of the (**$ amount**) deposit. Therefore, we are requesting a refund of (**$ amount**) be returned to us at the address above.

We apologize for any inconvenience this cancellation will cause. We anticipate receiving your check within a few days.

Sincerely,

RETURNING GIFTS (CANCELED EVENT)

Dear (**name of invited guest, sponsor, or donor**):

It is with particular regret that (**I/we**) inform you of the cancellation of (**wedding/benefit/charity event/auction**) scheduled for (**day/date**), at (**location**).

In view of (**circumstances forcing cancellation**), we must return (**your lovely gift/the gift you donated to benefit sponsored group/individuals**).

Your understanding is deeply appreciated, and your kindness will be long remembered.

Warmest regards,

REGRETS TO INVITED GUESTS

Dear (**name of invited guest**):

The (**sponsoring organization**) regrets to inform you of the cancellation of the (**event**) planned in honor of (**special guest**) on (**day/date/time**) at (**location**).

In consideration of (**circumstances prompting cancellation**), it is the consensus of (**the planning committee/membership/other**) that a (**event**) would be inappropriate at this time.

We appreciate your understanding and assure you that an alternate date will be decided upon very soon.

Thank you for your continued interest and support of our organization.

Sincerely,

Chapter 18

SOCIAL SECURITY

Requesting Application for Social Security Number
Reporting Lost Social Security Card
Change of Name
Requesting Information on Earnings Record
Applying for Benefits
Requesting Direct Deposit of Social Security Checks
Canceling Direct Deposit of Social Security Checks
Change of Address
Appealing Determination of Benefits Entitlement
Terminating Benefits—Death of Spouse
Disputing Termination of Benefits
Applying for Disability Benefits

Social Security is a program that affects the lives of nearly every American. Although it is usually thought of as a retirement program, it is actually a package of benefits to help you and your family when you retire, become severely disabled, or die.

Although it is possible to go to your local Social Security office or to call Social Security's toll-free number (1-800-234-5772), writing to your local or regional office is often a more effective way of obtaining the response you need. The letters in this chapter offer you guidelines for getting information and making requests. Be sure to include in your letter your Social Security number in order to assist your recipient in responding promptly.*

REQUESTING APPLICATION FOR
SOCIAL SECURITY NUMBER

Dear Sir:

I wish to apply for a Social Security number.

Please send the necessary information and forms to

    (Your name)
    (Your address)
    (City, state, zip code)

Thank you for your assistance.

Sincerely,

REPORTING LOST SOCIAL SECURITY CARD

Dear Sir:

I have lost my Social Security card and would like to obtain a replacement card.

My Social Security number is (**your Social Security number**). My address is (**address, city, state, zip code**).

Please send me the appropriate forms and guidelines.

Thank you for your assistance.

Sincerely,

---

* See the Social Security Administration section of "Information Please . . ." for the addresses and phone numbers of regional offices and regional program service centers.

CHANGE OF NAME

Dear Sir:

Please be advised that my name has changed from (**complete former name**) to (**complete new name**) due to my recent (**marriage/divorce**).

Please change your records accordingly and issue me a new card. My Social Security number is (**number**). I have enclosed a copy of my old Social Security card.

Thank you for your assistance.

Sincerely,

REQUESTING INFORMATION ON EARNINGS RECORD

Dear Sir:

I am interested in finding out whether or not my wages have been reported properly by my employer. What wages, subject to Social Security, have been reported by my employer (**employer's name and federal identification number, if known**)?

In addition, I would like to know how much has been paid into the Social Security system by (**employer's name**) on my behalf.

Please let me know how to go about obtaining this information. My Social Security number is (**number**).

Thank you for your assistance.

Sincerely,

APPLYING FOR BENEFITS

Dear Sir:

I am approaching retirement and need to know how to go about obtaining Social Security benefits. What information do you need from me in order to apply? How do I find out how much I am entitled to receive? (**Is/are my wife/husband/children, if applicable**) eligible to receive benefits as well? If I decide to continue working part time after I retire, will I still be eligible to receive benefits?

I would appreciate your responding to my questions at your earliest convenience. My Social Security number is (**number**).

Thank you.

Sincerely,

REQUESTING DIRECT DEPOSIT OF SOCIAL SECURITY CHECKS

Dear Sir:

My Social Security number is (**number**), and I am currently receiving my monthly check at my home address: (**address**).

I would like to arrange to have my checks deposited directly to my bank account. My account number is (**account number**). The address of my bank is (**complete name and address of your bank**).

Please send me the appropriate forms and information.

Thank you.

Sincerely,

CANCELING DIRECT DEPOSIT OF SOCIAL SECURITY CHECKS

Dear Sir:

My Social Security number is (**number**). You have been mailing my monthly checks directly to my bank where they have been credited to my account (**your bank account number**). The address of my bank is (**complete name and address of your bank**).

I wish to cancel this arrangement and have my checks sent to me at my home address (**address where you want the checks sent**).

Thank you for your cooperation in making this change.

Sincerely,

CHANGE OF ADDRESS

Dear Sir:

My Social Security number is (**number**). You are currently sending my benefits checks to (**address**).

Effective (**date**), my new address will be (**address**). Starting with my (**month**) check, please mail my checks to my new address.

Thank you for your cooperation.

Sincerely,

APPEALING DETERMINATION OF BENEFITS ENTITLEMENT

Dear Sir:

I recently wrote you requesting information about the amount of Social Security benefits I will be entitled to receive when I retire next year. The monthly figure you came up with was (**$ amount**). After reviewing the information you sent, I computed a different figure: (**$ amount**).

Please review your computations and clarify for me which figure is correct. My Social Security number is (**number**).

Thank you for your assistance.

Sincerely,

TERMINATING BENEFITS—DEATH OF SPOUSE

Dear Sir:

My (**husband/wife**), (**name of spouse**), died on (**date**). Up until the time of (**his/her**) death, (**he/she**) was receiving a monthly Social Security check in the amount of (**$ amount**). I am enclosing the check I received shortly after (**his/her**) death.

As (**his widow/her widower**), I need to know whether or not I am eligible for survivor's benefits. If I am, please send me the necessary information so that I may apply. My (**husband's/wife's**) Social Security number was (**spouse's number**). My Social Security number is (**number**).

Thank you for your assistance.

Sincerely,

DISPUTING TERMINATION OF BENEFITS

Dear Sir:

I have received notification from your office that my Social Security benefits have been terminated. The reason given was that the wages I am currently earning exceed the limit.

When I returned to work, I checked with your office to be certain that my wages would not exceed the limit allowable. As you can see from the enclosed letter from you, I was assured that my wages were well under the limit. Therefore, I do not understand why my benefits checks have been terminated.

I would appreciate a response to my concerns as soon as possible.

Thank you.

Sincerely,

APPLYING FOR DISABILITY BENEFITS

Dear Sir:

I wish to apply for disability payments through Social Security. I am currently employed and not of retirement age. However, my (**son/daughter**), (**name of son/daughter**), has been disabled by (**briefly describe the disability**). It is my understanding that, since (**he/she**) is now 18, I am eligible to receive benefits based on (**his/her**) disability. My Social Security number is (**number**). My (**son/daughter's**) Social Security number is (**number**).

Please send me the necessary information and forms.

Thank you for your assistance.

Sincerely,

Chapter 19

TAXES

Most of us are familiar with the scene at local post offices during the first three months of every year: a long table piled high with stacks of Internal Revenue Service (IRS) tax forms. Indeed, the major way we communicate with our federal government is through forms, particularly at tax time. However, there are occasions when it is necessary to write a letter, even if the purpose is to request yet another form.

Most of the letters in this chapter address questions or problems that may arise with regard to your federal income tax. In order to expedite a timely response, address these letters to the IRS regional office nearest you (instead of the IRS office in Washington, D.C.)

In all your correspondence with the IRS, be sure to include your taxpayer identification number, which is usually the same as your Social Security number. Omitting that number can slow response time considerably.*

REQUESTING EXTENSION TO FILE (IRS)

Dear Sir:

I am hereby requesting an extension on filing my income tax return for the year (**1991/ 1992/other**).

Please send the appropriate forms and information to

(**Your name**)
(**Your address**)
(**City, state, zip code**)

Thank you for your assistance.

Sincerely,

DISPUTING AMOUNT OF REFUND (IRS)

Dear Sir:

I have just received your check in the amount of (**$ amount**), my refund on my (**1988/ 1989/1990/other**) taxes.

According to my records and the forms I submitted, the amount you owe me is (**$ amount**). I have rechecked my figures, and I still come up with this amount. If I have miscalculated, please let me know. If not, please send me a check for the additional amount you owe me: (**$ amount**).

---

* IRS regional office addresses are listed in "Information Please . . .," under Internal Revenue Service.

My tax return was submitted in my name, (**name**). My taxpayer identification number is (**Social Security number or other taypayer identification number**).

Thank you for your assistance with this matter.

Sincerely,

DISPUTING AMOUNT OF TAX DUE (IRS)

Dear Sir:

I have just received correspondence from you indicating that, on my (**1989/1990/1991/ other**) tax return, I owe you (**$ amount**). I am writing to dispute your claim that I owe this amount.

Your claim is in error because you have (**failed to credit taxes already withheld/failed to credit me with the correct number of dependents/other**).

Please make the necessary adjustments in your records and mail me my refund as soon as possible.

In addition to the (**copy of W-4 form/tax form indicating number of dependents/other**) that refutes your claim, I have enclosed the bottom half of the notice you sent, as requested. My taxpayer identification number is (**Social Security or other taxpayer identification number**).

Sincerely,

RESPONDING TO NOTIFICATION OF AUDIT (IRS)

Dear Sir:

I have received your notification that my (**1988/1989/other**) federal tax return is being audited.

As you requested, I have checked my records and enclosed the following items for your review:

    (**List items requested by IRS.**)

I hope these items will answer your questions. If not, please feel free to contact me at (**telephone number**). My taxpayer identifying number is (**Social Security or other taxpayer identification number**).

Sincerely,

REQUESTING INDEPENDENT REVIEW (IRS)

Dear Sir:

Your auditors have just completed their audit of my (**1988/1989/other**) federal tax return, taxpayer identification number (**Social Security or other taxpayer identification number**). They proposed the following change in my tax liabilities: (**insert proposed change**). I do not agree with this change and am therefore requesting an independent review of my case.

Please advise me as to the procedure I need to follow in order to obtain this review.

Thank you for your cooperation in this matter.

Sincerely,

CHALLENGING ASSESSMENT—REAL ESTATE

Dear (**name of property appraiser**):

My property at (**address**) was recently assessed at the appraisal value of (**$ amount**). After checking with the owners of some of the neighboring properties, I have discovered that this assessment is much higher than the assessment of other properties of comparable size and construction.

Therefore, I am hereby challenging this assessment and petitioning for a reassessment by a different appraiser.

Thank you for your prompt attention to this matter.

Sincerely,

PROTESTING INCREASE—FEDERAL TAXES

Dear (**Senator (or) Mr./Ms. for representative name**):

I am writing to protest the increase in (**cigarettes/gasoline/other**) taxes currently being considered by the (**Senate/House of Representatives**). (**State why you believe this increase is wrong or inequitable; e.g., those who smoke should not be penalized/those who must drive to get to work should not be penalized/other**).

Thank you for your attention to my views.

Sincerely,

PROTESTING INCREASE—STATE TAXES

Dear (**name of appropriate state official**):

I am writing to protest the recent increase in the state (**sales tax/income tax/other**). I believe this causes an undue hardship on a small segment of the population and that there are better ways to increase state revenues.

I realize that this increase has already been put into effect; however, this is a very unfair tax and I believe that it should be repealed in the very next session of the legislature.

Thank you for your attention to my concerns.

Sincerely,

Chapter 20

TRAVEL

Bereavement Travel
Private Vacation Rental
Guaranteeing a Reservation
Canceling a Reservation
Appreciation for Excellent Service
Reporting a Grievance
Passport Amendment—U.S. Passport Office
Inquiry: Visa Requirements
Inquiry: U.S. Customs
International Health Regulations
Medical Certification: Cruise Ship
Medical Clearance: International Air Carrier

A long-awaited reunion with an old friend, an emergency flight to support relatives in crisis, a family vacation by automobile, pursuit of a business lead in a distant city, a once-in-a-lifetime opportunity to sail to a romantic foreign port—regardless of the reason, destination, or method of transportation, thorough preparation is necessary if your journey is to be trouble-free.

Travelers to foreign countries should be familiar with health regulations, travel restrictions, customs, and laws of the area they are planning to visit. In addition, those with disabilities or health-related concerns should contact carriers, foreign offices of tourism, and travel agents to learn what services and accommodations are available to make their trip more enjoyable and what obstacles or restrictions, if any, they are likely to encounter along the way.

All travelers returning from abroad should be familiar with the guidelines established by U.S. Customs. Rules and regulations are clearly defined in numerous publications that are available through the various customs offices, offices of tourism, and travel agencies. Failure to comply could result in serious penalties and cast a pall upon an otherwise memorable adventure.*

BEREAVEMENT TRAVEL

Dear (name of airline customer service representative, corporate offices):

On (date) I traveled from (point of embarkation) to (destination) to attend the funeral of (relative). When I purchased my ticket, I was unaware of the special rates for bereavement travel. I understand the actual cost of the fare should have been ($ amount) rather than ($ amount), which I paid.

I have been advised that in order to obtain a credit refund, you require copies of the ticket and the obituary notice, both of which are enclosed.

I would appreciate receiving a travel credit in the amount of ($ amount—difference between two charges) to be applied to my next flight on (name of airline).

Thank you for your assistance and understanding.

Sincerely,

* For a listing of U.S. Customs and U.S. Passport services, see the appendix, "Information Please . . .," U.S. Customs Service and U.S. Passport Services.

PRIVATE VACATION RENTAL

Dear (**name of owner or rental agent**):

Pursuant to our telephone conversation on (**date**), I am enclosing (**my personal check/a cashier's check/a money order**) in the amount of (**$ amount**) to reserve (**type of accommodation**) at (**name of hotel/resort/other/location**) for (**specify exact days/dates you will arrive and depart**).

(**I/we**) will be (**arriving/checking in**) at approximately (**time**) on (**day/date**). Should our plans change unexpectedly, I will notify you in advance with a revised arrival date and time. I understand that if you are unable to comply with an alternate time, I am entitled to a refund of my deposit providing I notify you within (**amount of time granted by lessor**) of such a change.

Please send an acknowledgment of receipt of this deposit to my attention at the address above.

Thank you for your assistance. (**I/we**) (**am/are**) looking forward to (**my/our**) (**first visit/ return**) to (**hotel/resort/area**).

Sincerely,

GUARANTEEING A RESERVATION

Dear (**name of hotel/motel/inn/resort reservations representative or rental agent**):

I have reserved a (**type of accommodation**) for (**dates**), under the name of (**your name**), confirmation number (**#**).

I have just learned that my arrival will be delayed for several hours, and I do not anticipate checking in until (**revised time**).

I wish to guarantee the reservation with my personal (**credit card**), (**number**), expiration date of (**date**).

Please issue a revised confirmation to my attention at the address above.

Thank you for your prompt attention to this matter.

Sincerely,

CANCELING A RESERVATION

Dear (**name of hotel/motel/inn/resort reservations representative or rental agent**):

Due to (**briefly state reason**), I am forced to postpone my trip to (**city**) on (**day/date**) and must cancel my reservation at the (**name of hotel/inn/resort/other**). My confirmation number is (**number**).

Please issue a refund credit of (**$ amount**) for the reservation guarantee, which was charged to my (**credit card**), (**number**) on (**date reservation was made and guaranteed**).

Please forward a written verification of this cancellation and credit to my attention as soon as possible.

Thank you.

Sincerely,

APPRECIATION FOR EXCELLENT SERVICE

Dear (**name of guest host, manager**):

I would like to express my appreciation to you and your excellent staff for the kindness and consideration extended to me (**and my family**) during (**my/our**) recent stay at (**name of hotel/motel/inn/other**).

(**My/our**) arrival was delayed for several hours due to (**adverse weather conditions/ delayed flight/other**). Imagine (**my/our**) dismay when (**I/we**) learned (**my/our**) accommodations had been given to another party; yet within a very short time you arranged for (**me/us**) to occupy (**describe alternate accommodations**), at (**the same/less than the cost**) of the (**room/suite**) (**I/we**) had originally reserved.

Due to the lateness of the hour, (**I/we**) elected to "try (**my/our**) luck" once again and called for room service. The food was delivered promptly, served by a courteous attendant, and the fare was excellent!

Again, many thanks for going the extra mile for (**this/these**) weary traveler(s). You may be assured the (**name of hotel/motel/inn/other**) will be (**my/our**) first choice on (**my/our**) next visit to (**city**).

Sincerely,

NOTE: If appropriate, send a copy of this letter to the corporate headquarters of hotel/motel/ resort chain.

REPORTING A GRIEVANCE

Dear (**name of hotel/motel/inn/resort corporate marketing or operations official**):

On (**date**) I arranged to stay at (**name of hotel/inn/resort/other**), in (**city—include street address if more than one in the city**), from (**date**) to (**date**) to attend a (**business meeting/convention/festival/other**). Realizing that it would be difficult, if not impossible, to find a place to stay due to the large number of (**guests/visitors**) this event attracts, I made my reservation (**length of time**) prior to my arrival.

I specifically advised your (**reservation clerk/staff**) that I would require (**a single/ double room/suite/other**) and that I expected to arrive at (**time**). A few days later, on (**date**), I received the attached confirmation verifying my request.

However, when I did arrive I was informed that the accommodation I requested was not available, and I was assigned (**room/suite/other**) which offered none of the amenities I had previously requested.

As I suspected, I was unable to find a more suitable accommodation elsewhere and was forced to remain at the (**name of hotel/inn/resort/other**) for the duration of my stay.

Considering the circumstances, I believe I am justified in requesting a (**partial/total**) refund of the charges. I am attaching a copy of the final bill and look forward to hearing from you regarding this matter at your earliest convenience.

Sincerely,

NOTE: If applicable, send a copy to the corporate headquarters of hotel/motel/inn/other and/or to the corporate headquarters of organization you represent.

PASSPORT AMENDMENT—U.S. PASSPORT OFFICE

Dear (**name of passport representative**):

Due to my recent (**marriage/divorce/other**), I wish to amend my passport, originally issued (**month/year**), to reflect my correct name (**and other pertinent information, if necessary**).

Enclosed please find my passport, completed Form DSP-19, and a certified copy of (**marriage certificate/other legal document attesting to change**).

Please return the amended passport and enclosed documents to my attention at (**current address**).

Thank you for your assistance.

Sincerely,

NOTE: This letter should be sent to the nearest regional or local U.S. Passport office.

INQUIRY: VISA REQUIREMENTS

Dear (**name of representative**):

I wish to obtain a (**personal/student/business/other**) visa to visit (**city/province/country**) in (**month/year**). I plan to remain in (**country**) approximately (**length of anticipated stay**).

Please advise what documents I must submit to obtain a visa; what fees, if any, are required when entering or departing the country; and how long I must wait to travel to (**country**) once the visa has been approved.

Any additional information you can provide regarding travel restriction, health regulations, and customs pertaining to the area will be most helpful.

Thank you for your assistance.

Respectfully,

NOTE: This letter should be sent to the embassy, nearest consular office, or U.S. foreign-based office of tourism.

INQUIRY: U.S. CUSTOMS

Dear (**name of director/district director of customs**):

I am planning a trip to (**country or countries**) in (**month/year**) and would like to obtain a copy of your Publication No. 512 (Rev. 2/88), "Know Before You Go," and/or any other publications or information pertaining to customs restrictions and requirements for returning residents.

Thank you for your assistance.

Sincerely,

NOTE: This letter should be sent to the U.S. Customs Service, Washington, D.C., or the nearest regional office.

INTERNATIONAL HEALTH REGULATIONS

Dear (**name of superintendent**):

I plan to travel to several foreign countries in (**month/year**), and I am particularly interested in learning about immunization requirements and other health-related requirements and restrictions relative to these areas.

I would like to obtain a copy of "Health Information for International Travel", and I am enclosing (**check/money order**) in the amount of (**$ amount**) to cover the cost of this information.

Thank you for your assistance and prompt response.

Sincerely,

NOTE: This letter should be sent to Superintendent of Documents, U.S. Government Printing Office, Washington, D.C. At the time of publication, a copy of "Health Information for International Travel" could be obtained for a fee of $4.75; however, the price is subject to change. This publication may also be available through some local health care departments and physicians' offices.

MEDICAL CERTIFICATION: CRUISE SHIP

Dear (**name of travel agent**):

Enclosed please find a copy of (**name of physician**)'s statement certifying that my (**spouse/child/other**) is able to travel to (**destination**) aboard the (**name of vessel**), as required by (**name of cruise line**). Additional information pertaining to medications, as well as other medical data, will be made available to the ship's medical staff as soon as we board.

As we discussed earlier, we will require a stateroom with barrier-free access, located as close to the elevators and wheelchair ramps as possible.

If you have any questions or require additional information, please contact me at (**telephone number**).

Thank you for your efforts to make this trip a memorable one for (**name of passenger**).

Sincerely,

NOTE: A copy of this letter should be sent to the passenger's personal physician.

MEDICAL CLEARANCE: INTERNATIONAL AIR CARRIER

Dear (**name of medical officer, corporate headquarters of international carrier**):

I am planning to travel to (**city/country**) in (**month/year**), by way of (**airline**). I am confined to a (**hand-driven or battery-powered**) wheelchair as a result (**state nature and extent of disability**).

If a medical clearance is required by (**airline**), please send me an INCAD form at your earliest convenience.

Any additional information you can provide regarding special adaptive equipment, boarding assistance, or equipment storage and handling will be very helpful.

Thank you for your assistance.

Sincerely,

NOTE: If travel will involve more than one international carrier, travelers may request a permanent medical clearance card known as a FREMEC card, recognized by over 100 international air carriers of the International Air Transport Association.

Chapter 21

VETERANS AFFAIRS

Determination of Eligibility—Loan Guaranty Entitlement
Request for Duplicate Copy of Military Document
Request for Reclassification of Discharge
Employment: Federal Employment
Employment: Civil Service Preference
Notice of Disagreement
Beneficiary's Claim for Life Insurance Benefits
Requesting Government Reimbursement for Burial Monument
Educational Assistance for Dependents
Exchange and Commissary Privileges
Nonfee or Fee-Free Passport
Request for Information—MIA

The Department of Veterans Affairs is comprised of three divisions: the Veterans Health Services and Research Administration, the Veterans Benefits Administration, and the National Cemetery System. Collectively, they are responsible for the administration and management of 172 hospitals, 231 outpatient clinics, 117 nursing homes, 27 domiciliaries, and 112 national cemeteries. In addition, they provide financial compensation to disabled veterans, pensions for low-income veterans and survivors, educational assistance and vocational rehabilitation; operate the nation's fifth largest life insurance program; and have guaranteed in excess of 12 million home loans.

It is estimated that over 27 million veterans and 47 million dependents and survivors, or one in every three persons living in the United States, may be entitled to federal benefits.

If you have questions regarding your eligibility for VA-sponsored programs and benefits, contact the local Veterans Affairs office or regional Veterans Affairs office nearest you.*

DETERMINATION OF ELIGIBILITY— LOAN GUARANTY ENTITLEMENT

Dear (name of local Veterans Affairs Officer):

I am considering purchasing a home using my GI entitlement, and would like to receive a copy of VA form 26-1880, Request for Determination of Eligibility and Available Loan Guaranty Entitlement. I have never applied for a VA-guaranteed home loan.

I served in the (branch of service) from (date) until I was honorably discharged on (date), with the rank of (rank at time of discharge), (length of time) in excess of the 181 days of continuous active duty required to qualify for VA-guaranteed home loan. My service number is (number) and my Social Security number is (number).

Please forward the form to the address shown above. Thank you for your assistance and prompt response to this request.

Sincerely,

---

* A listing of national and regional addresses and telephone numbers is featured in the appendix, "Information Please . . .," Veterans Affairs. For local listings, check your telephone directory under U.S. government offices.

REQUEST FOR DUPLICATE COPY OF MILITARY DOCUMENT

Dear (**name of Personnel Records Center official**):

I am unable to locate the original of (**document**) that was issued (**date/event/time of separation from branch of service**). I would like to obtain a duplicate copy of this (**document/information**).

My full name is (**full name, including maiden name if married since enlistment**), and my (**service/Social Security**) number is (**number**). I served in the (**branch of service**) for (**length of time**), from (**date**) until (**date**). My legal signature is affixed below.

I appreciate your assistance in obtaining this (**document/information**) as soon as possible as I need it to (**apply for education benefits/obtain job preference consideration/special benefits/other**).

Sincerely,

REQUEST FOR RECLASSIFICATION OF DISCHARGE

Gentlemen:

In (**month/year**) I (**separated/was involuntarily separated**) from (**branch of service**) with a (**classification**) discharge. I feel the official reasons cited for this action and the subsequent discharge classification do not accurately reflect the circumstances in this situation.

I am submitting herewith the Department of Defense form (**DD-293/DD-149**) requesting a review and possible reclassification from (**current classification**) to Honorable. My (**service/Social Security**) number is (**number**).

If you have any questions or require additional information, please contact me at the address on the form or by telephone at (**number**).

Thank you for your time and consideration.

Sincerely,

NOTE: This request should be addressed to the appropriate discharge review board for the applicable branch of service. If more than 15 years have elapsed since discharge, the veteran, or those appealing the classification, should use form DD-149; if fewer than 15 years have elapsed, use form DD-293.

EMPLOYMENT: FEDERAL GOVERNMENT

Gentlemen:

As a (**veteran/spouse/widow/widower/mother of permanently and totally service connected disabled veteran**), I understand I may be entitled to certain employment considerations under the Vietnam Era Veterans Readjustment Assistance Act of 1974. (**I/ my husband/my wife/son/daughter**) served with the (**branch of service**) in the Vietnam conflict from (**date**) to (**date**) preceding (**his/her death**) (**my/his/her separation from service with a service connected disability**) in (**month/year**). (**My/his/her**) (**service/ Social Security**) number is (**number**).

I would appreciate receiving any information you can provide regarding employment benefits and job opportunities with the federal government in (**area/state**) where (**I/we**) currently reside.

Sincerely,

NOTE: This letter should be sent to U.S. Office of Personnel Management, Federal Job Information Center.

EMPLOYMENT: CIVIL SERVICE PREFERENCE

Dear (**name of local Veterans Affairs officer**):

I have recently retired from active duty with the (**branch of service**) and have applied to (**name of business or organization**) to work as a (**position**).

The personnel department indicated it would be to my advantage to provide a Civil Service Preference Certificate, which would be included with my application, and could possibly result in a faster response to my interest in employment with them.

Please advise how I may obtain this certificate as quickly as possible. Any forms or printed materials should be sent to my attention at the address shown above.

Thank you for your prompt response to this inquiry.

Sincerely,

NOTICE OF DISAGREEMENT

Dear (**name of VA regional office representative**):

I have received your notification of (**date issued**), copy enclosed, advising me that my claim, submitted on (**date**), for (**compensation/pension benefits/education benefits/ waiver of recovery of overpayment/reimbursement of unauthorized medical services/ other**) has been denied. I am convinced the claim is a valid one based upon (**verifiable dates of service/information contained in military medical records/other**). I am, therefore, requesting an appellate review of this matter and full disclosure of the reasons for my denial from the Department of Veterans Affairs office. My (**service/Social Security**) number is (**number**).

I understand I will need to file a Substantive Appeal within 60 days after receipt of their Statement of the Case, or within one year of the date of your denial in order to complete the appeal process.

Please direct this matter to the attention of the individual or department responsible for initiating the review I am requesting.

Sincerely,

BENEFICIARY'S CLAIM FOR LIFE INSURANCE BENEFITS

Gentlemen:

As the designated beneficiary of (**name of husband/wife/son/daughter/other**)'s National Service Life Insurance Policy, I am advising you of (**his/her**) recent demise on (**date**) and am requesting your assistance in obtaining the benefits provided under policy (**number**). (**His/her**) date of birth was (**date**), and (**his/her service/Social Security number**) was (**number**).

Enclosed is a certified copy of the death certificate issued by (**name of individual/title/ area/location**). Please advise if you require additional information, or forward any forms needed to complete this claim.

Thank you for your assistance and prompt response.

Sincerely,

NOTE: This letter should be sent to VA Regional Office/Insurance Center St. Paul, MN, or Philadelphia, PA.

REQUESTING GOVERNMENT REIMBURSEMENT FOR BURIAL MONUMENT

Dear (**name of director**):

My (**father/husband/son/daughter/other**), (**full name of deceased**), passed away on (**date**) and was interred at (**name of cemetery**) in (**city and state**). (**He/she**) served in (**branch of service**) from (**date**) until (**he/she**) was honorably discharged on (**date of separation**). (**His/her service/Social Security number**) was (**number**).

A marker for the gravesite was purchased from (**name of company**), at a cost of (**$ amount**). I understand that I am entitled to reimbursement based upon the average cost for a government monument and may apply for reimbursement by completing VA Form 21-8834, Application for Reimbursement of Headstone or Marker Expense.

Please send this form to my attention at the address shown above. Upon receipt, I will complete it and attach the invoice.

Thank you for your assistance.

Sincerely,

NOTE: This letter should be sent to the nearest VA regional office.

EDUCATIONAL ASSISTANCE FOR DEPENDENTS

Dear (**name of Veterans Affairs officer**):

I am interested in obtaining any information you can provide regarding educational assistance for dependents of personnel who (**have been designated missing in action/ were killed in action during (specific) campaign or conflict/died as a result of service related causes/other**).

My (**son/daughter/other relative of whom you are the legal guardian**) will graduate from high school (**month/year**) and plans to enter (**vocational/technical/college**) in (**month/year**) as a (**full-time/part-time**) student. (**His/her**) (**parent/guardian/other**), (**rank/name**), served in (**branch of service**) in (**area/location**) from (**date**) until (**he/she**) was (**officially declared missing in action/passed away**) on (**date**). (**His/her service/ Social Security number**) was (**number**).

Thank you for your assistance in this matter.

Sincerely,

NOTE: This letter should be sent to the nearest VA regional office.

EXCHANGE AND COMMISSARY PRIVILEGES

Dear (**name of director**):

I have been informed that as the widow of a veteran who died as a result of complications from a service connected disability during the (**conflict**) I may be entitled to exchange and commissary privileges.

I would appreciate your sending me DD Form 1172, Application for Uniformed Services Identification and Privilege Card, at your earliest convenience.

Thank you for your assistance.

Sincerely,

NOTE: This letter should be sent to the nearest VA regional office.

NONFEE OR FEE-FREE PASSPORT

Gentlemen:

In (**month/year**) my (**father/brother/son/daughter**) was killed in action while serving in the (**branch of service**) with the (**unit**) in (**location**) and was interred at (**name of American military cemetery**). (**His/her service/Social Security number**) is (**number**).

I plan to travel to (**location**) in (**month/year**) to visit this site. I understand that as (**his/her**) next of kin I may be eligible to apply for a nonfee or fee-free passport for this purpose.

I would appreciate any information you can provide regarding the correct procedure to apply for this document.

Thank you for your attention and prompt response to my inquiry.

Sincerely,

NOTE: This letter should be sent to the American Battle Monuments Commission.

REQUEST FOR INFORMATION—MIA

Gentlemen:

My (**father/son/other**), (**rank, full name, service number**), was declared missing in action while serving with the (**branch of service, unit, location**) in (**month/year**). I would like to contact anyone who knew him personally or served with his unit during that time. (**His/her service/Social Security number**) was (**number**).

Any information you have regarding veterans' activities or reunions for this group would be greatly appreciated.

Please contact me with any suggestions of information at the above address or by telephone at (**number**).

Sincerely,

NOTE: This letter should be sent to U.S. Department of Veterans Affairs, Washington, D.C.

Part II

Personal Letters

HOW TO WRITE PERSONAL LETTERS THAT CONVEY YOUR MESSAGE

The model letters featured in Part II represent a variety of occasions and opportunities to communicate with family, friends, acquaintances, and, occasionally, adversaries.

Unlike the structured guidelines of the business letter, which offer a degree of anonymity to the writer as well as the recipient, the personal letter allows the writer to rely upon his or her opinions, emotions, and convictions to persuade, console, refute, and request so as to obtain the results he or she desires.

This creative latitude does not, however, absolve the writer of responsibility toward his or her reader. Quite the contrary. Special care should be taken to ensure a precise balance between what the writer wishes to convey and the recipient's actual interpretation of the message. The consequences of a poorly constructed message and a misinterpretation can, at best, be an unfavorable response, and the worst possible scenario, a lifetime of misunderstanding.

The letters that follow are designed to offer you, the writer, a broad selection of appropriate messages for all occasions. Whether you choose to use them as they are written or as a guide to create your own, letters are your personal gifts to others, to be cherished, ignored, discarded, but seldom forgotten.

The best of all personal messages are those written and received without regrets.

STYLING AND FORMATTING THE PERSONAL LETTER

In this age of high-tech communications, there is still no substitute for a handwritten personal letter. Whether expressing sympathy, offering congratulations, or simply saying "thank you," a handwritten letter on carefully selected stationery lets your recipient know that you care.

For handwritten notes (see handwritten sample), a more informal format is not only acceptable, it is recommended. Use the following "rules of thumb" when writing a personal note:

1. Unless using preprinted stationery, omit your return address and the recipient's inside address.
2. Always include the date, so your recipient will know when you wrote the letter.
3. Use your recipient's first name in the salutation (greeting).
4. Place a comma after the salutation (greeting).
5. Indent the first line of each paragraph.
6. Use an appropriate, informal complimentary close (closing), for example, Fondly, Love, Affectionately.

Occasionally, it is appropriate to type a personal letter (see typed sample). These letters, although personal, lend themselves to a more formal style. Therefore they have been set up for you in accordance with the rules for full-block style (like the letters in Part I). In addition, we recommend that, if you are looking for a reply to your personal correspondence, keep a copy for your personal file.

SAMPLE OF HANDWRITTEN LETTER

June 16, 1991

Dear Vickie,

Congratulations on opening your own business! I know it has long been a dream of yours to have your own antique shop, and now, you have made your dream a reality. How proud and happy you must be!!

I'll be coming by your shop to celebrate your grand opening, and look forward to congratulating you in person then.

Love,

Anne

SAMPLE OF TYPED LETTER

2347 Fairfield Drive
Your Town, CA 23490

May 24, 1990

George S. Employer
Summerwork Electronics Corporation
2351 Alameda Boulevard
Any Town, CA 23490

Dear George,

I am writing this letter for a young friend of mine, Sally Teenager. Sally is a high school student who has been one of our main child sitters for the past two years. The school year will be over soon, and she is looking for a summer job.

Sally is one of the most responsible young people I have ever met. When she is caring for our son, Douglas, I never worry because I know that Sally can handle any situation that may arise. She is mature beyond her 16 years as well as warm-hearted and outgoing. In addition, she has had some experience working in a yogurt shop and doing volunteer work for a church secretary.

I know that during the summer you sometimes need extra help in your firm. I would appreciate it if you would take the time to talk with Sally. She will be calling you soon to set up an appointment.

Thank you for considering the possibility of hiring her. If you need additional information from me, please do not hesitate to call: 943-5551.

Sincerely,

Anne R. Hagler

Chapter 22

ACKNOWLEDGMENTS

Your Gift Arrived
Received Your Payment
Received Information You Promised
Met Your Friend

Letters of acknowledgment let the recipient know that something that was supposed to happen did indeed occur. The letters in this chapter provide just a few samples of occasions when an acknowledgment letter would be appropriate and helpful. This type of letter is not a full-fledged "thank you," but it is a way of telling the recipient that whatever he or she intended did in fact happen.

YOUR GIFT ARRIVED

Dear (**name**),

I knew you would want to know right away that your lovely gift arrived safely. The (**describe gift**) is (**beautiful/just what I/we needed/other**). How thoughtful of you to remember (**my/our**) (**anniversary/birthday/graduation/other**) in such a special way!

Fondly,

RECEIVED YOUR PAYMENT

Dear (**name**),

I received your check in today's mail and wanted to thank you for repaying your loan so quickly. I hope you know that I was happy to help you out and would be glad to do so again if you ever need it.

Fondly,

RECEIVED INFORMATION YOU PROMISED

Dear (**name**),

Thank you very much for sending me the (**college catalog/source of inexpensive camping gear/other**). As an (**alumna/alumnus/avid camper/other**), I knew you would be a good person to ask about (**college admissions procedures/sources of inexpensive camping equipment/other**). As I mentioned when we talked, this information will enable me to (**help my young friend/take a vacation next summer/other**).

Thank you for taking the time to find and mail the information.

Sincerely,

MET YOUR FRIEND

Dear (name),

I wanted you to know what a pleasure it was to meet your friend, (name of friend), while I was (where you met the friend). Thank you very much for giving me (his/her) name and number. We (describe what you did together). I enjoyed being with (name of friend) and can understand why the two of you are such good friends—you are both nice people!

Sincerely,

Chapter 23

ANNOUNCEMENTS

Birth or Adoption
Graduation of Son/Daughter
Engagement
Wedding of Son/Daughter
Class Reunion
Humanitarian Event
Seeking Volunteers
Moved to New Location
New Associate/Employee
Forming Special Interest Group/Club

Personal announcements proclaim events or accomplishments you would be likely to share with family, friends, and colleagues: an invitation to witness a marriage, a religious ceremony, the birth or adoption of a child, graduation from college, or a solicitation to work with you toward the attainment of a common goal. The letters featured in this chapter offer a variety of appropriate messages for all those special occasions you wish to share with those who mean the most to you.

BIRTH OR ADOPTION

Mr. and Mrs. (**parents**) announce, with joy and pride, the (**birth/adoption**) of their (**son/daughter**), (**name**).

(**He/she**) was (**born/given**) into the loving care of (**his/her**) parents, and (**brothers/sisters**), (**names of siblings**), on (**day/date**).

Family and friends are invited to a celebration of the occasion at the home of (**name of child**)'s (**grandparents/godparents/other**), (**names**), (**address**), on (**day/date**) from (**time**) until (**time**).

GRADUATION OF SON/DAUGHTER

Dear (**name**):

(**Spouse**) and I are throwing a "bash" on the (**date**) to celebrate (**son/daughter**)'s graduation from (**high school/college**). Family and friends are invited for (**event**) at our home beginning at (**time**).

We are so proud of (**him/her**), and delighted (**he/she**) (**has been accepted/has accepted**) at (**college/a position with (company/corporation/organization**)) in (**location**). It is what (**he/she**) has worked so hard for.

See you (**day**) evening!

Sincerely,

ENGAGEMENT

Mr. and Mrs. (**parents of the bride**) and Mr. and Mrs. (**parents of the groom**) are pleased to announce the engagement of their daughter, (**bride's name**), and son, (**groom's name**).

Families and friends of the couple are invited to a celebration of the occasion at a (**formal/informal**) (**event**) at (**location**) on (**day/date**) at (**time**).

Please respond with acceptance or regrets to (**friend/relative**) at (**telephone number**) by (**date**).

WEDDING OF SON/DAUGHTER

Dear (**name**),

We are pleased to announce to all of our friends the recent marriage, on (**date**), of our (**son/daughter**), (**name**), to (**name of bride or groom**) of (**city/state**).

(**Son/daughter**) and (**bride/groom**) will arrive on (**date**) for a visit, and we look forward to introducing you to our new (**son-in-law/daughter-in-law**).

Please join us for an informal gathering of family and friends at (**location**) on (**day/date**) at (**time**).

Sincerely,

CLASS REUNION

Dear Alumni,

The (**name of school**) graduating class of (**year**) will hold its (**number**) reunion on (**day/date**). In order to turn back the clock and recapture the magical night of our Senior Prom, we need your help.

We are asking everyone to submit photographs from (**year**) and other memorabilia which will be on display in the lobby and returned to you at the close of the evening. We are also enclosing a roster of our classmates and ask that you help in locating those whose addresses are not indicated beside their names.

Please take a few minutes and complete the brief questionnaire and return it with your photos and any information you can provide about other classmates to our function coordinator, (**name**), at (**address**), no later than (**date**).

Formal invitations will be mailed (**approximate date**). Please contact (**function coordinator**) if you fail to receive yours by (**deadline**).

So, mark your calendar, and plan to bring your best girl or guy to your second "Senior Prom."

Sincerely,

HUMANITARIAN EVENT

Dear Friends,

On (**day/date**) the (**faculty and students/staff**) of (**name of school/company**) will sponsor a (**event**) to benefit the family of (**teacher/fellow student/co-worker**).

As you probably know (**name**) was (**seriously injured in an automobile accident/ hospitalized with serious illness**) on (**date**). (**His/her**) (**recovery/rehabilitation**) is expected to be a lengthy and expensive process, and it will probably be several (**weeks/ months**) before (**name**) will be able to return to (**his/her**) friends here at (**name of school/ company**).

All proceeds from this event will be donated to the (**name of teacher/student/co-worker**) Fund, administered by (**name of trustee or financial institution**), to help defray the cost of (**his/her**) medical care.

Activities will take place at (**location**) to accommodate the expected turnout. In the event of inclement weather, it will be held at (**alternate location**).

Please contact (**function coordinator**), (**telephone number**), who has graciously volunteered to answer any questions or to accept donations for the (**name**) family.

We are counting on you!

The (**faculty and students/staff**) of (**name of school/company**)

SEEKING VOLUNTEERS

Dear Club Members,

The (**organization**) has issued an urgent request for volunteers whom they can call upon should a (**natural disaster/emergency situation**) threaten our immediate area.

As you are all aware, (**area**) is particularly vulnerable to (**nature of frequent or possible emergencies**). With such a large number of (**elderly citizens/students/other**) (**residing in health care facilities/dormitories/other**), emergency evacuation to safer locations can be a problem without the help of people like you.

There is a critical need for volunteers trained in (**transportation services/first aid/possessing a medical background/other**) who would be willing to (**transport/staff evacuation centers/dispense food and bedding**).

If you are willing to work under impossible conditions, without pay, but with the heartfelt gratitude of those in need, please contact (**name and title**) at (**telephone number**) as soon as possible.

Thank you for caring.

MOVED TO NEW LOCATION

Dear (name of patron):

The (organization) is proud to announce the opening of its new (type of facility) at (location).

You are cordially invited to a grand opening reception at the (center/facility/other) on (day/date) beginning at (time).

Volunteers will be on hand to provide tours and explain the many new and exciting innovations made possible by your efforts and generosity. Refreshments will be served in the (specific area) throughout the evening.

Come and help us celebrate the culmination of (number) years of planning and hard work.

Sincerely,

NEW ASSOCIATE/EMPLOYEE

Dear (name),

(Partner) and I are pleased to announce the appointment of a new associate, (name), to (company/firm). We are looking forward to introducing (him/her) to our friends and colleagues and hope that you and (spouse/guest) will join us at a reception at (location) on (day/date) at (time).

(Name of new associate) is a very (personable/charming) young (man/woman), and we are confident (he/she) will soon establish (himself/herself) as an invaluable asset to the (company/firm) and the community.

Please join us in making (name) feel welcome.

Kind regards,

FORMING SPECIAL INTEREST GROUP/CLUB

Dear (name),

(Name) has told me of your interest in (hobby/special interest) and has asked that I contact you with information about a new group we would like to establish for (participants) throughout the area.

We plan to meet at **(location)** on **(scheduled times)** to discuss our work, exchange ideas on how to improve marketing techniques, and offer encouragement and support to one another. We also hope to secure guest speakers who would be willing to share their success stories and offer suggestions and advice.

Our first meeting will be held **(day/date)** at **(location)** beginning at **(time)**. Refreshments will be available, and we anticipate **(number)** guests to attend.

Please come and share your ideas.

Sincerely,

Chapter 24

APOLOGIES

Forgot Special Occasion
Overlooked Anniversary of Employment
Sorry I Haven't Written
Impulsive Statement
Defusing an Unpleasant Situation
Unseemly Behavior of Guest
Withdrawing from a Voluntary Commitment
Unable to Attend a Function
Late Payment
Bounced Check
Failure to Supply Information
Damage to Property

Personal apologies are intended to correct oversights, repair unintentional damage, defuse volatile situations, and reclaim words spoken in anger and are almost always prompted by circumstances we wish had never occurred. Even though we may attempt to convince ourselves such incidents will be forgotten, they niggle our conscience and linger for months, years, even a lifetime.

An expression of regret that begins "I apologize, but . . ." is instantly stripped of its validity. If your sincere and forthright apology is refused, do not belabor the point. The anticipated outcome is no reason to delay. The passage of time will not guarantee a favorable response nor lessen accountability on your part.

FORGOT SPECIAL OCCASION

Dear (name),

How could I have forgotten your (birthday/anniversary)! You can't imagine how embarrassed I was to discover the day had slipped past and I had failed to send a card or call you. You *must* let me make it up to you.

Are you free for lunch on (day)? There is an excellent restaurant on (street address) that features (special item), which, if I recall, is your favorite.

I will call you on (day) to confirm a time. I hope there will be no conflict with another commitment. I look forward to seeing you soon.

Affectionately,

OVERLOOKED ANNIVERSARY OF EMPLOYMENT

Dear (name),

Imagine (my/our) dismay when (I/we) realized (I/we) had overlooked your (anniversary) here at (company/club/school) on (date). The oversight was not intentional, (I/we) assure you.

In fact, (I/we) have been so impressed with your work and dedication to team effort, it seems you have been with us much longer than (number) (year(s)).

Please accept (my/our) belated good wishes and sincere thanks for a super job. (I/we) are glad to have you on board and count you as a good friend.

Best regards,

SORRY I HAVEN'T WRITTEN

Dear (**name**),

Please forgive me for not writing sooner to thank you for your gracious hospitality when I visited (**town/city**). My intentions were the best, but circumstances refused to cooperate. Things have been so hectic since I arrived back in (**town/city**).

I will be leaving for (**town/city**) within the week and promise a long letter when I return, but I just could not let any more time go by without a note to say how wonderful it was to be with my very dear friend(**s**) again.

Keep in touch, and I will do the same.

Affectionately,

IMPULSIVE STATEMENT

Dear (**name**),

Please accept my apology for the inappropriate remarks I made at the meeting on (**day or date**).

As you suggested, I looked into the situation further, and discovered I was indeed in error, and your observations were correct.

I will, of course, amend my statements to the other members at our next meeting. I hope we can put this unfortunate incident behind us and work together for the good of the organization and those who depend on us for leadership.

My sincere thanks for your understanding.

Best regards,

DEFUSING AN UNPLEASANT SITUATION

Dear (**name**),

For the past several (**days/weeks/months**) we have continued to disagree regarding information I was certain I had forwarded to you, and you were equally convinced I had not. It now appears you were right all along, and I am enclosing (**document**), with my apologies.

If you require additional information, feel free to contact me with the assurance of my full cooperation.

Respectfully,

UNSEEMLY BEHAVIOR OF GUEST

Dear (name(s)),

(Name of other person sharing your message) and I hope you will accept our apology for the unfortunate incident that occurred at our (home/party) last (day) evening.

We felt the remarks made by (name of individual) were most inappropriate and do not reflect our (beliefs/opinion).

We regret any embarrassment it may have caused you and assure you it will not occur again.

We are having a small get-together on the (date), beginning at (time), and look forward to sharing a pleasant evening with you.

Sincerely,

WITHDRAWING FROM A VOLUNTARY COMMITMENT

Dear (name),

I regret to inform you that I must withdraw from the (type) committee for the (organization/event).

An unexpected personal situation requires my full attention at this time, and I must ask you to find someone else to assume my duties. I apologize for this inconvenience and appreciate your understanding.

I am sure the (event) will be an outstanding success under your expert guidance, and I look forward to working with you again next year.

Sincerely,

UNABLE TO ATTEND A FUNCTION

Dear (name),

Thank you for the kind invitation to your (number) anniversary party on (day), (date). Unfortunately, due to another commitment, we will be unable to attend. We regret the conflict in scheduling, but look forward to celebrating with you next year.

Congratulations on reaching this impressive milestone. We wish you (joy/happiness/success/good fortune) in the year ahead.

Fondly,

LATE PAYMENT

Dear (name),

Enclosed please find my (personal check/money order), in the amount of (amount), to cover the cost of my membership fee for the month of (month and year).

I apologize for the delay in getting this to you. However, I was unexpectedly called out of town on a (business/personal) matter and returned to (city/area) only yesterday.

I will be sending my next payment on (date).

Thank you for your (patience/understanding).

Sincerely,

BOUNCED CHECK

Dear (name),

Thank you for contacting me so promptly concerning the payment for (service/item/fees). I apologize for any inconvenience my (carelessness/oversight) may have caused.

I am enclosing a (money order/cashier's check) to cover the cost of (service/item/fee) plus an additional (amount) overdraft fee. Also, for your convenience, I am enclosing a self-addressed stamped envelope for the return of the original check.

Again, my thanks and apologies. I assure you it will not happen again.

Sincerely,

FAILURE TO SUPPLY INFORMATION

Dear (**name**),

Enclosed please find a copy of (**requested document**) that I promised to send to you several (**days/weeks/months**) ago. I apologize for the (**delay/oversight**) and hope it has not caused you any inconvenience.

If you need additional information, or have any questions regarding (**situation relating to document being forwarded**), please telephone me at (**number**) for clarification. I will call in a few days to make certain you received this material.

Again, my apologies. I promise to do better next time.

Sincerely,

DAMAGE TO PROPERTY

Dear (**name**),

I feel very bad about the damage to (**item**). You were very kind to say it was only an accident, but I will not be satisfied until it is returned to its original condition.

I have taken the liberty of contacting (**repairperson/company**) and have asked them to telephone you to arrange a time they may come by and obtain an estimate for repairs. With your permission, they will begin work as soon as it is convenient for you.

Sincerely,

Chapter 25

CHILDREN

Like most adults, children also enjoy receiving mail. The letters in this chapter reflect a wide variety of situations that might offer you the opportunity to write to a child. Letters to children under the age of nine should be printed or typed since children are not usually comfortable reading cursive writing until at least third grade.

INVITATION FOR A HOLIDAY VISIT

Dear (name of child),

It's been such a long time since we've seen you, and (name of your child) really misses you! (He/she) and I were talking about you the other day, and (name of your child) suggested that you come to visit us for the (name of holiday) holidays. Do you think you could come? We would love to have you with us.

Please talk with your folks about our invitation, and write and let us know what you think.

We're hoping to see you soon!

Affectionately,

INVITATION TO ACCOMPANY SON/DAUGHTER ON FAMILY VACATION

Dear (name of child),

We will be going to (destination) for our vacation this (summer/winter/spring/fall). (Name of child) has asked if you could come with us, and we would love to have you. We will be leaving on (date) and returning (date).

Talk the idea over with your folks, and let us know if you can come, so we can include you in our plans.

We are looking forward to hearing from you soon.

Affectionately,

ENJOYED YOUR VISIT

Dear (name of child),

It was wonderful to have you with us for the (name of holiday) holidays! We hope you enjoyed being with us as much as we enjoyed being with you. (Name of child) especially liked having you here. We hope you can come back again soon.

Affectionately,

HAPPY BIRTHDAY

Dear (name of child),

I looked at my birthday calendar and realized that your birthday is coming up soon. Birthdays are very special, and we wanted to be a part of your celebration by wishing you a super day and a wonderful year ahead. We'll be thinking of you especially on (date of child's birthday).

Affectionately,

THANK YOU FOR YOUR THOUGHTFULNESS

Dear (name of child),

It was so good of you to remember (name of person and/or occasion)! What a thoughtful person you are! It really meant a lot to (him/her) to hear from you on this special day. (Name of occasion) is an important event in a person's life, and we are grateful that you wanted to be a part of (his/her) celebration. (Name of person) shared your (card/letter) with us)—it reminds us of what a good friend you are. (He/she) will be (writing/calling) you soon to thank you (himself/herself) and to tell you all about (his/her) (name of occasion).

Affectionately,

GOOD FOR YOU!

Dear (name of child)

Your (Aunt Susan/Uncle Joe/grandparents/other) sent us the (newspaper/other announcement) about your (type of accomplishment). What an accomplishment! I know it took a lot of time and effort to get this kind of recognition. Hurray for you! We wish we could have been there to see you do your (type of accomplishment).

Keep up the good work!

Affectionately,

SYMPATHY—LOSS OF PET

Dear (name of child),

How sad we were to hear about the death of your (kind of animal), (name of pet). This must be a tough time for you, and we wanted you to know that you are in our thoughts. Remember all the good times you and (name of pet) shared, and let those memories bring you joy in the midst of your sadness. (Name of pet) was a wonderful (kind of animal), and we believe that if there is a heaven for (kind of animal), (name of pet) is surely there.

Please let us know if we can do anything to help you through this difficult time.

Affectionately,

RELIGIOUS OCCASION

Dear (name of child),

We are writing to congratulate you on your (confirmation/baptism/bar mitzvah/bat mitzvah). We know that this is both a solemn and joyous occasion—a real milestone in your religious growth. Even though we could not be there to celebrate with you, we wanted you to know how proud we are of your dedication and accomplishment. May you always remember this day as one of the most important in your life.

Affectionately,

Chapter 26

CLERGY

A minister, priest, or rabbi can play a significant role in a person's life. In these stressful times, he or she can provide a personal reference, give comfort, or perform a particularly meaningful service.

The letters in this chapter cover a variety of situations when you may want to share your feelings or put your request in writing.*

WELCOMING NEW SPIRITUAL LEADER TO COMMUNITY

Dear   :

Welcome to (**name of community**)! We are looking forward to making you a part of our congregational family. I know it is not always easy to get acclimated to a new community. Please know that my family and I will be happy to help in any way we can. We have lived here many years and are familiar with names of good doctors, the best places to shop, and so on. After you have had a chance to get settled in, we plan to invite you and your family for dinner.

Our thoughts and prayers are with you and your family.

Sincerely,

APPRECIATION FOR BEAUTIFUL CEREMONY

Dear   :

Thank you for helping to make my (**daughter's/son's**) wedding ceremony such a beautiful one. From beginning to end, the service ran smoothly. In addition, your special words to my (**daughter/son**) and (**son/daughter**)-in-law and the selections you chose to read made the service a memorable one for all those in attendance.

I truly appreciate your time and dedication.

Sincerely,

* See Forms of Address in the appendix for proper salutation.

APPRECIATION FOR INSPIRING SERMON/MESSAGE

Dear   :

Thank you for your inspiring sermon last Sunday. You preached a message that I really needed to hear, and your words have lingered with me throughout the week. Your sermon gave me the sustenance I needed in order to carry me through my weekly activities. I know that it must not be easy to write meaningful weekly sermons, and I am grateful for your time and careful preparation.

Sincerely,

APPRECIATION FOR COMFORT IN TIME OF SORROW

Dear   :

I want to thank you for your comfort and support at the time of my (**occasion of grief**). Your prayers and kind words helped me to cope with my sadness and loss. I honestly don't know how I would have made it through the past few weeks without you. You were there for me, and I am deeply grateful.

Sincerely,

APPRECIATION FOR EXCELLENT HOLIDAY PROGRAM

Dear   :

I wanted to let you know how much I appreciated the special programs you provided during the (**name of season**) season. I found the (**type of service**) service particularly meaningful. That service helped me to (**describe your reaction to the service**). Thank you for making the (**name of season**) season so meaningful for me.

Sincerely,

REQUESTING PERSONAL CHARACTER REFERENCE

Dear   :

I am currently seeking employment and would appreciate your giving me a character reference. I have been a member of (**name of church**) for (**number**) years and have been involved in the following programs and activities: (**list programs and activities**).

It would be helpful if you would write the letter "To Whom It May Concern" so that I can use the reference for any job I apply for.

Thank you for your assistance.

Sincerely,

REQUESTING GUEST SPEAKER

Dear   :

I belong to (**name of club/organization**). On behalf of the officers of our (**club/organization**), I am cordially inviting you to be the speaker at our meeting on (**date**) at (**time**). We are interested in hearing you talk about (**topic, or list possible topics**). If you are willing to accept this invitation, please call me at (**number**). If you are unable to come, can you suggest someone else who would be a good speaker on the (**topic(s)**) listed? Or, perhaps you could come at another time.

I look forward to hearing from you and thank you for considering our invitation.

Sincerely,

REQUESTING COUNSELING

Dear   :

I am having some personal problems and believe that pastoral counseling would be helpful. Would you be willing to see me to discuss these problems? If so, please call me at (**number**) so we can set up a mutually convenient time. If you cannot see me, would you recommend another minister who might be willing to spend time with me?

Thank you for your assistance. I would appreciate hearing from you as soon as possible.

Sincerely,

VOLUNTEERING FOR A SPECIAL PROGRAM OR COMMITTEE

Dear (**name of committee or program chairperson**):

I would appreciate the opportunity to serve on the (**name of committee or program**). I believe that my concerns and skills will enable me to make a valuable contribution to the work and goals of this (**committee/program**). Please let me know if you can use me.

Thank you.

Sincerely,

OFFERING PLEDGE OR DONATION TO SPECIAL FUND

Dear   :

I am writing to offer a (**pledge/donation**) to the (**name of fund**) Fund at (**name of church**). I strongly believe in the goals of this project and want to contribute (**$ amount**) toward the attainment of those goals. I would like to pay my (**pledge/donation**) in monthly installments of (**$ amount**). Please let me know how to make out my checks so that the money will go to the correct fund.

Sincerely,

Chapter 27

COMPUTERS

Remove My Name from Your Mailing List
Unwanted Merchandise
Billed in Error
Bill Already Paid
Is Anyone Out There?

In this computer age, you have no doubt encountered the problem of trying to get past the computer to the person running it. Somehow you must get the attention of a real person before you can begin to get your problem resolved. The letters in this chapter are designed to assist you in doing just that. Adapt the problems you have encountered to fit the approach and style of these letters, and you will improve your chances of getting the results you want.

REMOVE MY NAME FROM YOUR MAILING LIST

Dear Sir:

Your computer has somehow put my name on your mailing list and I want it removed. The literature that you have been sending is of no interest to me. I have attached one of your mailing labels so that there will be no question of which address to remove.

(Tape, glue, or staple address label here.)

Thank you for your prompt attention to this matter.

Sincerely,

UNWANTED MERCHANDISE

Dear Computer:

YOU ARE HEREBY INSTRUCTED TO TAKE THIS LETTER TO YOUR HUMAN!

Dear Human:

Your computer has been programmed in ERRORinERRORinERRORinERROR. It has sent me (**describe merchandise**) that I (1) did not order, (2) do not want, and (3) cannot use. This matter must be corrected immediately. FIX YOUR COMPUTER! The address label from the package is enclosed to help you track down your error.

I will return the merchandise upon receipt of your payment for return postage in the amount of (**$ amount**) or will ship merchandise C.O.D. as you direct.

Please respond immediately as I do not have room to store (**this/these**) item(s) for you. After two (2) weeks, I will be forced to dispose of (**it/them**).

Thank you for your prompt attention to this matter.

Sincerely,

BILLED IN ERROR

Dear Computer:

You have a major error in your program. You have billed me for merchandise that I (1) did not purchase, (2) did not receive, (3) do not have, and (4) do not want. You must contact your programmer immediately and have your program corrected. The incorrect billing that you have sent me must be erased from your memory. I have enclosed the bill so that your programmer will know which bill to erase.

Please send me a letter confirming that your error has been corrected.

Sincerely,

BILL ALREADY PAID

Dear Computer:

Please contact your data entry clerk. You have billed me (**$ amount of bill**), an amount that I have already paid. Your clerk must enter that fact at once. My canceled check (copy enclosed) has been returned to me by my bank proving that you received and cashed it.

You have my account listed as follows:

(Name on account)
Account number (**your account number**)
My check number (**your check number**)
Amount of check (**amount of check payment**)
Date you cashed the check (**date stamped on back of check**)

Please send me a revised statement showing that you have corrected your error.

Sincerely,

IS ANYONE OUT THERE?

To whomever can read:

I have written repeatedly, but you have never replied. Your computer just keeps sending me more (**incorrect bills/unordered merchandise/advertisements/whatever is annoying you**). *FIX YOUR COMPUTER! CORRECT YOUR RECORDS! ENOUGH IS ENOUGH!* If I receive anything more from you other than an apology, I will pursue other means to force you to take corrective action.

Your latest mailing label is attached.

(Cut out and attach mailing label here.)

At the end of my patience,

Chapter 28

CONDOLENCE
AND ENCOURAGEMENT
AND SUPPORT

• CONDOLENCE •

Friends, On Death of Child
Student, On Death of Parent
Coworker, On Death of Relative
Coworker, On Death of Relative (Belated)
Friend, On Death of Colleague
Colleague, On Death of Spouse

• ENCOURAGEMENT AND SUPPORT •

Student on Graduation
Athlete in Training for an Event
Coworker in Hospital
Get Well Soon—Teacher
Friend/Coworker on Demotion
Coworker on Loss of Job
Politician Campaigning for Office
Politician—Approving an Issue
Politician on Election Defeat
Stricter Laws/Regulations

CONDOLENCE

Of all the letters we will ever write, none finds us a at a more distressing loss for words than an expression of sorrow and support for a grieving friend, acquaintance, colleague, or loved one.

If distance precludes a personal visit, then a simple communication conveying how deeply you care and your willingness to share their burden is appropriate. Such messages should, understandably, be brief: the sharing of a fond remembrance, a simple offer of assistance or support, omitting any reference to their personal "loss," or their loved one's "suffering."

However awkward your attempt may seem, this endearing gesture will be remembered long after the initial pain of their grief has begun to diminish.

FRIENDS ON DEATH OF CHILD

Dearest (names),

(Name of person sharing your message) and I want so much to help you if we can. We know there is little we can say to ease your terrible burden, only listen if you need to talk.

(Name of deceased) was, and is, so very special to us. There are many memories we will always cherish of a (beautiful/handsome) (girl/boy) that we felt was almost our own.

We do not wish to intrude upon your solitude, but we want to see you both when you are ready to receive visitors. (Name of other relative/neighbor) has promised to let us know how you are, and if there is anything you need.

God bless you both.

With love,

STUDENT ON DEATH OF PARENT

Dear (name),

All of your friends at (school or class) want you to know our (prayers/thoughts) are with you at this very difficult time.

Your wonderful stories about your (mother/father) made us all feel as if we knew (her/him) personally. While we cannot ease the weight of your burden, we, nevertheless, are saddened by (her/his) passing.

We hope the caring and concern of your many friends will sustain you in the days ahead.

Affectionately,

COWORKER ON DEATH OF RELATIVE

Dear (name),

So many times we have heard you speak of your (relationship/name of deceased) and the special bond the two of you shared. Though we never met (him/her) personally, we all felt we knew (him/her). What a remarkable person (he/she) was to have such a devoted (recipient's relationship to deceased).

We trust the memory of (his/her) love and special strength will comfort and sustain you in the difficult days ahead.

God bless you and your family. Our (thoughts/prayers) are with you.

Affectionately,

COWORKER ON DEATH OF RELATIVE (BELATED)

Dear (name),

I have just learned of the recent passing of your (recipient's relationship to deceased). You have always spoken so highly of (him/her), and I am particularly saddened over your loss.

In time, the memories the two of you shared will ease your pain, and tears will give way to smiles again.

I will call you in a few days to see how you are. I hope I may help you in some way at this very difficult time.

Please extend my personal regards to your family.

Sincerely,

FRIEND ON DEATH OF COLLEAGUE

Dear (name),

I was shocked and saddened to learn of the unexpected passing of (name of colleague) on (date). I know how much you valued (him/her), not only as a partner but as a personal friend.

Though I was not personally acquainted with (**spouse of deceased**), please convey my sympathy to (**him/her**) and their children.

If there is any way I may be of help to you during the difficult days ahead, please feel free to call on me.

Sincerely,

COLLEAGUE ON DEATH OF SPOUSE

Dear (**name**),

(**Name of other person sharing your message**) and I have shared so many pleasant times with you and (**name of deceased**) over the (**years/months**), memories we cherish now more than ever before. There are no adequate words to ease the burden of your grief or our own.

We embrace you in our hearts, and trust you will draw strength from your many friends who want to help you through this very difficult time.

God bless you, my friend.

ENCOURAGEMENT AND SUPPORT

Messages of encouragement and support can take many forms: praise for someone who has attained a personal goal, encouragement when another appears to lack initiative to continue, best wishes for a quick recovery from an illness, or requests to a local politician to support a bill that directly impacts your neighborhood.

Whatever the reason, your offer of help and encouragement should be confined to tasks you are able to accomplish, and requests for intervention should be clearly stated and realistic. Be genuine in your offers of assistance, reasonable in your expectations, and generous with well-deserved praise.

STUDENT ON GRADUATION

Dear (**name**),

We are all looking forward to your graduation from (**name of college/school**) on (**date**). You have worked very hard to make your dreams come true, and soon all the effort and sacrifices will take on a new meaning. You made it!

We are very proud of your determination, and we share your enthusiasm as you begin your new career as a (**title**).

We will all be there to applaud your accomplishment on (**date**).

Affectionately,

ATHLETE IN TRAINING FOR AN EVENT

Dear (**name**),

On (**date**) all your friends here in (**location**) will be adding our cheers to those lucky enough to be present at the (**event**).

Your years of determination and hard work have paid off at last, and have earned you a place among the finest athletes representing our country today.

We all feel such a tremendous sense of pride in your accomplishments. You have shown us the true meaning of dedication and perseverance, and have gained the respect and admiration of everyone who knows you.

Good luck in (**location**). We're looking forward to a great victory!

Best regards,

COWORKER IN HOSPITAL

Dear (**name**),

I have just learned of your recent admission to (**name of facility**), and I wanted to let you know how concerned we all are and offer whatever help would be of value to you at this time.

You will be missed during this temporary absence, and we are counting on your speedy recovery and return to work.

I would like to come by and visit with you when you are feeling better. Please let me know when it will be convenient.

All of us at the office send our best.

Warmest regards,

GET WELL SOON—TEACHER

Dear (name),

(Name of child/other) has just told me of your (accident/illness) and that you will be away from school for some time. How unfortunate for you, and for your class.

Although I am certain suitable arrangements will be made for a qualified substitute, you will be missed by the students and the parents who depend upon you and appreciate the excellent job you are doing at (name of school or class).

I understand several of the parents plan to contact the school to volunteer their time and help your replacement adjust to a classroom of little strangers.

If I may help you in some way, please do not hesitate to call on me.

Take care, and hurry back. (Name of child) misses you already.

Sincerely,

FRIEND/COWORKER ON DEMOTION

Dear (name),

Although your appointment was on an interim basis, everyone here at (company, branch, club, or organization) was surprised to learn the position of (position/title) has been filled by (name of appointee).

We all felt you did a splendid job, and given the opportunity, we would have supported your permanent promotion to (title). We are confident, however, that your qualifications have been recognized and that your fine efforts will be rewarded soon.

Many thanks for your hard work and dedication. Your presence made our jobs easier.

Best regards,

COWORKER ON LOSS OF JOB

Dear (name),

It is especially difficult to say good-bye to someone I have worked alongside for (length of time). I am sure this unexpected change has temporarily unsettled you, but I have no doubt that, with your excellent qualifications, you will soon find yourself concentrating on a new position.

I have taken the liberty of mentioning your name to (**name of individual**) of (**name of company**), who is looking for someone with your qualifications. (**He/she**) asked that you contact (**him/her**) at (**telephone number**) when you are ready to consider another position.

In the meantime, if there is anything further I can do, please call me.

Sincerely,

POLITICIAN CAMPAIGNING FOR OFFICE

Dear (**name**),

(**Name of your club/organization**) applauds your decision to campaign for the office of (**mayor/councilperson/commissioner/other**).

We have followed your political career with great interest, and we feel that your views, dedication, and concern for your fellow citizens of (**city/county/state**) qualify you as the best choice for this position.

Once elected, we encourage you to continue your efforts on behalf of (**cause**).

Good luck in your pursuit of this very worthwhile goal.

Respectfully,

NOTE: If you represent an organization, include your title and affiliation.

POLITICIAN—APPROVING AN ISSUE

Dear (**name**),

I would like to add my voice to the many others who support your position on the (**cause**) issue.

While it has not always been a popular topic among some members of your constituency, your honesty and perseverance on behalf of (**cause**) has been most refreshing and has lent credibility to a difficult and confusing situation.

I urge you to continue to stand firm against those who oppose you. I am confident that your proposed legislation will benefit the majority of our citizens, and their approval will be reflected in the results of the next election.

Sincerely,

POLITICIAN ON ELECTION DEFEAT

Dear (name),

As a member of your reelection committee, I would like to express my personal regrets on the outcome of the recent polling.

Those who supported you applaud your determination to adhere to your own convictions, and we do not view this temporary setback as an adverse reflection on your dedication and excellent qualifications.

We are confident you will soon find favor with those who opposed your views, and we look forward, with great enthusiasm, to working for your successful election next term.

Warm personal regards,

STRICTER LAWS/REGULATIONS

Dear (name),

I am sure you are familiar with the proposed bill to enforce observance of (**state nature of problem/legislation**).

To date, statistics show (**problems, number of incidents**) have occurred in this area as a result of (**who/what is responsible for occurrences**). Can we afford yet another tragedy?

Stricter regulations and enforcement of (**actions to correct the problem**) would greatly reduce the chances of potential harm to the residents of (**location**).

I urge you to support this legislation at the next (**meeting/session**) of (**governing board**), and hope it will result in prompt action to correct this problem.

Thank you for your concern and assistance.

Sincerely,

Chapter 29

CONGRATULATIONS

Friend on Opening Own Business
Colleague on Completion of Difficult Project
Politician on Passage of Sponsored Legislation
Acquaintance or Colleague on Special Appointment
Friend on Achieving Personal Goal
Student on Graduating from High School
Student on Graduating from College
Coworker on Promotion
Acquaintance on Public Recognition
Acquaintance on Special Achievement (Belated)

People appreciate it when their accomplishments are acknowledged by their friends, colleagues, or acquaintances. Sometimes, you can find a greeting card that expresses what you want to say; however, there are times when no card articulates your feelings accurately. The letters in this chapter are designed to fill that gap and help you to say what is in your heart or on your mind.

FRIEND ON OPENING OWN BUSINESS

Dear (name),

Congratulations on opening your own business! I know it has long been a dream of yours to have your own (type of business), and, now, you have made your dream a reality. How proud and happy you must be!

I'll be coming by your shop to celebrate your grand opening, and look forward to congratulating you in person then.

Love,

COLLEAGUE ON COMPLETION OF DIFFICULT PROJECT

Dear (name),

Congratulations on finally completing (name/type of project)! I know it's been a long haul for you, gathering all the information you needed and then putting it all together in just the right way. I appreciated the chance to look over this project, and I think you have done a super job. You were certainly the right person to handle this difficult assignment. I'll be eager to hear how it is received.

Again, my compliments on a job well done.

Sincerely,

POLITICIAN ON PASSAGE OF SPONSORED LEGISLATION

Dear (name),

I am writing to congratulate you on the recent passage of the (type of legislation) bill you sponsored in the (congress/senate/assembly/other). I have followed with interest the progress of the bill as it has been reported in the newspapers. According to these reports, this bill has not been an easy one to push through. I admire your perseverance and dedication.

(Type of legislation) issues are at the forefront of my personal concerns, and I know that this concern is shared by many others in your constituency. Thank you for not giving up in the face of formidable and frustrating odds. I know that the specific sections of this bill will benefit all the people of our area, including those who were against its passage.

The passage of this bill has confirmed my belief in you as a **(congressman/woman/ senator/other)** who is committed to serving the people of **(town/county/state)**. Again, congratulations!

Sincerely,

ACQUAINTANCE OR COLLEAGUE ON SPECIAL APPOINTMENT

Dear **(name)**,

I want to congratulate you on your recent appointment to the **(name of committee/ commission of appointment)**. This appointment is an honor you richly deserve. Your hard work and creative ideas have already helped to improve **(subject of committee/ commission)**. I am glad that your imaginative approaches have earned you **(national/ state/other)** recognition. Your work on this **(committee/commission)**, I hope, will enable you to effect changes in **(subject of committee/commission)** **(nation/state/county/ town)**-wide.

I wish you all the best in this endeavor.

Sincerely,

FRIEND ON ACHIEVING PERSONAL GOAL

Dear **(name)**,

Congratulations! You made it! You are now the proud **(briefly describe goal)**. I know it hasn't been easy, juggling all of the demands on your time while still pursuing your dream. You have had to make many sacrifices in order to achieve this goal, and I admire your perseverance and commitment—to say nothing of the long hours it has required.

Pat yourself on the back, and give yourself a well-deserved rest.

Love,

STUDENT ON GRADUATING FROM HIGH SCHOOL

Dear (name),

Congratulations! You have reached a milestone in your educational life! I am proud of you and know that you are proud of yourself. Graduation is a good time to look back and assess your accomplishments. It is also a good time to look ahead, to decide how you can best use your skills to create the kind of future you want for yourself.
I wish you all the best.

Sincerely,

STUDENT ON GRADUATING FROM COLLEGE

Dear (name),

Congratulations on your graduation from college! This must be a time of mixed emotions for you—saying "good-bye" to the past and "hello" to the future. You can look back with pride on your accomplishments of the last four years, and you can look forward with anticipation to the accomplishments you will achieve in the years ahead.
I wish you all the best.

Affectionately,

COWORKER ON PROMOTION

Dear (name),

Congratulations on being promoted to the position of (title)! I can't think of anyone who deserves this position more. Your contributions to the work of our (company/agency) have been exemplary. You have not only devoted yourself to improving the quality of our (service/product), but you have also demonstrated a supervisory style that has won you the respect of all those who have worked with you. I am glad you have been given the opportunity to use your talents and skills in this new position.
I look forward to continuing to work with you.

Sincerely,

ACQUAINTANCE ON PUBLIC RECOGNITION

Dear (name),

Congratulations on being named (type of public recognition)! What a perfect recognition of your outstanding contributions to the community! Although I do not know you well, I am very much aware of your efforts to make our (state/county/town) a better place to live. I applaud the (name of organization) for acknowledging your dedication and commitment in such a special way.

Sincerely,

ACQUAINTANCE ON SPECIAL ACHIEVEMENT (BELATED)

Dear (name),

I am sorry to take so long to congratulate you on (type of special achievement). From what I understand, this achievement is the fulfillment of a dream you have had for a long time. You must be feeling a tremendous sense of satisfaction.

Please accept my belated congratulations. May you reap the benefits of this achievement for many years to come!

Sincerely,

Chapter 30

FROM THE HEART

At times we tend to procrastinate when it comes to writing letters to those near and dear to our hearts. Busy schedules, unexpected business trips, or studying for exams cause us to postpone our letters home or to close friends who have moved away.

Messages from the heart are very special ones, filled with shared memories, an offering of encouragement, a recounting of childhood secrets, laughter, anger, and tears. It is difficult to devise a model letter that is perfectly suited for any particular situation; instead, the letters featured in this chapter are designed to offer inspiration for the writer and encouragement not to delay any longer.

However you choose to use them, do not put off writing that letter to parents, children, and friends. Someone very special is waiting to hear from you.

THANK YOU FOR EXPRESSION OF SYMPATHY

Dear (name),

Thank you so much for your kind expression of caring at the passing of our beloved (relative), (name). Since we received your letter, we have had an opportunity to go through (his/her) personal effects and discovered several letters that you had written to (him/her) over the years, as well as some treasured photographs of the two of you when you were school friends in (town/city/neighborhood). We feel that (relative) would want you to have them, and we are sending them to you under separate cover.

We plan to return to (city/state/neighborhood) on (date) and would like to call on you while we are there. We are sure you have many delightful stories to tell of the two of you, and we would love to hear them all.

Again, our thanks for your thoughtfulness. We look forward to meeting (relative)'s dear friend, (pet name)

Sincerely,

ENCOURAGING A TROUBLED FRIEND

Dear (name),

I was very sorry to learn of your recent troubles and want you to know I am thinking of you, and hoping to be able to help in some way.

We have not seen much of each other recently, but you have never been far from my thoughts. I have always admired your inner strength and courage and your belief in yourself. While those traits must surely have been sorely tested, they have not deserted you. I am confident you will overcome this temporary setback.

If there is anything I can do to help ease your burden, or if you simply need to talk, call any time.

Affectionately,

"MISS YOU" TO A FRIEND WHO HAS MOVED AWAY

Dear (name),

(Season) has come to (area) once again, and it is at this time of year that you are so often in (my/our) thoughts. It was at the (seasonal occasion/holiday) that (spouse/friend) and (I/we) first met you and (spouse/friend) and began the first of our many holiday celebrations together.

Change comes slowly to the old neighborhood, and it is probably much as you remember it. (Name) now occupy your (house/apartment), and you will be pleased to know, they care for it as much as you.

We have thought of selling our home and moving to a warmer climate when (spouse/friend) retires. However, with each change of season, and each year that passes, we become less willing to leave family and friends behind. (Spouse/friend) insists we are becoming stodgy, but I prefer to believe we have come to realize we have the best of everything, right here in (neighborhood).

Having you and (spouse/friend) close by would make it perfect. If we cannot entice you to return permanently, can we at least persuade you to spend your vacation with us? It's been too long since we last saw you.

Fondly,

THANKING A VOLUNTEER

Dear (name),

I would like to extend my sincere thanks to you for the kindness you have shown to my (relative/friend), (name), who is a resident at (facility).

It is not always possible for me to be there when (he/she) needs someone to talk with or to accompany (him/her) on outings.

Your interest in (his/her) welfare has added so much enjoyment to (his/her) days. (He/she) looks forward to your visits and speaks so well of you.

I look forward to meeting you on my next trip to (**location**) and thanking you personally for your caring.

Respectfully,

MAKING AMENDS

Dear (**name**),

For some reason that I cannot explain, you have been on my mind a lot lately. Perhaps I feel guilty for having let this situation continue, and a bit angry that you have done the same.

It proves one thing, at least. We are both stubborn. With that in mind, it is doubtful we will ever agree on (**family dispute/opposing viewpoint/personal goals/political views/other**).

We have been (**friends/relatives**) (**all our lives/number of years**), long before this situation occurred. We did not begin with it, and I don't believe we must end with it.

You are very special to me. I have missed you.

Friends, again (?),

LOVE AND APPRECIATION TO PARENTS

Dear Mom and Dad,

Today is our special day once again, my birthday, and I cannot think of two nicer people to spend it with, even though I must do so through this letter.

Tonight (**friend/spouse/family**) (**is/are**) taking me to dinner, and I know we will have a wonderful time. But, for a while this afternoon I am taking a few moments alone to reflect upon those special times you and I have spent together.

Each year my appreciation of you becomes stronger, and my love deeper. Even though it was not always laughter and good times, I want to thank you for treasured memories, and those yet to come.

You are the very best. Happy birthday to the three of us!

All my love,

LETTER TO HOMESICK SON/DAUGHTER

Dearest (name),

We have just received your letter, and though we were happy to hear from you, we are disturbed by the "sound" of it. You see, dear, we can "hear" you, even if it's in a letter.

Even though you are physically away from home, you are always with us. We feel your presence whenever we walk into your room or watch a program on TV that you always liked. Sometimes we forget that you are not here to answer the phone on the first ring, and by the time we remember, the caller hangs up!

It is, I think, very common to feel more homesick than usual as a holiday approaches, but soon you will be home with us and your friends again.

We are so eager to see you, and your (mother/father) is already planning ways to keep you close to home. (She/he) declares that within an hour of your arrival, you will be back at (favorite spot) with your (friends/buddies), just like the "good old days."

Everyone sends their love. See you soon.

BLANKET INVITATION—FAMILY REUNION

Dear Loved Ones,

As you all know, (parents/grandparents) will celebrate their (silver/golden/other) wedding anniversary on (date). (Number) of years of devotion should not go unrecognized, agreed?

We have often talked of getting the family together, and what better time than a surprise reunion to celebrate (parents/grandparents) anniversary. (Name of relative living close by) thinks it is a wonderful idea and has agreed to make arrangements for accommodations at (name of hotel/motel) and dinner at (restaurant/club).

(He/she) will send you the details, including your share of expenses, within a few days.

Imagine their surprise when (family member/friend) takes them to dinner and they discover (number) unexpected guests have arrived also.

Love to all. See you in (town/city/neighborhood) on (date).

Chapter 31

INTRODUCTIONS

Son/Daughter of Friend to College Admissions Committee
Friend/Acquaintance Seeking Employment
Domestic Help
Volunteer to Political Candidate
Student Applying for Summer Job
Relative to Friend
Student Applying to College

One of the favors you are occasionally asked to do for a friend or relative is to write a letter of introduction. An introductory letter can help to open the door to employment, volunteer work, or college admission. Although not usually considered a formal reference letter, it is important for your letter of introduction to indicate your relationship to the person being introduced and to point out that person's desirable traits. When your letter is going to a college or business, you should include an inside address.

SON/DAUGHTER OF FRIEND TO COLLEGE ADMISSIONS COMMITTEE

Dear (**name of member of college admissions committee**):

I am writing this letter for (**name**) of (**city/state**). (**First name**), who is the (**son/daughter**) of my good friend, (**name of friend**), has applied for admission to your college. In every contact with (**first name**), I have found (**him/her**) to be one of the brightest and most conscientious and thoughtful young people I have ever met. For the past several years, (**he/she**) (**describe an interesting or outstanding activity or accomplishment of the prospective student**), demonstrating a strong sense of responsibility as well as a determination to succeed.

As a graduate of (**name of college**), I am aware of the kind of student you are looking for. I believe that (**first name**) would make an exceptionally fine addition to your freshman class. I would appreciate your giving (**his/her**) application careful consideration.

Sincerely,

FRIEND/ACQUAINTANCE SEEKING EMPLOYMENT

Dear (**name**),

This letter will introduce my good friend, (**name**), who will soon be moving to your area. I am hoping that you will be willing to talk with (**him/her**) about the possibilities of employment in your organization.

(**Name**) is a (**brief educational background of person being introduced**). Recently, (**he/she**) has worked (**brief employment background applicable to this business**). (**He/she**) also (**brief description of other social/community activities**). (**He/she**) has often mentioned that (**his/her**) goal was to find employment with an organization such as yours.

I know that there are times when you have positions available for a talented person. If this is one of them, I hope you will give (**name**) serious consideration. I am certain that you will find (**him/her**) to be a conscientious worker, a willing learner, and an asset to your company.

If you do not have any openings, I would appreciate your steering (**him/her**) toward other businesses that might be interested in hiring a capable (**man/woman**) with professional potential. If you have any questions concerning (**name**), please do not hesitate to call me.

I often think of the many good times we spent together and how much I enjoyed (**briefly describe any activities that you shared with the person you are writing to**). I hope you and your family are well and happy.

Sincerely,

DOMESTIC HELP

Dear (**name**),

I am writing this letter for (**name**) who served as my (**housekeeper/sitter/nanny/cook/other**). (**He/she**) will be moving to your area in (**month**) and will be looking for employment there. When (**you last wrote/we last talked**), you told me that you were looking for a (**housekeeper/cook/other**).

(**Name**) was a simply wonderful (**housekeeper/cook/other**). I could not have asked for better. I recommend (**him/her**) to you without reservation.

I have given (**name**) your address and phone number, and (**he/she**) will be in touch with you as soon as (**he/she**) has arrived in your area. If you have not already hired a (**housekeeper/cook/other**), (**name**) just might be the person you are looking for. If you have, perhaps you could steer (**him/her**) in the direction of others who might have needs similar to yours.

I remember with joy the time when we were living in the same town. We must be sure to get together the next time one of us is in the other's area.

Fondly,

VOLUNTEER TO POLITICAL CANDIDATE

Dear (**political candidate**):

My friend, (**name**), mentioned to me that (**he/she**) is looking for an opportunity to do political volunteer work. I told (**him/her**) about your running for (**mayor/governor/other**), and (**he/she**) expressed interest in working for you.

(**Name**) has had experience as a (**typist/receptionist/other**) and is a hard worker who always follows through on any assignment (**he/she**) is given. Moreover, (**he/she**) is (loyal/outgoing/responsible/other). (He/she) is also dedicated to many of the causes that you have publicly espoused. I think that (he/she) would be a valuable addition to your volunteer staff.

I have suggested that (he/she) get in touch with you and hope that you will be willing to talk with (him/her).

Good luck with your campaign. You already have my vote!

Sincerely,

STUDENT APPLYING FOR SUMMER JOB

Dear (name),

I am writing this letter for a young friend of mine, (name). (Name) is a high school student who has expressed an interest in working at (name of company or business) during the summer.

(Name) is one of the most responsible young people I have ever met. (He/she) is mature beyond (his/her) (age) years as well as (loyal/dependable/outgoing/other). In addition, (he/she) has had some experience working in (fast food service/retail sales/other) and doing volunteer work for (his/her) (church/father's office/other).

I know that during the summer you sometimes need extra help in your (firm/company/office/other). I would appreciate it if you would take the time to talk with (name). (He/she) will be calling you soon to set up an appointment.

Thank you for considering the possibility of hiring (him/her).

Sincerely,

RELATIVE TO FRIEND

Dear (friend),

I am writing this letter for my (relationship), (name of relative being introduced). (He/she) is planning a move to your area and is in the process of seeking employment there. Since you have lived in the (name of place) for some time, it occurred to me that you might be of some help to (him/her).

(Name)'s background is in (computer programming/office management/financial/other). (He/she) has (brief description of awards, accomplishments, or promotions).

I know that your work as a (**type of work done by friend**) brings you into contact with people in many different fields. I would appreciate it if you would be willing to put (**name**) in touch with anyone who might make use of (**his/her**) special expertise. I have given (**name**) your address and have suggested that (**he/she**) send you a resume as well as a letter laying out (**his/her**) career goals.

I miss you and your family and wish we lived close enough to see one another more often. I hope that your business is doing well and that you and your family are happy and healthy.

Fondly,

STUDENT APPLYING TO COLLEGE

Dear (**admissions officer**):

A young friend of mine, (**name**), told me that (**he/she**) has applied for admission to your college. (**Name**) is my (**student/baby sitter/other**). (**He/she**) is an exceptional young person who possesses (**intelligence/sensitivity/leadership potential/other**). (**His/her**) comments are always well thought out and clearly articulated. I have also been impressed with (**his/her**) ability to (**resolve conflicts between friends/follow through on an assigned task/other**).

I believe that (**name**) would make a valuable addition to your upcoming freshman class and hope you will give (**his/her**) application favorable consideration.

Sincerely,

Chapter 32

INVITATIONS AND SPECIAL REQUESTS

Birthday Party—No Gifts, Please
Shower—Bridal or Baby
Private Wedding at Home
Informal Gathering
Reception/Cocktail Party
Attend a Benefit
House Guest
Join a Social Club
Guest Speaker
Chair a Fund Raiser
Sponsor an Event
Serve on a Panel
Serve on a Committee
Requesting Bids from Vendors
Oppose a Political Issue

Whether it is a birthday celebration, private wedding at home, persuading someone to chair a fund raiser, or inviting bids from competing vendors, how clearly you phrase your invitation or request determines how successful you are likely to be.

A cordial and informative message indicating the purpose of a function, or the reason for a request will more often than not ensure an acceptance, whereas a vague and confusing one will result in regrets or an outright refusal.

Simply select the most appropriate message for your needs from the variety of model letters featured in this chapter and wait for a positive response.

BIRTHDAY PARTY—NO GIFTS, PLEASE

Dear (name),

I have actually accomplished the impossible! My reluctant "better half" has agreed to a bash in honor of (his/her) (year)th birthday. But, here's the catch—absolutely NO GIFTS!

We will launch this affair at (time), (day/date), at poolside. Bring your swimsuits and get ready for a "whale" of a time.

No regrets, no excuses. Don't miss this once-in-a-lifetime opportunity!

SHOWER—BRIDAL OR BABY

Dear (name),

On (day/date) at (time), the (department) will host a surprise (bridal/baby) shower for (name).

Refreshments will be served in (specific area) from (time) until (time).

Since several of her coworkers have expressed a preference for individual gifts rather than a collective effort, a ($ amount) limit has been placed on all personal gifts. In the interest of fairness to others, please make a special effort not to exceed this amount.

Contact (name and telephone number) if you will be unable to attend; otherwise, we look forward to seeing you there.

Sincerely,

PRIVATE WEDDING AT HOME

Dear (name(s)),

On (day/date) at (time) (name of bride) and (name of groom) will be married in a private candlelight ceremony at home. We would be honored to have you share in the happiness of this occasion as they begin their new life together.

The ceremony and reception will be held at (address). (Name of clergy or official) will officiate.

Please favor us with a reply to (name), (telephone number), by (date).

Sincerely,

Mr. and Mrs. (bride's parents)
            and
Mr. and Mrs. (groom's parents) (or other designated persons)

AN INFORMAL GATHERING

Dear (name),

The (organization) will hold its annual (seasonal event) on (day/date), at (area/facility), beginning at (time).

You and your (family/guest) are urged to attend and bring (memorabilia) to display in the (area.)

Lunch will be served at 12:00 noon, followed by (swimming/tennis/other). Lifeguards will be in attendance for swimmers throughout the day.

Please contact (function coordinator) at (telephone number) with acceptance or regrets no later than (date).

Please join us for good food and fellowship!

Sincerely,

RECEPTION/COCKTAIL PARTY

Dear Member:

The (organization) board of directors would like to extend a personal invitation to you, and a guest, to attend a (formal/informal) reception honoring (name), guest speaker for our (annual event).

The reception will be held in the (**specific area**) of the (**facility**), beginning at (**time**), (**day/date**).

This is an excellent opportunity for our members to meet our special guest and extend a warm welcome to our city.

Please RSVP by returning the enclosed card to (**function coordinator**) no later than (**date**).

We look forward to seeing you on (**date**).

Cordially,

ATTEND A BENEFIT

Dear (**name**),

The (**sponsoring group**) would like to extend a personal invitation to you to attend our annual (**event**) on (**day**) evening, the (**date**) of (**month**), at the (**hall/hotel/club/other**).

The festivities will begin with a reception in the (**specific area**) at (**time**), with dinner and dancing in the (**specific area**) beginning at (**time**).

Traditionally, a (**donation/pledge**) of (**$ amount**) to the (**recipient's**) fund accompanies each acceptance. We know you will appreciate the importance of this event and honor us with your presence.

Please return the enclosed reservation card with your (**donation/pledge**) to (**function coordinator**) by (**day/date**).

Respectfully,

HOUSE GUEST

Dear (**guest**),

(**Name of friend/relative/child**) has informed us that your (**spouse/parents/other**) will be traveling to (**destination**) on (**date**). We would like very much to have you join us for the (**season**) holiday here in (**town/city**).

(**Name of friend/relative/child**) has told us so much about you we feel as if we have already met, and look forward to having you join us for this occasion. (**He/she**) can fill you in on the activities we have planned. We think you will find your first trip to (**town/city**) a most enjoyable one.

We look forward to having you with us.

Sincerely,

JOIN A SOCIAL CLUB

Dear (name),

A mutual friend, (name), told me of your recent move to our area from (location), and your keen interest in (activity).

The (area) chapter of (national organization) has earned numerous awards for their (performances/services/accomplishments), and we are always seeking out new talent to enhance our (group).

We would be delighted to have you accompany (name) to our next meeting on (day/date) at (time), in the hope we can persuade you to continue your interest in (activity) with our chapter.

We meet the (designated day/week/month), at (time), in the (designated area).

Again, welcome. I look forward to meeting you personally on (date).

Sincerely,

GUEST SPEAKER

Dear (name),

The (organization) of (location) will hold its annual (event) at the (facility) on (day/date), beginning at (time).

Our membership is comprised of approximately (number) of (vocation/profession) who actively pursue their interest in (area of expertise or nature of interest), both as a profession and as a hobby.

Each year the members are asked to submit the names of persons whose accomplishments earn them special recognition, and whom they would like to meet personally. As a result of this impartial polling, we are pleased to extend a special invitation to you to be our honored guest and (after dinner/other) speaker at this year's annual gathering.

As our guest, you will be provided accommodations at (hotel), and all incidental expenses including air and ground transportation will be paid by the (organization).

There is no time requirement imposed upon our speakers, though generally presentations rarely exceed one hour.

Please allow sufficient time for questions from the audience; I am sure there will be many.

If you are able to favor us with an acceptance, please contact me at your earliest convenience so that we can make the necessary arrangements to ensure that your visit is a most enjoyable one.

I am certain you will find the (**organization**) to be a most enthusiastic audience and very appreciative of your expertise.

Sincerely,

CHAIR A FUND RAISER

Dear (**name**),

The (**organization**) is planning to sponsor a (**event**) to raise money for a monument in honor of (**veterans/sportsmen/humanitarian/other**) to be unveiled (**occasion**) at (**location**) on (**date**).

As a (**prominent figure in the financial community/veteran/advocate of related cause/ other**), we would be pleased if you will agree to chair this event. We need your expertise. Won't you help us in this endeavor?

I am enclosing the initial plans we have drawn up. Any ideas or suggestions you might be able to provide will be greatly appreciated.

I will telephone your office on (**date/day**) at (**time**) to discuss this with you personally.

Sincerely,

SPONSOR AN EVENT

Dear (**name**),

On (**date**) the (**area**) High School (**sports/scholastic/music group**) will travel to (**destination**) to compete for the title of (**award or honor**) in the (**state/region/United States**).

In order to make this trip, these remarkable young (**athletes/scholars/musicians**) must raise (**$ amount**) by (**deadline**). We are asking all businesses in the area to pledge (**$ amount**) toward the cost of their expenses.

Won't you join with other leaders in the community to help our youth in their quest for this impressive honor? Donations may be (**made/sent in person/by mail**) to the school administration office.

Your support will be greatly appreciated by the students, faculty, and families.

Kindest regards,

SERVE ON A PANEL

Dear (name),

The (name of civic committee/club) of (area) is very concerned about the impact of the proposed addition of yet another (project) at (location). We believe indiscriminate overbuilding has already overtaxed our water supply, utilities, public roadways, and seriously threatens our ecological environment.

We are forming a panel to study this issue so that we may present a convincing rebuttal to the zoning board to bar further development of this vital area.

Your expertise in the areas of (recognized work) would lend indisputable credibility to our position. We urgently seek your help, and hope you will agree to serve on this panel.

I am enclosing additional information that clearly supports our claims. I will contact you later in the week to discuss this matter further.

Sincerely,

SERVE ON A COMMITTEE

Dear (name),

As chairman of (organization), I would like to invite you to serve on our committee for (project) and work with us to devise better ways and means to assure (objective).

Your reputation as a (recognized effort) expert, and your related work with (similar organizations), would do much to promote our cause.

The (organization) meets (number of times weeks/month) at (location) to discuss current events and legislation pertaining to our program.

Please contact me if you have any questions. I would be pleased to convey your acceptance to the other committee members.

Best regards,

REQUESTING BIDS FROM VENDORS

Dear (name),

The members of (school/club/organization) will host its annual (group) Appreciation Dinner on (day/date). Each year we present a gift to the (school/club/organization) in honor of these dedicated (volunteers/professionals/employees/public servants). This year we are planning to contribute (**item**), and we are currently accepting bids from various (**manufacturers/craftsmen/vendors**) in the area. We would be pleased to accept a bid from (**name of company**) before the (**date**) deadline.

We are enclosing a list of area specifications and equipment which the (**school/club/ organization**) needs. The Association committee members will review each bid and announce their decision at the next meeting on (**date**).

Thank you for your interest in this project.

Sincerely,

OPPOSE A POLITICAL ISSUE

Dear association member,

On (**date**) the (**Congress of the United States or other governing body**) will cast a critical vote that could adversely affect your right to (**state rights or privileges in question**) for years to come. Passage of (**legislation**) will enable our (**national/state/local**) government to (**assess/dictate/revoke/restrict**) our (**income/regulations/privileges/freedoms**), a move that would clearly not be beneficial to (**senior citizens/special interest groups/labor and professional groups/others**).

Together, our combined voices will be heard in (**Washington or city/county/state**), staunchly opposing the passage of this (**unfair/unwarranted/ludicrous/ill conceived**) bill.

Exercise your constitutional right to a voice in the government of the (**United States of America or city/county/state**). Resolve to write your (**congressperson or other official**) today. Tomorrow may be too late!

Best regards,

Chapter 33

DECLINING INVITATIONS
AND SPECIAL REQUESTS

Previous Commitment
Unexpected Emergency (Belated)
Volunteering Time/Services
Host a Dinner Party
Chair a Committee
Attend a Fund Raiser
Attend a Boring Affair
Support a Political Candidate
Ask for a Raincheck
Loan of a Personal Item

We often look forward with anticipation to a gathering with friends, acquaintances, and colleagues, yet there are times when conflicting schedules or unexpected emergencies make it necessary to decline an invitation to an affair, or, for personal reasons, choose to say "no" to a request.

A thoughtful and timely response expressing regret, or a plausible explanation for why you are unable to comply, lessens the other person's disappointment and ensures their goodwill, particularly if you are able to offer an alternate time to get together, or a solution to a request for assistance or the loan of a personal item.

PREVIOUS COMMITMENT

Dear (name),

You cannot imagine how gratified I was to be offered the opportunity to speak to the (organization) at their (event) in (location) on (date). It is with particular regret that I must decline, as I do have a previously scheduled commitment on that date.

All (vocation/profession members) enjoy a special camaraderie in their dedication and pursuit of this noble profession. I am certain the opportunity to come together in a bond of common fellowship and sharing will ensure a memorable occasion for everyone.

Please convey my very best wishes to all, and my sincere hope that you will favor me with another invitation in the future.

Warmest regards,

UNEXPECTED EMERGENCY (BELATED)

Dear (name),

Please accept our belated good wishes on your recent promotion and our apologies for our absence at your celebration party.

We learned just that afternoon (of the arrival of unexpected guests/of a family emergency/other), and in our haste to (prepare for their arrival/leave for destination), we failed to telephone and let you know we would be unable to attend. We hope you will forgive the oversight.

Again, congratulations on well deserved recognition.

Sincerely,

VOLUNTEERING TIME/SERVICES

Dear (**name**),

Thank you for your inquiry of (**date**) regarding the (**event/program/project**).

Being a volunteer for the past (**number**) (**months/years**) has been a very rewarding personal experience, and I especially regret that I will be unable to help out this time.

I have decided to resume my (**studies/work**) at (**location**) and do not feel I would have sufficient spare time to do justice to (**event/program/project**).

Please contact me again next (**month/year/term**). I hope I shall be in a better position to help at that time.

Sincerely,

HOST A DINNER PARTY

Dear (**name**),

Thank you for the kind compliment in requesting the use of our home as the site for the (**event**). At any other time we would be delighted to act as the official host for (**special guest**)'s visit; however, the date conflicts with (**a previously scheduled event/family gathering/other**), and we must decline as it is too late to make other arrangements.

If I may suggest an alternate choice, I am sure (**name**) would be pleased to entertain our visitor from (**location**).

I am sure it will be a very successful affair, and I regret we will be unable to attend.

Kindest regards,

CHAIR A COMMITTEE

Dear (**name**),

I appreciate your confidence in my ability to chair the (**committee**) for the (**tenure**) term, and I truly wish that I could help you out.

However, I (**just recently agreed to serve on another committee/am working with a member of the opposing side/other**), and I believe there might be a potential conflict of interest involved. I am certain you will find a suitable candidate who will provide the leadership the committee needs.

Again, I am very gratified by your offer, but considering the circumstances, I must reluctantly defer to someone else at this time.

Kind regards,

ATTEND A FUND RAISER

Dear **(name)**,

Thank you for your kind invitation to the reception at **(location)** on **(day/date)** to meet **(special guest)**. Unfortunately, I **(am still feeling the effects of a stubborn virus/have scheduled another commitment on that date)** and will be unable to join you and your other guests.

I am certain the board's decision to award the design contract for the **(project)** to **(special guest)**'s firm is a sound and prudent one, and to show my support of their selection, I am enclosing a donation in the amount of **($ amount)** to be applied to the project.

I look forward to reviewing **(guest)**'s final plans and specifications at the board meeting next month.

Cordially,

ATTEND A BORING AFFAIR

Dear **(name)**,

How nice of you to invite **(spouse)** and me to your party on **(day)** night to review the slide presentation of your trip to **(location)**. We have looked forward to seeing you since you returned, but, unfortunately, **(we are unable to find a sitter/must attend other function)**.

Let's plan to meet for **(lunch/dinner)** soon. I am eager to try that new **(type)** restaurant on **(location)**. My treat!

I'll be in touch later in the week.

Fondly,

TO SUPPORT A POLITICAL CANDIDATE

Dear (name),

In response to your request for a personal endorsement of (candidate), I regret that I must decline based upon our opposing views on the (nature of dispute) question.

While I respect and admire the work (he/she) has done on other issues, I find (his/her) position on (nature of dispute) to be far too (liberal/conservative) and potentially damaging to the majority of (his/her) constituency.

Should (his/her) position change to a more (liberal/conservative) stance, I would be amenable to supporting (his/her) candidacy. However, at the present time, such an endorsement would compromise my personal convictions, and I cannot, in good conscience, disregard my own principles.

Sincerely,

ASK FOR A RAINCHECK

Dear (name),

I know how delighted you must be that your (friend/relative) will be visiting next week. I so wanted to meet (name) after hearing so much about (him/her). Just my luck, I have to leave for (destination) the day before (he/she) arrives, and will not return until (date).

Please extend my apologies, and let's plan to get together when (he/she) visits again at (holiday/occasion).

Affectionately,

LOAN OF A PERSONAL ITEM

Dear (name),

I am very flattered that you would want to borrow (item) for (event) and wish that I could say "yes." I know you would take excellent care of it, however, (it is very old and fragile/family heirloom/I have never used it myself/it actually belongs to someone else/other), and I must decline.

I do have (alternate item) that I am sure would suit just as well, and you are welcome to borrow it if you think it would serve the purpose. Please let me know so that I can have it ready in time for (event).

Sincerely,

Chapter 34

REFERENCES

Personal Recommendation on Behalf of Acquaintance/Friend
Applicant for Club/Organization Membership
Domestic Employee
Nominating a Candidate for an Award
Student Applying to School
Endorsing a Guest Speaker
Declining to Offer a Reference

Offering a professional or personal reference on behalf of another individual is your personal endorsement of that person's capabilities or character. To safeguard your credibility, great care should be given to the wording of your response to a reference request. If you feel your comments could be detrimental to the person you are referencing, you may wish to confine your remarks to the positive aspects of his or her work performance or character which you have observed firsthand.

Avoid the tendency to embellish your message with lavish praise or obscure flaws and weaknesses with complicated phraseology. An astute businessperson or perceptive membership chairman will recognize this ploy very quickly.

If your personal knowledge of a person's work performance or personal character is limited, you may, of course, refuse to offer a reference. Instead, acknowledge your lack of familiarity with the individual in question, and suggest an alternate source for a more accurate assessment of his or her capabilities.

PERSONAL RECOMMENDATION ON BEHALF OF ACQUAINTANCE/FRIEND

Dear (**name**),

I am pleased to offer this recommendation on behalf of (**full name**), who recently applied for the position of (**title**) with our company.

I was previously associated with (**Mr./Ms.**) (**name**) during my tenure with (**previous employer**). During the (**number**) (**months/years**) we worked together, I found (**him/her**) to be dedicated to (**his/her**) (**vocation/profession**), proficient in (**his/her**) job duties, and consistently willing to go beyond what was expected to accomplish (**his/her**) professional goals and objectives.

(**He/she**) is a very pleasant and thoughtful person, and (**his/her**) genuine concern for others is reflected in the positive attitudes of clients and coworkers alike.

I would not hesitate to recommend (**full name**) for any position (**he/she**) feels qualified to seek, and I encourage your favorable consideration of (**his/her**) application.

Sincerely,

APPLICANT FOR CLUB/ORGANIZATION MEMBERSHIP

Dear (**name**),

I am pleased to offer this recommendation on behalf of (**name**), who has applied for membership in this organization.

I have known (name) as a personal friend, and professional associate, for (length of time). I can attest to (his/her) personal integrity as well as (his/her) genuine interest in the (goals/objectives) of (club/organization).

I would be honored to sponsor (name) as a candidate for membership and request your favorable consideration of (his/her) application.

Respectfully,

DOMESTIC EMPLOYEE

Dear (name),

In response to your inquiry of (date), I am pleased to offer this personal recommendation on behalf of (name), who was in my employ for a period of (length of employment), from (date) to (date).

During the (number) (months/years) (he/she) worked for me, I found (him/her) to be loyal, trustworthy, and extremely personable.

(His/her) performance of (his/her) duties was unfailingly superior, and I would not hesitate to offer (him/her) employment should (he/she) decide to return to (area) at some future time.

Sincerely,

NOMINATING A CANDIDATE FOR AN AWARD

Dear (name),

I would like to nominate (name) as a candidate for the (title) award to be presented at (event) on (day/date).

(Name) is known to the majority of our membership for (his/her) loyalty, dedication, and hard work on behalf of (sponsored event/charitable works). (He/she) has always been among the first to volunteer for (tasks/responsibilities); specifically, (list specific examples of candidate's actions that qualify him/her for this particular honor).

I am sure you will agree, (name) is deserving of this prestigious recognition.

Respectfully,

STUDENT APPLYING TO SCHOOL

Dear (**name of dean of admissions**):

I am pleased to offer this recommendation on behalf of (**student**). I have been acquainted with (**name**) since (**he/she**) joined our staff as a (**position**) for (**length of time**) prior to (**his/her**) graduation from (**name of school**).

During that time I was able to observe (**his/her**) job skills as well as (**his/her**) interaction with other employees. I found (**his/her**) performance consistently superior in both instances.

(**He/she**) displayed an outstanding aptitude for learning and applying (**his/her**) knowledge in a manner far superior to my initial expectations.

I believe (**he/she**) would approach (**his/her**) studies with the same determination and enthusiasm (**he/she**) displayed while in our employ.

Should you have any questions, or require additional information, please do not hesitate to contact me at (**telephone number**).

Respectfully,

ENDORSING A GUEST SPEAKER

Dear (**name**),

I understand your organization is seeking a guest speaker to address (**group**) at your annual convention on the subject of (**topic**). I believe you will find (**name**) of (**school/organization**) to be just the person you are looking for.

I recently had the pleasure of attending a (**lecture/seminar/other**) and hearing (**name**) speak on (**topic**). Even though (**his/her**) message was brief, it was delivered with the confidence of someone thoroughly familiar with the subject, in a manner that was both entertaining and informative. The most surprising aspect was the obvious disappointment of the audience—that it ended too soon!

If you would like to contact (**name**), (**he/she**) may be reached at (**address and/or telephone number**). I suggest you might want to speak with (**him/her**) at your earliest convenience as (**he/she**) is in great demand and a few days' delay could mean a missed opportunity.

Sincerely,

DECLINING TO OFFER A REFERENCE

Dear (name),

I have received your inquiry of (date) regarding (name of applicant). (Our records indicate/I can verify) (he/she) was employed by (friends/company) for approximately (length of time) in (approximate dates/year).

I cannot personally attest to the reason for (his/her) (resignation/termination of employment), and I feel it would be inappropriate to speculate. Perhaps (applicant) can provide you with another reference more familiar with (his/her) job skills and performance.

Sincerely,

Chapter 35

GENTLE REMINDERS

Call or Visit a Friend
Repair Damage Caused by Pets or Children
Return a Borrowed Item
Repay a Personal Loan
Pay Share of Cost
Pay Dues or Fees
Submit Plans or Ideas, as Promised
Support a Candidate
Promised Favor for a Friend or Relative
Attend a Meeting

"So little time, and so much to do!" has become a commonplace lament in our fast-paced society today. Offices and homes boast an assortment of calendars, message recorders, and hastily scrawled notes to remind us of a deadline, to return a borrowed item, to return library books, to visit a friend, or to attend a meeting. Just as we tend to overlook obligations from time to time, so others need an occasional reminder.

You will surely recognize many of the situations depicted in the model letters that follow. Perhaps some will remind you of something you have forgotten.

CALL OR VISIT A FRIEND

Dear **(name)**,

I have just returned from visiting with our mutual friend, **(name)**, at **(facility)**. **(Recovery/rehabilitation)** can be a long and tedious process, and **(he/she)** appears to be progressing well at this point.

(He/she) spoke often of you and **(his/her)** other friends at **(work/school/club/church/ organization)**. I am certain your busy schedule does not allow you a great deal of flexibility, but a brief visit would do so much to brighten **(his/her)** day. Won't you please telephone **(him/her)** and plan to stop by soon? Visiting hours are **(days and time)**.

Please telephone me after your visit, and let me know how **(name)** is getting along. I may be reached at **(telephone number)**.

Sincerely,

REPAIR DAMAGE CAUSED BY PETS OR CHILDREN

Dear **(name of parents/owners)**,

I am enclosing a written estimate from **(name of repair shop/company)** to **(repair/clean)** the **(item)** in my **(room)**.

(If damage was caused by child)

I am certain the incident that occurred on **(day)** was not an intentional act of mischief. Please reassure **(name of child)** the damage can readily be repaired.

I appreciate your kind offer to pay the cost of restoring the **(item)** to its original condition and have informed **(owner or representative of shop/company)** to expect your call approving the work within the week. The telephone number is shown on the estimate.

Sincerely,

RETURN A BORROWED ITEM

Dear (name),

On (date), at your request, I loaned my (item) to (school/club/organization) for (event). I was assured it would be returned the day after.

This (item) is a cherished family heirloom, and, naturally, I am eager to have it returned as promised. I would very much appreciate your assistance in locating it and having it delivered to my home by (day).

Thank you for your prompt attention to my request.

Sincerely,

REPAY PERSONAL LOAN

Dear (name),

I have not received your check for ($ amount) toward your personal loan of (total $ amount), which I advanced to you on (date). From time to time we all find ourselves preoccupied with other matters and fail to remember an obligation. I am sure this is merely an oversight since you are always so prompt.

If you sent the payment in time to have reached me by now, you may wish to contact your bank and arrange to have a "stop payment" placed on the original check so that another may be issued.

Thanks for your prompt attention to this matter. I look forward to hearing from you soon.

Sincerely,

PAY SHARE OF COST

Dear (name),

I am enclosing a copy of the invoice from (store) for the (items) (club or organization) donated to (group/school/facility).

The total amount for (number) of (sets/pairs) is ($ amount). Each member is responsible for ($ amount of individual donation) of the cost. I will need your check by (date) to satisfy this obligation before it becomes past due.

Thanks so much for participating in this very worthy project. Your kindness and generosity will be remembered and appreciated long after the (**holiday season/special occasion**) has passed.

Sincerely,

PAY DUES OR FEES

Dear (**name**),

Our records indicate you have not paid your (**annual/monthly**) membership (**dues/fee**) of (**$ amount**); therefore, since (**number of weeks/months**) have elapsed, we must assume that you do not wish to (**renew/continue**) your membership in (**club/organization/class**). We will note on the record that this is a VOLUNTARY LAPSE.

Should you decide to (**continue/renew**) your privileges, you will need to submit the full amount currently due plus an additional reinstatement fee of (**$ amount**).

If you have paid the (**annual/monthly**) (**dues/fee**), we will require a copy of your canceled check or a receipt if you paid cash. We will be happy to correct our records and offer our apologies for the error.

We hope you will plan to join us again soon and look forward to welcoming you back to (**club/organization/class**).

Sincerely,

SUBMIT PLANS AND IDEAS, AS PROMISED

Dear (**name**),

the (**organization**) show planning committee will meet at (**location**) on (**date**) at (**time**) to make final arrangements for this season's (**event**).

We must have plans and specifications from all participants no later than (**date**) so that (**spaces/booths**) may be appropriately assigned to ensure the most favorable exposure to all contributing members.

To date we have not received yours, and since you have always been one of our most enthusiastic supporters, we are certain you will want to submit your requirements as quickly as possible.

We look forward to working with you again this year and appreciate your continued interest and participation in this exciting event.

Cordially,

SUPPORT A CANDIDATE

Dear **(name)**,

I would like to encourage you to attend the next **(organization)** meeting at **(location)** on **(day/date)** at **(time)**.

We will be casting our ballots for association officers, and I urge your favorable consideration of **(name of candidate)**, who would make a very fine **(office/position)**

(Name of candidate) has volunteered **(his/her)** time as a **(role)** and has served on the committees of several of the **(organization's)** fund raising events over the past **(number)** years. In addition to **(his/her)** involvement with **(organization)**, **(his/her)** background in **(vocation)** provides the professional expertise needed in this vital position.

Please lend your support to this very deserving candidate by voting for **(name of candidate)** for **(office)** on **(date)**.

Sincerely,

PROMISED FAVOR FOR A FRIEND OR RELATIVE

Dear **(name)**,

Just a brief note to let you know my **(friend/relative)**, **(name)**, has just arrived in town and would like to talk with you regarding her interest in **(specific goal/club/school)**.

As we discussed earlier, **(name)** is **(very talented/quite experienced)** in **(nature of talent or interest)**, and I am confident you will quickly recognize **(he/she)** has much to offer the **(goal/club/school)**.

I appreciate your kind offer to sponsor **(name)**, and I look forward to introducing the two of you at a mutually convenient time.

If I may reciprocate, do not hesitate to contact me.

Sincerely,

ATTEND A MEETING

Dear **(name)**,

The **(club/organization)** will hold its monthly board meeting on **(date)** at **(location)**, beginning at **(time)**.

The agenda will include (**topics for discussion**). With so many topics to be discussed, it is imperative that we begin the meeting on time, so please be prompt. Your cooperation will be beneficial to everyone.

If you are unable to attend this very important session, please contact (**function coordinator**) at (**telephone number**) no later than (**date**), and give (**him/her**) the name of the member whom you have designated to vote your preferences on the various issues.

Sincerely,

Chapter 36

SPECIAL OCCASIONS
AND HOLIDAYS

Anniversary of Business Partnership
Birthday of Son/Daughter
Baptism/Christening
Confirmation
Bar/Bat Mitzvah
Christmas
Hanukkah
Mother's Day
Father's Day
Grandparent's Day

The magic of holidays and those special occasions that touch our hearts offer a welcome respite from the hectic pace of our day to day routines. It is a time to pause and take stock of who we are, give thanks for what we have, reaffirm our faith and love for one another, and through our own personal letters, embrace those at a distance.

While the moment may seem to pass all too quickly, the memories will linger for others in the messages you cared enough to write.

ANNIVERSARY OF BUSINESS PARTNERSHIP

Dear (name),

It has been (number) (months/years) since we formally entered into a partnership to start (name of business). Without question, I consider it one of the most important and gratifying decisions I ever made.

Though times were not always easy, and the rewards did not seem to justify our efforts, I still remember how thrilled we both were when the ink turned from red to black!

I believe we surprised ourselves more than anyone else, and I could not have done it without your encouragement and determination.

Thanks, partner, for being my friend through the bad times as well as the good. I look forward to celebrating many more anniversaries in the future.

Warmest personal regards,

BIRTHDAY OF SON/DAUGHTER

Dearest (name),

So many times your (mother/father) and I have heard you say how happy you would be to reach your (number) birthday! Well, this is it. We hope it is all you expected.

(Mom/Dad) and I have reflected upon this day with mixed emotions. It hardly seems possible so much time has passed since we first brought you home. Little did we realize at the time that we were about to embark upon a journey of such magnitude and wonder!

From kindergarten, to scouts, your learner's permit, your first (girl/boy) friend, and finally college, we survived it all. Oh, there were mishaps and stumbling blocks along the way, but always there was love and pride.

You are the best of both of us, and we are well pleased. If ever there was a testament of our love for one another, it is you.

Happy birthday, sweetheart. We love you.

BAPTISM/CHRISTENING

Dear (parents),

How we wish we could be present at (church/cathedral) on (date) for the (christening/baptism) of your (beautiful/wonderful) little (daughter/son).

As (she/he) grows, each day will bring new discoveries and surprises, and you will always remember the joy that filled your hearts on this special day.

May God's love embrace each of you and bless you in the years to come.

Our deepest affection to you and (name of child).

CONFIRMATION

Dearest (name),

We have watched you grow into a lovely young girl and witnessed so often the beauty of your gentle and caring ways. On this special day, as you are received into the loving shelter of God's embrace, our hearts are filled with love and pride.

Even though we cannot be present to share in the joy and celebration of this special time in your life, you will be in our hearts and prayers.

Fondly,

BAR/BAT MITZVAH

Dear (name),

It seems only yesterday we first shared your parents' joy at the birth of their (son/daughter). Now we have cause to rejoice once again as you prepare to celebrate (Bar/Bat) Mitzvah.

Even though the years have passed too quickly, they have been filled with love, laughter, and pride in all that you are and will become.

We congratulate you, and pray that God's wisdom and blessings will guide you in the years to come.

With love,

CHRISTMAS

To all our family and friends . . .

This is a very special time of year when we pause to rededicate ourselves to our faith, reaffirm our love for family and friends, and reflect upon the memories of those who are no longer with us.

It is a time of mixed blessings, joy and sadness, triumphs and tears, but, above all, a time to give thanks for all that we have.

We cherish each and every one of you in our hearts, and hope the coming year will find you richly blessed in every way.

Merry Christmas to all, and God bless you and yours.

With deepest love and affection,

HANUKKAH

Dear (name),

At this special holiday season we pause to remember all our many friends and to give thanks for the many ways they enrich our lives.

As we each rededicate ourselves to our faith, we are ever mindful of the hopes, dreams, and common purposes that guide us all.

We rejoice in your celebration and cherish you in our hearts.

God bless.

Affectionately,

MOTHER'S DAY

Dear (name),

We could not let Mother's Day pass without pausing for a moment to tell you how very special you are to all of us, and how our lives have been enriched by your many kindnesses through the years.

We cannot recall a time when you haven't been there with a kind word, a helping hand, and encouragement when it was needed most.

Your sweet and gentle nature fills our lives with sunshine, our yesterdays with gold, and tomorrow with promise.

Thank you for all the memories, and those yet to come. You are very dear to us all.

With love,

FATHER'S DAY

Dear (name),

On this special day, we pause to pay tribute and give thanks for those very special men whose strength, patience, and wisdom guide and protect us throughout our lives.

Your kindness and irrepressible humor have enriched us in so many ways. We cherish our memories and look forward to many more wonderful years together.

Happy Father's Day to our favorite ("Dad"/"Uncle"/other).

With deepest affection

GRANDPARENT'S DAY

Dear (Grandmother/Grandfather),

How wonderful it is to have a special day to honor our grandparents. I am so privileged and blessed to have the two of you. You have always been there to love, guide, and protect me.

(If from an adopted child)

Though I was not born into this family, I never felt that I was different or unwanted. When Mom and Dad chose me to be their own, they gave me more than shelter and care; they gave me love, and, most important, they gave me you.

How can I ever thank you for all you have done for me, or make you understand how deeply you are loved and cherished?

Yours,

Chapter 37

THANKS AND
APPRECIATION

Gift
Encouragement
Favor for Friend or Family Member
Expression of Sympathy/Support
Being Honest
Constructive Advice
Help in Resolving a Problem

A personal note is often more meaningful to the recipient than a well-chosen greeting card, especially when a "thank you" is in order. Your handwritten note lets the recipient know how much you appreciated his or her gift, whether tangible or intangible. Your friends give you their sympathy, support, assistance, honesty, encouragement, or advice willingly and freely, and your "thank you" is like a return gift of kindness.

GIFT

Dear (**name**),

Thank you for the lovely gift you sent for my (**wedding/retirement/birthday/other**). As always, you picked out a perfect gift! The (**describe gift**) is (**beautiful/just what I hoped for/other**)! Every time I see it, I will think of you and remember your thoughtfulness. How lucky I am to have you for a friend!

Love,

ENCOURAGEMENT

Dear (**name**),

You probably don't realize how much your encouragement has meant to me as I have been (**struggling to resolve the conflicts between my son and me/trying to meet my editor's deadline/working to complete a difficult project/other**). You have lifted me up when I felt down on myself, you have pointed to the light at the end of the tunnel when I was buried in darkness, and you got me off dead center when I felt stuck. It felt so good to know that you were there for me whenever I needed you. Thank you for being my friend.

Love,

FAVOR FOR FRIEND OR FAMILY MEMBER

Dear (**name**),

Thank you for helping (**name of relative or friend**) with (**his/her**) (**describe favor**). I knew you were the right person to ask since (**give reason for asking this person**). On (**his/her**) behalf, I want you to know how much (**he/she**) appreciates all that you did for (**him/her**). It was good of you to assist (**him/her**) in this area where (**he/she**) did not know where to turn.

Sincerely,

EXPRESSION OF SYMPATHY/SUPPORT

Dear (**name**),

Thank you for your recent letter. Your support means a great deal to me during this difficult time. As you know, I was not prepared for (**describe problem/situation**), and it has not been easy for me to adjust. Your faith in me is one of the things that is helping me to (**describe how you are being helped**). Thanks for reminding me that any problem carries with it an opportunity to grow in new ways. It means a lot to know that you are there for me.

Love,

BEING HONEST

Dear (**name**),

I want to thank you for being straightforward and honest with me when we were discussing my problems. When I am involved in an emotionally charged situation, it is difficult for me to see clearly what is happening. I came to you because I needed honest feedback on my behavior, and that is exactly what I got. Some of your comments were not easy to take, but I am still grateful for them because they helped me to clarify what I am doing and how I need to change.

I value your friendship and appreciate your willingness to risk being upfront with me.

Love,

CONSTRUCTIVE ADVICE

Dear (**name**),

Thanks so much for your helpful advice about (**describe subject**). Since you have recently made a similar decision, I knew you would be a good person to turn to. In addition, you know (**me/us**) well enough to help (**me/us**) assess (**my/our**) needs. It made such a difference to (**me/us**) to hear your constructive feedback on (**me/our**) thoughts and ideas. Your input has certainly helped (**me/us**) in making this critical decision.

As always, (**I/we**) appreciate your time and concern.

Love,

HELP IN RESOLVING A PROBLEM

Dear (**name**),

I wanted to let you know how much I appreciated it when you helped (**name**) and me resolve our disagreement about (**describe cause**). (**He/she**) and I were both equally adamant about the best way to proceed, and there seemed to be no way that we could combine our two opposing ideas. You came up with a third idea that we both could agree upon. Your intervention enabled us to work together on (**describe project/situation**) instead of being at odds. Thanks to you, our work is proceeding on schedule.

Sincerely,

Appendix

"INFORMATION PLEASE . . ."
A Directory of Selected Federal, State, and National Resources

Aging
Banking Authorities
Better Business Bureaus
Broadcast Networks (Major)
Consumer Protection Offices
Education
Environmental Protection Agencies
Federal Trade Commission
Health and Human Services, Department of
Health-Related Organizations
Insurance Regulators
Internal Revenue Service
Medicare Carriers
Medicare Peer Review Organizations
Occupational Safety and Health Administration
Small Business Administration
Social Security Administration
U.S. Customs Service
U.S. Government Offices
U.S. Passport Services
Utility Commissions
Veterans Affairs

AGING

State Agencies

Alabama Commission on Aging
136 Catoma Street
Montgomery, Alabama 36130
(205) 261-5743
1-800-243-5463 (toll free in Alabama)

Older Alaskans Commission
Post Office Box C, MS 0209
Juneau, Alaska 99811
(907) 465-3250

Department of Economic Security
Aging and Adult Administration
1400 West Washington Street
Phoenix, Arizona 85007
(602) 254-4446

Division of Aging and Adult Services
Donaghey Plaza South, Suite 1417
7th and Main Streets
Post Office Box 1437/Slot 1412
Little Rock, Arkansas 72203-1437
(501) 682-2441

Department of Aging
1600 K Street
Sacramento, California 95814
(916) 322-3887

Aging and Adult Services
Department of Social Services
1575 Sherman Street, 10th Floor
Denver, Colorado 80203-1714
(303) 866-5905

Department on Aging
175 Main Street
Hartford, Connecticut 06106
(203) 566-7772
1-800-443-9946 (toll free in Connecticut)

Division of Aging
Department of Health and Social Services
1901 North Dupont Highway
New Castle, Delaware 19720
(302) 421-6791

Office on Aging
Executive Office of the Mayor
1424 K Street, N.W., 2nd Floor
Washington, D.C. 20005
(202) 724-5626
(202) 724-5622

Florida Department of Insurance
The Capitol
Tallahassee, Florida 32301
1-800-342-2762

Office of Aging
Department of Human Resources
878 Peachtree Street, N.E., Room 632
Atlanta, Georgia 30309
(404) 894-5333

Executive Office on Aging
335 Merchant Street, Room 241
Honolulu, Hawaii 96813
(808) 548-2593

Office on Aging
Statehouse, Room 114
Boise, Idaho 83720
(208) 334-3833

Department on Aging
421 East Capitol Avenue
Springfield, Illinois 62701
(217) 785-2870

Department of Human Services
251 North Illinois
Post Office Box 7083
Indianapolis, Indiana 46207-7083
(317) 232-1139

Department of Elder Affairs
Jewett Building, Suite 236
914 Grand Avenue
Des Moines, Iowa 50319
(515) 281-5187

Department on Aging
122-S Docking State Office Building
915 S.W. Harrison
Topeka, Kansas 66612-1500
(913) 296-4986

Division for Aging Services
Department for Social Services
275 East Main Street
Frankfort, Kentucky 40621
(502) 564-6930

Governor's Office of Elderly Affairs
Post Office Box 80374
Baton Rouge, Louisiana 70898-0374
(504) 925-1700

Maine Committee of Aging
State House, Station 127
Augusta, Maine 04333
(207) 289-3658

State Agency on Aging
301 West Preston Street
Baltimore, Maryland 21201
(301) 225-1102

Executive Office of Elder Affairs
38 Chauncy Street
Boston, Massachusetts 02111
(617) 727-7750
1-800-882-2003 (toll free in Massachusetts)

Office of Services to the aging
Post Office Box 30026
Lansing, Michigan 48909
(517) 373-8230

Minnesota Board on Aging
Metro Square Building, Suite 204
121 East 7th Street
St. Paul, Minnesota 55101
(612) 296-2770

Council on Aging
301 West Pearl Street
Jackson, Mississippi 39203-3092
(601) 949-2070
1-800-222-7622 (toll free in Mississippi)

Missouri Division of Insurance
Truman Building 630
Post Office Box 690
Jefferson City, Missouri 65102-0690
1-800-235-5503 (toll free in Missouri)

Department of Family Services
Post Office Box 8005
Helena, Montana 59604
(406) 444-5900

Department on Aging
Legal Services Developer
State Office Building
301 Centennial Mall South
Lincoln, Nebraska 68509
(402) 471-2306

Department of Human Resources
Division for Aging Services
505 East King Street, Room 101
Carson City, Nevada 89710
(702) 885-4210

Department of Health and Human Services
Division of Elderly and Adult Services
6 Hazen Drive
Concord, New Hampshire 03301
(603) 271-4390

Department of Community Affairs
Division on Aging
South Broad and Front Streets
CN 807
Trenton, New Jersey 08625-0807
(609) 292-0920

Agency on Aging
La Villa Rivera Building, 4th Floor
224 East Palace Avenue
Santa Fe, New Mexico 87501
(505) 827-7640
1-800-432-2080 (toll free in New Mexico)

State Office for the Aging
Agency Building
#2 Empire State Plaza
Albany, New York 12223-0001
(518) 474-5731
1-800-342-9871 (toll free in New York)

Department of Human Resources
Division of Aging
1985 Umstead Drive
Raleigh, North Carolina 27603
(919) 733-3983

Department of Human Services
Aging Services Division
State Capitol Building
Bismarck, North Dakota 58505
(701) 224-2577

Department of Aging
50 West Broad Street, 9th Floor
Columbus, Ohio 43266-0501
(614) 466-1220

Department of Human Services
Aging Services Division
Post Office Box 25352
Oklahoma City, Oklahoma 73125
(405) 521-2327

Department of Human Resources
Senior Services Division
313 Public Service Building
Salem, Oregon 97310
(503) 378-4636
1-800-232-3020 (toll free in Oregon)

Department of Aging
231 State Street
Barto Building
Harrisburg, Pennsylvania 17101
(717) 783-1550

Department of Elderly Affairs
79 Washington Street
Providence, Rhode Island 02903
(401) 277-2858

Commission on Aging
400 Arbor Lake Drive, Suite B-500
Columbia, South Carolina 29223
(803) 735-0210

Agency on Aging
Adult Services and Aging
Richard F. Kneip Building
700 Governors Drive
Pierre, South Dakota 57501-2291
(605) 773-3656

Commission on Aging
Commerce and Insurance Department
Volunteer Plaza
James Robinson Parkway
Nashville, Tennessee 37219-5573
(615) 741-2241

Department on Aging
Post Office Box 12786
Capitol Station
Austin, Texas 78711
(512) 444-2727

Division of Aging and Adult Services
120 North 200 West
Post Office Box 45500
Salt Lake City, Utah 84145-0500
(801) 538-3910

Office on Aging
Waterbury Complex
103 South Main Street
Waterbury, Vermont 05676
(802) 241-2400

Department for the Aging
101 North 14th Street, 18th Floor
Richmond, Virginia 23219
(804) 225-2271
1-800-552-4464 (toll free in Virginia)

Aging and Adult Services Administration
Department of Social and Health Services
Mail Stop OB-44-A
Olympia, Washington 98504
(206) 586-3768

Commission on Aging
State Capitol Complex
Holly Grove
Charleston, West Virginia 25305
(304) 348-3317
1-800-642-3671 (toll free in West Virginia)

Bureau on Aging
Department of Health and Social Services
Post Office Box 7851
Madison, Wisconsin 53707
(608) 266-2536
1-800-242-1060 (toll free in Wisconsin)

Commission on Aging
Hathaway Building, 1st Floor
Cheyenne, Wyoming 82002
(307) 777-7986
1-800-442-2766 (toll free in Wyoming)

Division of Senior Citizens
Department of Public Health and
    Social Services
Post Office Box 2816
Agana, Guam 96910
(617) 734-2942

Governors Office of Elderly Affairs
Gericulture Commission
Post Office Box 11398
Santurce, Puerto Rico 00910
(809) 722-2429 or 722-0225

Department of Human Services
Barbel Plaza South
Charlotte Amalie
St. Thomas, Virgin Islands 00802
(809) 774-0930

Other Organizations

American Association of Retired Persons
    (AARP)
3200 East Carson Street
Lakewood, California 90712

Commissioner, Administration on Aging
Office of Human Development Services
Department of Health and Human Services
200 Independence Avenue, S.W.
Washington, D.C. 20201

Employment and Training Administration
Department of Labor
200 Constitution Avenue, N.W.
Washington, D.C. 29201

BANKING AUTHORITIES

Superintendent of Banks
166 Commerce Street, 3rd Floor
Montgomery, Alabama 36130
(205) 261-3452

Director of Banking
Corporations and Securities
Post Office Box D
Juneau, Alaska 99811
(907) 465-2521

Superintendent of Banks
3225 North Central, Suite 815
Phoenix, Arizona 85012
(602) 255-4421
1-800-544-0708 (toll free in Arizona)

Bank Commissioner
Tower Building
323 Center Street, Suite 500
Little Rock, Arkansas 72201
(501) 371-1117

Superintendent of Banks
111 Pine Street, Suite 1100
San Francisco, California 94111-5613
(415) 557-3535
1-800-622-0620 (toll free in California)

State Bank Commissioner
Division of Banking
First West Plaza, Suite 650
303 West Colfax
Denver, Colorado 80204
(303) 620-4358

Banking Commissioner
44 Capitol Avenue
Hartford, Connecticut 06106
(203) 566-4560
1-800-842-2220 (toll free in Connecticut)

State Bank Commissioner
555 E. Loockerman Street, Suite 210
Dover, Delaware 19901
(302) 736-4235

Superintendent of Banking and
    Financial Institutions
1250 I Street, N.W., Suite 1003
Washington, D.C. 20005
(202) 727-1563

State Comptroller
State Capitol Building
Tallahassee, Florida 32399-0350
(904) 488-0286
1-800-848-3792 (toll free in Florida)

Commissioner, Banking and Finance
2990 Brandywine Road, Suite 200
Atlanta, Georgia 30341
(404) 986-1633

Commissioner, Financial Institutions
Post Office Box 2054
Honolulu, Hawaii 96805
(808) 548-5855

Department of Finance
700 West State Street, 2nd Floor
Boise, Idaho 83720
(208) 334-3319

Commissioner of Banks and
  Trust Companies
117 South 5th Street, Room 100
Springfield, Illinois 62701
(217) 785-2837
1-800-634-5452 (toll free in Illinois)
(credit card rate information only)

Department of Financial Institutions
Indiana State Office Building, Room 1024
Indianapolis, Indiana 46204
(317) 232-3955
1-800-382-4880 (toll free in Indiana)

Superintendent of Banking
200 East Grand, Suite 300
Des Moines, Iowa 50309
(515) 281-4014

State Bank Commissioner
700 Jackson Street, Suite 300
Topeka, Kansas 66603
(913) 296-2266

Commissioner, Department of Financial
  Institutions
911 Leawood Drive
Frankfort, Kentucky 40601
(502) 564-3390

Commissioner Financial Institutions
Post Office Box 94095
Baton Rouge, Louisiana 70804
(504) 925-4660

Superintendent of Banking
State House Station #36
Augusta, Maine 04333
(207) 582-8713

Bank Commissioner
34 Market Place
Baltimore, Maryland 21202
(301) 333-6262
1-800-492-7521 (toll free in Maryland)

Commissioner of Banks
100 Cambridge Street
Boston, Massachusetts 02202
(617) 727-3120

Commissioner, Financial Institutions Bureau
Post Office Box 30224
Lansing, Michigan 48909
(517) 373-3460

Deputy Commissioner of Commerce
500 Metro Square Building, 5th Floor
St. Paul, Minnesota 55101
(612) 296-2135

Department of Banking and Consumer
  Finance
Post Office Box 23729
Jackson, Mississippi 39225
(601) 359-1031
1-800-826-2499 (toll free in Mississippi)

Commissioner of Finance
Post Office Box 716
Jefferson City, Missouri 65102
(314) 751-3242

Commissioner of Financial Institutions
1520 East 6th Avenue, Room 50
Helena, Montana 59620-0542
(406) 444-2091

Director of Banking and Finance
301 Centennial Mall, South
Lincoln, Nebraska 68509
(402) 471-2171

Commissioner, Financial Institutions
406 East 2nd Street
Carson City, Nevada 89710
(702) 885-4260

Bank Commissioner
45 South Main Street
Concord, New Hampshire 03301
(603) 271-3561

Commissioner of Banking
20 West State Street
CN 040
Trenton, New Jersey 08625
(609) 292-3420
1-800-421-0069 (toll free in New Jersey)

Director, Financial Institutions Division
Bataan Memorial Building, Room 307
Santa Fe, New Mexico 87503
(505) 827-7740

Superintendent of Banks
Two Rector Street
New York, New York 10006
(212) 618-6642
1-800-522-3330 (toll free in New York)

Commissioner of Banks
Post Office Box 29512
Raleigh, North Carolina 27626-0512
(919) 733-3016

Commissioner of Banking and Financial
  Institutions
600 East Boulevard, 13th Floor
Bismarck, North Dakota 58505
(701) 224-2256

Superintendent of Banks
77 South High Street
Columbus, Ohio 43266-0549
(614) 466-2932

Bank Commissioner
Malco Building
4100 North Lincoln Boulevard
Oklahoma City, Oklahoma 73105
(405) 521-2783

Division of Finance and Corporate Securities
Labor and Industries Building, Room 21
Salem, Oregon 97310
(503) 378-4140

Secretary of Banking
333 Market Street, 16th Floor
Harrisburg, Pennsylvania 17101
(717) 787-6991
1-800-PA-BANKS (toll free in Pennsylvania)

Superintendent of Banking and Securities
233 Richmond Street, Suite 231
Providence, Rhode Island 02903-4231
(401) 277-2405

Commissioner of Banking
1026 Sumter Street, Room 217
Columbia, South Carolina 29201
(803) 734-1050

Director of Banking and Finance
State Capitol Building
Pierre, South Dakota 57501
(605) 773-2236

Commissioner, Financial Institutions
John Sevier Building, 4th Floor
Nashville, Tennessee 37219
(615) 741-2236

Banking Commissioner
2601 North Lamar
Austin, Texas 78705
(512) 479-1200

Commissioner, Financial Institutions
Post Office Box 89
Salt Lake City, Utah 84110
(801) 530-6502

Commissioner, Banking and Insurance
State Office Building
Montpelier, Vermont 05602
(802) 828-3301

Commissioner, Financial Institutions
Post Office Box 2-AE
Richmond, Virginia 23205
(804) 786-3657
1-800-552-7945 (toll free in Virginia)

Supervisor of Banking
General Administration Building, Room 219
Olympia, Washington 98504
(206) 753-6520

Commissioner of Banking
State Capitol Complex
Building 3, Room 311
Charleston, West Virginia 25305
(304) 348-2294
1-800-642-9056 (toll free in West Virginia)

Commissioner of Banking
131 West Wilson, 8th Floor
Madison, Wisconsin 53703
(608) 266-1621

State Examiner
Herschler Building, 3rd Floor East
Cheyenne, Wyoming 82002
(307) 777-6600

Department of Revenue and Taxation
Post Office Box 2796
Agana, Guam 96910

Commissioner of Banking
G.P.O. Box 70324
San Juan, Puerto Rico 00936
(809) 721-7064

Chairman of the Banking Board
Kongens Garde 18
St. Thomas, Virgin Islands 00802
(809) 774-2991

BETTER BUSINESS BUREAUS

National

Council of Better Business Bureaus Inc.
4200 Wilson Boulevard
Arlington, Virginia 22203
(703) 276-0100

Local Bureaus

Better Business Bureau
1214 South 20th Street
Birmingham, Alabama 35205
(205) 558-2222

Better Business Bureau
Post Office Box 383
Huntsville, Alabama 35804
(205) 533-1640

Better Business Bureau
707 Van Antwerp Building
Mobile, Alabama 36602
(205) 433-5494
(205) 433-5495

Better Business Bureau
Commerce Street, Suite 810
Montgomery, Alabama 36104
(205) 262-5606

Better Business Bureau
3380 C Street, Suite 100
Anchorage, Alaska 99503
(907) 562-0704

Better Business Bureau
4428 North 12th Street
Phoenix, Arizona 85014
(602) 264-1721

Better Business Bureau
50 West Drachman Street, Suite 103
Tucson, Arizona 85705
(602) 622-7651 (inquiries)
(602) 622-7654 (complaints)

Better Business Bureau
1415 South University Avenue
Little Rock, Arkansas 72204
(501) 664-7274

Better Business Bureau
705 18th Street
Bakersfield, California 93301
(805) 322-2074

Better Business Bureau
Post Office Box 970
Colton, California 92324
(714) 825-7280

Better Business Bureau
6101 Ball Road, Suite 309
Cypress, California 90630
(714) 527-0680

Better Business Bureau
5070 North Sixth, Suite 176
Fresno, California 93710
(209) 222-8111

Better Business Bureau
510 16th Street, Suite 550
Oakland, California 94612
(415) 839-5900

Better Business Bureau
400 S Street
Sacramento, California 95814
(916) 443-6843

Better Business Bureau
525 B Street, Suite 301
San Diego, California 92101-4408
(619) 234-0966

Better Business Bureau
33 New Montgomery Street Tower
San Francisco, California 94105
(415) 243-9999

Better Business Bureau
1505 Meridian Avenue
San Jose, California 95125
(408) 978-8700

Better Business Bureau
Post Office Box 294
San Mateo, California 94401
(415) 347-1251

Better Business Bureau
Post Office Box 746
Santa Barbara, California 93102
(805) 963-8657

Better Business Bureau
1111 North Center Street
Stockton, California 95202
(209) 948-4880, 4881

Better Business Bureau
Post Office Box 7970
Colorado Springs, Colorado 80933
(719) 636-1155

Better Business Bureau
1780 South Belleaire, Suite 700
Denver, Colorado 80222
(303) 758-2100 (inquiries)
(303) 758-2212 (complaints)

Better Business Bureau
1730 South College Avenue, #303
Fort Collins, Colorado 80525
(303) 484-1348

Better Business Bureau
432 Broadway
Pueblo, Colorado 81004
(719) 542-6464

Better Business Bureau
2345 Black Rock Turnpike
Fairfield, Connecticut 06430
(203) 374-6161

Better Business Bureau
2080 Silas Deane Highway
Rock Hill, Connecticut 06067-2311
(203) 529-3575

Better Business Bureau
100 South Turnpike Road
Wallingford, Connecticut 06492
(203) 269-2700 (inquiries)
(203) 269-4457 (complaints)

Better Business Bureau
Post Office Box 300
Milford, Delaware 19963
(302) 422-6300 (Kent)
(302) 856-6969 (Sussex)

Better Business Bureau
Post Office Box 5361
Wilmington, Delaware 19808
(302) 996-9200

Better Business Bureau
1012 14th Street, N.W.
Washington, D.C. 20005
(202) 393-8000

Better Business Bureau
13770 58th Street, North, #309
Clearwater, Florida 33520
(813) 535-5522

Better Business Bureau
2976-E Cleveland Avenue
Fort Myers, Florida 33901
(813) 334-7331, 7152

Better Business Bureau
3100 University Boulevard, South, #23
Jacksonville, Florida 32216
(904) 721-2288

Better Business Bureau
2605 Maitland Center Parkway
Maitland, Florida 32751-7147
(407) 660-9500

Better Business Bureau
16291 N.W. 57th Avenue
Miami, Florida 33014-6709
(305) 625-0307 (inquiries for Dade County)
(305) 625-1302 (complaints for Dade County)
(305) 524-2803 (inquiries for Broward
County)
(305) 527-1643 (complaints for Broward
County)

Better Business Bureau
250 School Road, Suite 11-W
New Port Richey, Florida 34652
(813) 842-5459

Better Business Bureau
Post Office Box 1511
Pensacola, Florida 32597-1511
(904) 433-6111

Better Business Bureau
1950 Port St. Lucie Boulevard, #211
Port St. Lucie, Florida 34952
(407) 878-2010
(407) 337-2083

Better Business Bureau
1111 North Westshore Boulevard, Suite 207
Tampa, Florida 33607
(813) 875-6200

Better Business Bureau
2247 Palm Beach Lakes Boulevard, #211
West Palm Beach, Florida 33409-3408
(407) 686-2200

Better Business Bureau
1319-B Dawson Road
Albany, Georgia 31707
(912) 883-0744

Better Business Bureau
100 Edgewood Avenue, Suite 1012
Atlanta, Georgia 30303
(404) 688-4910

Better Business Bureau
Post Office Box 2085
Augusta, Georgia 30903
(404) 722-1574

Better Business Bureau
Post Office Box 2587
Columbus, Georgia 31902
(404) 324-0712 (inquiries)
(404) 324-0713 (complaints)

Better Business Bureau
6606 Abercorn Street, Suite 108-C
Savannah, Georgia 31416
(912) 354-7521

Better Business Bureau
1600 Kapiolani Boulevard, Suite 704
Honolulu, Hawaii 96814
(808) 942-2355

Better Business Bureau
409 West Jefferson
Boise, Idaho 83702
(208) 342-4649
(208) 467-5547

Better Business Bureau
545 Shoup, Suite 210
Idaho Falls, Idaho 83402
(208) 523-9754

Better Business Bureau
211 West Wacker Drive
Chicago, Illinois 60606
(312) 444-1188 (inquiries)
(312) 346-3313 (complaints)

Better Business Bureau
109 S.W. Jefferson Street, #305
Peoria, Illinois 61602
(309) 673-5194

Better Business Bureau
515 North Court Street
Rockford, Illinois 61110
(815) 963-2222

Better Business Bureau
Post Office Box 405
Elkhart, Indiana 46515
(219) 262-8996

Better Business Bureau
119 S.E. Fourth Street
Evansville, Indiana 47708
(812) 422-6879

Better Business Bureau
1203 Webster Street
Fort Wayne, Indiana 46802
(219) 423-4433

Better Business Bureau
4231 Cleveland Street
Gary, Indiana 46408
(219) 980-1511
(219) 769-8053
(219) 926-5669

Better Business Bureau
Victoria Centre
22 East Washington Street
Indianapolis, Indiana 46204
(317) 637-0197

Better Business Bureau
320 South Washington Street, #101
Marion, Indiana 46952
(317) 668-8954, 8955

Better Business Bureau
Whitinger Building, Room 150
Muncie, Indiana 47306
(317) 285-5668

Better Business Bureau
509 85 U.S. #33, North
South Bend, Indiana 46637
(219) 277-9121

Better Business Bureau
2435 Kimberly Road, #110 North
Bettendorf, Iowa 52722
(319) 355-6344

Better Business Bureau
1500 Second Avenue, S.E., #212
Cedar Rapids, Iowa 52403
(319) 366-5401

Better Business Bureau
615 Insurance Exchange Building
Des Moines, Iowa 50309
(515) 243-8137

Better Business Bureau
318 Badgerow Building
Siouxland, Iowa 51101
(712) 252-4501

Better Business Bureau
501 Jefferson, Suite 24
Topeka, Kansas 66607
(913) 232-0455

Better Business Bureau
300 Kaufman Building
Witchita, Kansas 67202
(316) 263-3146

Better Business Bureau
154 Patchen Drive, Suite 90
Lexington, Kentucky 40502
(606) 268-4128

Better Business Bureau
844 Fourth Street
Louisville, Kentucky 40203
(502) 583-6546

Better Business Bureau
1605 Murray Street, Suite 117
Alexandria, Louisiana 71301
(318) 473-4494

Better Business Bureau
2055 Wooddale Boulevard
Baton Rouge, Louisiana 70806
(504) 926-3010

Better Business Bureau
300 Bond Street
Houma, Louisiana 70361
(504) 868-3456

Better Business Bureau
Post Office Box 30297
Lafayette, Louisiana 70593
(318) 234-8341

Better Business Bureau
Post Office Box 1681
Lake Charles, Louisiana 70602
(318) 433-1633

Better Business Bureau
141 De Siard Street, Suite 300
Monroe, Louisiana 71201
(318) 387-4600, 4601

Better Business Bureau
1539 Jackson Avenue
New Orleans, Louisiana 70130
(504) 581-6222

Better Business Bureau
1401 North Market Street
Shreveport, Louisiana 71101
(318) 221-8352

Better Business Bureau
812 Stevens Avenue
Portland, Maine 04103
(207) 878-2715

Better Business Bureau
2100 Huntingdon Avenue
Baltimore, Maryland 21211-3215
(301) 347-3990

Better Business Bureau
Eight Winter Street
Boston, Massachusetts 02108
(617) 482-9151 (inquiries)
(617) 482-9190 (complaints)

Better Business Bureau
106 State Road, Suite 4
North Dartmouth, Massachusetts 02747
(508) 999-6060

Better Business Bureau
One Kendall Street, Suite 307
Framingham, Massachusetts 01701
(508) 872-5585

Better Business Bureau
78 North Street, Suite 1
Hyannis, Massachusetts 02601
(508) 771-3022

Better Business Bureau
316 Essex Street
Lawrence, Massachusetts 01840
(508) 687-7666

Better Business Bureau
293 Bridge Street, Suite 324
Springfield, Massachusetts 01103
(413) 734-3114

Better Business Bureau
Post Office Box 379
Worcester, Massachusetts 01601
(508) 755-2548

Better Business Bureau
150 Michigan Avenue
Detroit, Michigan 48226
(313) 962-7566 (inquiries)
(313) 962-6785 (complaints)

Better Business Bureau
620 Trust Building
Grand Rapids, Michigan 49503
(616) 774-8236

Better Business Bureau
1745 University Avenue
St. Paul, Minnesota 55104
(612) 646-7700

Better Business Bureau
2917 West Beach Boulevard, #103
Biloxi, Mississippi 39531
(601) 374-2222

Better Business Bureau
105 Fifth Street
Columbus, Mississippi 39701
(601) 327-8594

Better Business Bureau
Post Office Box 390
Jackson, Mississippi 39205-0390
(601) 948-8222

Better Business Bureau
306 East 12th Street, Suite 1024
Kansas City, Missouri 64106
(816) 421-7800

Better Business Bureau
5100 Oakland, Suite 200
St. Louis, Missouri 63110
(314) 531-3300

Better Business Bureau
205 Park Central East, #509
Springfield, Missouri 65806
(417) 862-9231

Better Business Bureau
719 North 48th Street
Lincoln, Nebraska 68504
(402) 467-5261

Better Business Bureau
1613 Farnam Street
Omaha, Nebraska 68102
(402) 346-3033

Better Business Bureau
1022 East Sahara Avenue
Las Vegas, Nevada 89104
(702) 735-6900, 1969

Better Business Bureau
Post Office Box 21269
Reno, Nevada 89505
(702) 322-0657

Better Business Bureau
410 South Main Street
Concord, New Hampshire 03301
(603) 224-1991
1-800-852-3757 (toll free in New Hampshire)

Better Business Bureau
1700 Whitehorse—Hamilton Square
Trenton, New Jersey 08690
(609) 588-0808 (Mercer County)
(201) 536-6306 (Monmouth County)
(201) 329-6855 (Middlesex, Somerset, and
   Hunterdon counties)

Better Business Bureau
34 Park Place
Newark, New Jersey 07102
(201) 642-INFO

Better Business Bureau
Two Forest Avenue
Paramus, New Jersey 07652
(201) 845-4044

Better Business Bureau
1721 Route 37, East
Toms River, New Jersey 08753
(201) 270-5577

Better Business Bureau
4600-A Montgomery, N.E., #200
Albuquerque, New Mexico 87109
(505) 884-0500
1-800-445-1461 (toll free in New Mexico)

Better Business Bureau
308 North Locke
Farmington, New Mexico 87401
(505) 326-6501

Better Business Bureau
2407 West Picacho, Suite B-2
Las Cruces, New Mexico 88005
(505) 524-3130

Better Business Bureau
1210 Luisa Street, Suite 5
Santa Fe, New Mexico 87502
(505) 988-3648

Better Business Bureau
346 Delaware Avenue
Buffalo, New York 14202
(716) 856-7180

Better Business Bureau
266 Main Street
Farmingdale, New York, 11735
(516) 420-0500

Better Business Bureau
257 Park Avenue, South
New York, New York 10010
(212) 533-6200

Better Business Bureau
1122 Sibley Tower
Rochester, New York 14604
(716) 546-6776

Better Business Bureau
100 University Boulevard
Syracuse, New York 13202
(315) 479-6635

Better Business Bureau
120 East Main Street
Wappinger Falls, New York 12590
(914) 297-6550

Better Business Bureau
30 Glenn Street
White Plains, New York 10603
(914) 428-1230, 1231

Better Business Bureau
801 BBB&T Building
Asheville, North Carolina 28801
(704) 253-2392

Better Business Bureau
1130 East 3rd Street, Suite 400
Charlotte, North Carolina 28204
(704) 332-7151
1-800-532-0477 (toll free in North Carolina)

Better Business Bureau
3608 West Friendly Avenue
Greensboro, North Carolina 27410
(919) 852-4240, 4241, 4242

Better Business Bureau
Post Office Box 1882
Hickory, North Carolina 28603
(704) 464-0372

Better Business Bureau
3120 Poplarwood Drive, Suite 101
Raleigh, North Carolina 27604-1080
(919) 872-9240

Better Business Bureau
2110 Cloverdale Avenue, #2-B
Winston-Salem, North Carolina 27103
(919) 725-8348

Better Business Bureau
Post Office Box 80596
Akron, Ohio 44308
(216) 253-4590

Better Business Bureau
1434 Cleveland Avenue, N.W.
Canton, Ohio 44703
(216) 454-9401

Better Business Bureau
898 Walnut Street
Cincinnati, Ohio 45202
(513) 421-3015

Better Business Bureau
2217 East 9th Street, Suite 200
Cleveland, Ohio 44115
(216) 241-7678

Better Business Bureau
527 South High Street
Columbus, Ohio 43215
(614) 221-6336

Better Business Bureau
40 West Fourth Street, #1250
Dayton, Ohio 45402
(513) 222-5825
1-800-521-8357 (toll free in Ohio)

Better Business Bureau
Post Office Box 269
Lima, Ohio 45802
(419) 223-7010

Better Business Bureau
Post Office Box 1706
Mansfield, Ohio 44910
(419) 522-1700

Better Business Bureau
425 Jefferson Avenue, Suite 909
Toledo, Ohio 43604
(419) 241-6276

Better Business Bureau
345 North Market
Wooster, Ohio 44691
(216) 263-6444

Better Business Bureau
Post Office Box 1495
Youngstown, Ohio 44501
(216) 744-3111

Better Business Bureau
17 South Dewey
Oklahoma City, Oklahoma 73102
(405) 239-6860 (inquiries)
(405) 239-6081 (inquiries)
(405) 239-6083 (complaints)

Better Business Bureau
6711 South Yale, Suite 230
Tulsa, Oklahoma 71436
(918) 492-1266

Better Business Bureau
601 S.W. Alder Street, Suite 615
Portland, Oregon 97205
(503) 226-3981

Better Business Bureau
528 North New Street
Bethlehem, Pennsylvania 18018
(215) 866-8780

Better Business Bureau
6 Marion Court
Lancaster, Pennsylvania 17602
(717) 291-1151
(717) 232-2800 (Harrisburg)
(717) 846-2700 (York County)

Better Business Bureau
Post Office Box 2297
Philadelphia, Pennsylvania 19103
(215) 496-1000

Better Business Bureau
610 Smithfield Street
Pittsburgh, Pennsylvania 15222
(412) 456-2700

Better Business Bureau
Post Office Box 993
Scranton, Pennsylvania 18501
(717) 342-9129

Better Business Bureau
Post Office Box 1300
Warwick, Rhode Island 02887-1300
(401) 785-1212 (inquiries)
(401) 785-1213 (complaints)

Better Business Bureau
1830 Bull Street
Columbia, South Carolina 29201
(803) 254-2525

Better Business Bureau
311 Pettigru Street
Greenville, South Carolina 29601
(803) 242-5052

Better Business Bureau
Post Office Box 8603
Myrtle Beach, South Carolina 29578-8603
(803) 448-6100

Better Business Bureau
Post Office Box 1176 TCAS
Blountville, Tennessee 37617
(615) 323-6311

Better Business Bureau
1010 Market Street, Suite 200
Chattanooga, Tennessee 37402
(615) 266-6144
(615) 479-6096 (Bradley County only)
(615) 266-6144 (North Georgia counties of
    Whitfield and Murray)

Better Business Bureau
Post Office Box 10327
Knoxville, Tennessee 37939-0327
(615) 522-2552
(615) 522-2130
(615) 522-2139

Better Business Bureau
Post Office Box 41406
Memphis, Tennessee 38174-1406
(901) 272-9641

Better Business Bureau
One Commerce Place, Suite 1830
Nashville, Tennessee 37239
(615) 254-5872

Better Business Bureau
3300 South 14th Street, Suite 307
Abilene, Texas 79605
(915) 691-1533

Better Business Bureau
Post Office Box 1905
Amarillo, Texas 79106
(806) 358-6222

Better Business Bureau
1005 American Plaza
Austin, Texas 78701
(512) 476-1616

Better Business Bureau
Post Office Box 2988
Beaumont, Texas 77704
(409) 835-5348

Better Business Bureau
202 Varisco Building
Bryan, Texas 77801
(409) 823-8148, 8149

Better Business Bureau
4535 South Padre Island Drive
Corpus Christi, Texas 78411
(512) 854-2892

Better Business Bureau
2001 Bryan Street, Suite 850
Dallas, Texas 75201
(214) 220-2000

Better Business Bureau
1910 East Yandell
El Paso, Texas 79903
(915) 545-1212, 1264

Better Business Bureau
106 West Fifth Street
Fort Worth, Texas 76102
(817) 332-7585

Better Business Bureau
2707 North Loop West, Suite 900
Houston, Texas 77008
(713) 868-9500

Better Business Bureau
Post Office Box 1178
Lubbock, Texas 79401
(806) 763-0459

Better Business Bureau
Post Office Box 60206
Midland, Texas 79711
(915) 563-1880
1-800-592-4433 (toll free in Texas)

Better Business Bureau
Post Office Box 3366
San Angelo, Texas 76902-3366
(915) 653-2318

Better Business Bureau
1800 Northeast Loop 410, #400
San Antonio, Texas 78217
(512) 828-9441

Better Business Bureau
Post Office Box 6652
Tyler, Texas 75711-6652
(214) 581-5704

Better Business Bureau
Post Office Box 7203
Waco, Texas 76714-7203
(817) 772-7530

Better Business Bureau
Post Office Box 69
Weslaco, Texas 78596
(512) 968-3678

Better Business Bureau
1106 Brook Avenue
Wichita Falls, Texas 76301
(817) 723-5526

Better Business Bureau
385 24th Street, Suite 717
Ogden, Utah 84401
(801) 399-4701

Better Business Bureau
1588 South Main
Salt Lake City, Utah 84115
(801) 487-4656
(801) 377-2611 (Provo)

Better Business Bureau
3608 Tidewater Drive
Norfolk, Virginia 23509
(804) 648-0016

Better Business Bureau
701 East Franklin, Suite 712
Richmond, Virginia 23219
(804) 648-0016

Better Business Bureau
121 West Campbell Avenue, S.W.
Roanoke, Virginia 24011
(703) 342-3455

Better Business Bureau
127 West Canal Drive
Kennewick, Washington 99336
(509) 582-0222

Better Business Bureau
2200 Sixth Avenue, Suite 828
Seattle, Washington 98121-1857
(206) 448-8888

Better Business Bureau
South 176 Stevens Street
Spokane, Washington 99204
(509) 747-1155

Better Business Bureau
Post Office Box 1274
Tacoma, Washington 98401
(206) 383-5561

Better Business Bureau
Post Office Box 1584
Yakima, Washington 98907
(509) 248-1326

Better Business Bureau
740 North Plankinton Avenue
Milwaukee, Wisconsin 53202
(414) 273-1600 (inquiries)
(414) 273-0123 (complaints)

Better Business Bureau/Idaho Falls
Lincoln Park and Teton counties
(208) 523-9754

Better Business Bureau/Fort Collins
All other Wyoming counties
1-800-873-3222 (toll free)

Better Business Bureau
G.P.O. Box 70212
San Juan, Puerto Rico 00936
(809) 756-5400

BROADCAST NETWORKS (MAJOR)

Audience Services

ABC Television Network
1330 Avenue of the Americas
New York, New York 10019
(212) 887-7478

CBS Broadcast Group
524 West 52nd Street
New York, New York 10019
(212) 975-3166

NBC, Inc.
30 Rockefeller Plaza
New York, New York 10112
(212) 664-2333

Turner Broadcasting System, Inc.
Post Office Box 7500 (WTBS)
Atlanta, Georgia 30357
1-800-257-1234 (toll free outside Georgia)

CONSUMER PROTECTION OFFICES

Consumer Protection Division
Office of Attorney General
11 South Union Street
Montgomery, Alabama 36130
(205) 261-7334
1-800-392-5658 (toll free in Alabama)

Consumer Protection Section

Office of Attorney General
1031 West Fourth Avenue, Suite 110-B
Anchorage, Alaska 99501
(907) 279-0428

Office of Attorney General
100 Cushman Street, Suite 400
Fairbanks, Alaska 99701
(907) 456-8588

Financial Fraud Division
Office of Attorney General
1275 West Washington Street
Phoenix, Arizona 85007
(602) 542-3702 (fraud only)
1-800-352-8431 (toll free in Arizona)

Financial Fraud Division
Office of Attorney General
402 West Congress Street, Suite 315
Tucson, Arizona 85701
(602) 628-5501

Consumer Protection Division
Office of Attorney General
200 Tower Building
4th and Center Street
Little Rock, Arkansas 72201
(501) 682-2007 (voice/TDD)
1-800-482-8982 (toll free voice/TDD in
  Arkansas)

California Department of Consumer Affairs
1020 N Street
Sacramento, California 95814
(916) 445-0660 (complaint assistance)
(916) 445-1254 (consumer information)
(916) 522-1700 (TDD)

Public Inquiry Unit
Office of Attorney General
1515 K Street, Suite 511
Post Office Box 944255
Sacramento, California 94244-2550
(916) 322-3360
1-800-952-5225 (toll free in California)
1-800-952-5548 (toll free TDD in California)

Bureau of Automotive Repair
California Department of Consumer Affairs
10240 Systems Parkway
Sacramento, California 95827
(916) 366-5100
1-800-952-5210 (toll free in California—auto
  repair only)

Consumer Protection Unit
Office of Attorney General
1525 Sherman Street, 3rd Floor
Denver, Colorado 80203
(303) 866-5167

Consumer and Food Specialist
Department of Agriculture
1525 Sherman Street, 4th Floor
Denver, Colorado 80203
(303) 866-3561

Department of Consumer Protection
State Office Building
165 Capitol Avenue
Hartford, Connecticut 06106
(203) 566-4999
1-800-842-2649 (toll free in Connecticut)

Antitrust/Consumer Protection
Office of Attorney General
110 Sherman Street
Hartford, Connecticut 06105
(203) 566-5374

Division of Consumer Affairs
Department of Community Affairs
820 North French Street, 4th Floor
Wilmington, Delaware 19801
(302) 571-3250

Economic Crime/Consumer Rights Division
Office of Attorney General
820 North French Street
Wilmington, Delaware 19801
(302) 571-3849

Department of Consumer and Regulatory
  Affairs
614 H Street, N.W.
Washington, D.C. 20001
(202) 727-7000

Department of Agriculture and Consumer
  Services
Division of Consumer Services
218 Mayo Building
Tallahassee, Florida 32399
(904) 488-2226
1-800-342-2176 (toll free TDD in Florida)
1-800-327-3382 (toll free information and
  education in Florida)
1-800-321-5366 (toll free lemon law in
  Florida)

Consumer Protection Division
Office of Attorney General
401 N.W. 2nd Avenue, Suite 921-N
Miami, Florida 33128
(305) 377-5619

Governor's Office of Consumer Affairs
2 Martin Luther King, Jr., Drive, S.E.
Plaza Level—East Tower
Atlanta, Georgia 30334
(404) 656-7000, 3790
1-800-282-5808 (toll free in Georgia)

Office of Consumer Protection
Department of Commerce and Consumer
  Affairs
828 Fort Street Mall
Post Office Box 3767
Honolulu, Hawaii 96812-3767
(808) 548-2560 (administration and legal in
  Hawaii)
(808) 548-2540 (complaints and
  investigations in Hawaii)

Office of Consumer Protection
Department of Commerce and Consumer
  Affairs
75 Aupuni Street
Hilo, Hawaii 96720
(808) 961-7433

Office of Consumer Protection
Department of Commerce and Consumer
  Affairs
3060 Eiwa Street
Lihue, Hawaii 96766
(808) 245-4365

Office of Consumer Protection
Department of Commerce and Consumer
  Affairs
54 High Street
Post Office Box 1098
Wailuku, Hawaii 96793
(808) 244-4387

Governor's Office of Citizens Assistance
201 West Monroe Street
Springfield, Illinois 62706
(217) 782-0244
1-800-642-3112 (toll free in Illinois)

Consumer Protection Division
Office of Attorney General
100 West Randolph, 12th Floor
Chicago, Illinois 60601
(312) 917-3580
(312) 793-2852 (TDD)

Department of Citizen Rights
100 West Randolph, 13th Floor
Chicago, Illinois 60601
(312) 917-3289
(312) 917-7123 (TDD)

Consumer Protection Division
Office of Attorney General
219 State House
Indianapolis, Indiana 46204
(317) 232-6330
1-800-382-5516 (toll free in Indiana)

Iowa Citizens' Aide/Ombudsman
215 East 7th Street
Capitol Complex
Des Moines, Iowa 50319
(515) 281-3592
(515) 242-5065 (TDD)
1-800-358-5510 (toll free in Iowa)

Consumer Protection Division
Office of Attorney General
1300 East Walnut Street, 2nd Floor
Des Moines, Iowa 50319
(515) 281-5926

Consumer Protection Division
Office of Attorney General
Kansas Judicial Center
Topeka, Kansas 66612
(913) 296-3751
1-800-432-2310 (toll free in Kansas)

Consumer Protection Division
Office of Attorney General
209 Saint Clair Street
Frankfort, Kentucky 40601
(502) 564-2200
1-800-432-9257 (toll free in Kentucky)

Consumer Protection Division
Office of Attorney General
107 South 4th Street
Louisville, Kentucky 40202
(502) 588-3262
1-800-432-9257 (toll free in Kentucky)

Consumer Protection Section
Office of Attorney General
State Capitol Building
Post Office Box 94005
Baton Rouge, Louisiana 70804
(504) 342-7013

Office of Agro-Consumer Services
Department of Agriculture
325 Loyola Avenue, Room 317
New Orleans, Louisiana 70112
(504) 568-5472

Bureau of Consumer Credit Protection
State House Station No. 35
Augusta, Maine 04333
(207) 582-8718

Consumer and Antitrust Division
Office of Attorney General
State House Station No. 6
Augusta, Maine 04333
(207) 289-3716 (9 A.M.–1 P.M.)

Mediation Consumer Service
Office of Attorney General
991 Forest Avenue
Portland, Maine 04104
(207) 797-8978 (1 P.M.–4 P.M.)

Consumer Protection Division
Office of Attorney General
7 North Calvert Street
Baltimore, Maryland 21202
(301) 528-8662 (9 A.M.–2 P.M.)
(202) 470-7534 (Washington, D.C.,
  metro area)
(301) 576-6372 (voice/TDD in Baltimore
  area)
1-800-492-2114, (toll free in Maryland)

Licensing and Consumer Services
Motor Vehicle Administration
6601 Ritchie Highway, N.E.
Glen Burnie, Maryland 21062
(301) 768-7420

Consumer Protection Division
Office of Attorney General
State Office Complex
Route 50 and Cypress Street
Salisbury, Maryland 21801
(301) 543-6620

Consumer Protection Division
Office of Attorney General
138 East Antietam Street, Suite 210
Hagerstown, Maryland 21740
(301) 791-4780

Consumer Protection Division
Department of Attorney General
131 Tremont Street
Boston, Massachusetts 02111
(617) 727-8400 (information and referral
  only)

Consumer Affairs and Business Regulation
One Ashburton Place, Room 1411
Boston, Massachusetts 02108
(617) 727-7780 (information and referral
  only)

Consumer Protection Division
Department of Attorney General
436 Dwight Street
Springfield, Massachusetts 01103
(413) 784-1240

Consumer Protection Division
Office of Attorney General
670 Law Building
Lansing, Michigan 48913
(517) 373-1140

Michigan Consumers Council
414 Hollister Building
106 West Allegan Street
Lansing, Michigan 48933
(517) 373-0947
(517) 373-0701 (TDD)

Bureau of Automotive Regulation
Michigan Department of State
Lansing, Michigan 48918
(517) 373-7858
1-800-292-4204 (toll free in Michigan)

Office of Consumer Services
Office of Attorney General
117 University Avenue
St. Paul, Minnesota 55155
(612) 296-2331

Consumer Services Division
Office of Attorney General
320 West 2nd Street
Duluth, Minnesota 55802
(218) 723-4891

Consumer Protection Division
Office of Attorney General
Post Office Box 220
Jackson, Mississippi 39205
(601) 354-6018

Department of Agriculture and Commerce
500 Greymont Avenue
Post Office Box 1609
Jackson, Mississippi 39215
(601) 354-7063

Gulf Coast Regional Office
of the Attorney General
Post Office Box 1411
Biloxi, Mississippi 39533
(601) 436-6000

Department of Economic Development
Post Office Box 1157
Jefferson City, Missouri 65102
(314) 751-4962

Trade Offense Division
Office of Attorney General
Post Office Box 899
Jefferson City, Missouri 65102
(314) 751-2616
1-800-392-8222 (toll free in Missouri)

Consumer Affairs Unit
Department of Commerce
1424 Ninth Avenue
Helena, Montana 59620
(406) 444-4312

Consumer Protection Division
Department of Justice
2115 State Capitol
Post Office Box 98920
Lincoln, Nebraska 68509
(402) 471-4723

Department of Commerce
State Mail Room Complex
Las Vegas, Nevada 89158
(702) 486-4150

Consumer Affairs Division
Department of Commerce
201 Nye Building, Capitol Complex
Carson City, Nevada 86710
(702) 885-4340

Consumer Protection and Antitrust Division
Office of Attorney General
State House Annex
Concord, New Hampshire 03301
(603) 271-3641

Division of Consumer Affairs
1100 Raymond Boulevard, Room 504
Newark, New Jersey 07102
(201) 648-4010

Division of Law
Office of Attorney General
1100 Raymond Boulevard, Room 316
Newark, New Jersey 07102
(201) 648-4730

Department of the Public Advocate
Justice Complex
CN 850
Trenton, New Jersey 08625
(609) 292-7087
1-800-792-8600 (toll free in New Jersey)

Consumer and Economic Crime Division
Office of Attorney General
Post Office Drawer 1508
Santa Fe, New Mexico 87504
(505) 872-6910
1-800-432-2070 (toll free in New Mexico)

Consumer Protection Board
99 Washington Avenue
Albany, New York, 12210
(518) 474-8583

Bureau of Consumer Frauds and Protection
Office of Attorney General
State Capitol
Albany, New York 12224
(518) 474-5481

Consumer Protection Board
250 Broadway, 17th Floor
New York, New York 10007-2593
(212) 587-4908

Bureau of Consumer Frauds and Protection
Office of Attorney General
120 Broadway
New York, New York 10271
(212) 341-2300

Consumer Protection Section
Office of Attorney General
Department of Justice Building
Post Office Box 629
Raleigh, North Carolina 27602
(919) 733-7741

Office of Attorney General
600 East Boulevard
Bismarck, North Dakota 58505
(701) 224-2210
1-800-472-2600 (toll free in North Dakota)

Consumer Fraud Division
Office of Attorney General
600 East Boulevard
Bismarck, North Dakota 58505
(701) 224-3404
1-800-472-2600 (toll free in North Dakota)

Consumer Frauds and Crimes Section
Office of Attorney General
30 East Broad Street
State Office Tower, 25th Floor
Columbus, Ohio 43266-0410
(614) 466-4986 (complaints)
1-800-282-0515 (toll free in Ohio)
(614) 466-1393 (TDD)

Consumers' Counsel
77 South High Street, 15th Floor
Columbus, Ohio 43266
(614) 466-9605 (voice/TDD)
1-800-282-9448 (toll free in Ohio)

Consumer Affairs
Office of Attorney General
112 State Capitol Building
Oklahoma City, Oklahoma 73105
(405) 521-3921

Department of Consumer Credit
4545 Lincoln Boulevard, Suite 104
Oklahoma City, Oklahoma 73105
(405) 521-3653

Financial Fraud Section
Department of Justice
Justice Building
Salem, Oregon 97310
(503) 378-4320

Bureau of Consumer Protection
Office of Attorney General
Strawberry Square, 14th Floor
Harrisburg, Pennsylvania 17120
(717) 787-9707
1-800-441-2555 (toll free in Pennsylvania)

Office of Consumer Advocate—Utilities
Office of Attorney General
Strawberry Square, 14th Floor
Harrisburg, Pennsylvania 17120
(717) 783-5048 (utilities only)

Bureau of Consumer Protection
Office of Attorney General
27 North 7th Street
Allentown, Pennsylvania 18101
(215) 821-6690

Bureau of Consumer Protection
Office of Attorney General
919 State Street, Room 203
Erie, Pennsylvania 16501
(814) 871-4371

Bureau of Consumer Protection
Office of Attorney General
IGA Building, Route 219 North
Post Office Box 716
Ebensburg, Pennsylvania 15931
(814) 949-7900

Bureau of Consumer Protection
Office of Attorney General
1009 State Office Building
1400 West Spring Garden Street
Philadelphia, Pennsylvania 19130
(215) 560-2414

Bureau of Consumer Protection
Office of Attorney General
Manor Building, 4th Floor
564 Forbes Avenue
Pittsburgh, Pennsylvania 15219
(412) 565-5135

Bureau of Consumer Protection
Office of Attorney General
State Office Building, Room 358
100 Lackawanna Avenue
Scranton, Pennsylvania 18503
(717) 963-4913

Consumer Protection Division
Department of Attorney General
72 Pine Street
Providence, Rhode Island 02903
(401) 277-2104
(401) 274-4400, ext. 354 (voice/TDD)
1-800-852-7776 (toll free in Rhode Island)

Consumer Fraud and Antitrust Section
Office of Attorney General
Post Office Box 11549
Columbia, South Carolina 29211
(803) 734-3970

Department of Consumer Affairs
Post Office Box 5757
Columbia, South Carolina 29250
(803) 734-9452
(803) 734-9455 (TDD)
1-800-922-1594 (toll free in South Carolina)

Office of Executive Policy and Program
1205 Pendleton Street, Room 308
Columbia, South Carolina 29201
(803) 734-0457

Division of Consumer Affairs
Office of Attorney General
State Capitol Building
Pierre, South Dakota 57501
(605) 773-4400

Antitrust and Consumer Protection Division
Office of Attorney General
450 James Robertson Parkway
Nashville, Tennessee 37219
(615) 741-2672

Division of Consumer Affairs
Department of Commerce and Insurance
500 James Robertson Parkway, 5th Floor
Nashville, Tennessee 37219
(615) 741-4737
1-800-342-8385 (toll free in Tennessee)

Consumer Protection Division
Office of Attorney General
Capitol Station
Post Office Box 12548
Austin, Texas 78711
(512) 463-2070

Office of Consumer Protection
State Board of Insurance
One Republic Plaza
333 Guadalupe, Box 44
Austin, Texas 78701
(512) 495-6448

Consumer Protection Division
Office of Attorney General
714 Jackson Street, Suite 700
Dallas, Texas 75202
(214) 742-8944

Consumer Protection Division
Office of Attorney General
6090 Surety Drive, Room 260
El Paso, Texas 79905
(915) 772-9476

Consumer Protection Division
Office of Attorney General
1019 Congress Street, Suite 1550
Houston, Texas 77002
(713) 223-5886

Consumer Protection Division
Office of Attorney General
1208 14th Street, Suite 801
Lubbock, Texas 79401
(806) 747-5238

Consumer Protection Division
Office of Attorney General
3600 North 23rd Street, Suite 305
McAllen, Texas 78501
(512) 682-4547

Consumer Protection Division
Office of Attorney General
200 Main Plaza, Suite 400
San Antonio, Texas 78205
(512) 225-4191

Division of Consumer Protection
Department of Commerce
160 East 3rd South
Post Office Box 45802
Salt Lake City, Utah 84145
(801) 530-6601

Consumer Affairs
Office of Attorney General
115 State Capitol
Salt Lake City, Utah 84114
(801) 538-1331

Public Protection Division
Office of Attorney General
109 State Street
Montpelier, Vermont 05602
(802) 828-3171

Consumer Assurance Section
Department of Agriculture
116 State Street
Montpelier, Vermont 05602
(802) 828-2436

Antitrust and Consumer Litigation Section
Office of Attorney General
Supreme Court Building
101 North 8th Street
Richmond, Virginia 23219
(804) 786-2116
1-800-451-1525 (toll free in Virginia)

Office of Consumer Affairs
Department of Agriculture and Consumer
  Services
Washington Building, Room 101
1100 Bank Street
Richmond, Virginia 23219
(804) 786-2042
1-800-552-9963 (toll free in Virginia)

Office of Consumer Affairs
Department of Agriculture and Consumer
  Services
100 North Washington Street, Suite 412
Falls Church, Virginia 22046
(703) 532-1613

Consumer and Business
Fair Practices Division
Office of Attorney General
North 122 Capitol Way
Olympia, Washington 98501
(206) 753-6210

Consumer and Business Fair Practices
  Division
Office of Attorney General
710 2nd Avenue, Suite 1300
Seattle, Washington 98104
(206) 464-7744
1-800-551-4636 (toll free in Washington)

Consumer and Business
Fair Practices Division
Office of Attorney General
West 1116 Riverside Avenue
Spokane, Washington 99201
(509) 456-3123

Consumer and Business
Fair Practices Division
Office of Attorney General
1019 Pacific Avenue, 3rd Floor
Tacoma, Washington 98402
(206) 593-2904

Consumer Protection Division
Office of Attorney General
812 Quarrier Street, 6th Floor
Charleston, West Virginia 25301
(304) 348-8986
1-800-368-8808 (toll free in West Virginia)

Division of Weights and Measures
Department of Labor
1800 Washington Street, East
Building #3, Room 319
Charleston, West Virginia 25305
(304) 348-7890

Division of Trade and Consumer Protection
Department of Agriculture
801 West Badger Road
Post Office Box 8911
Madison, Wisconsin 53708
(608) 266-9836
1-800-362-3020 (toll free in Wisconsin)

Office of Consumer Protection and Citizen
   Advocacy
Department of Justice
Post Office Box 7856
Madison, Wisconsin 53707
(608) 266-1852
1-800-362-8189 (toll free in Wisconsin)

Division of Trade and Consumer Protection
Department of Agriculture
927 Loring Street
Altoona, Wisconsin 54720
(715) 839-3848

Division of Trade and Consumer Protection
Department of Agriculture
200 North Jefferson Street, Suite 146A
Green Bay, Wisconsin 54301
(414) 436-4087

Division of Trade and Consumer Protection
Department of Agriculture
3333 North Mayfair Road, Suite 114
Milwaukee, Wisconsin 53222-3288
(414) 257-8956

Office of Consumer Protection
Department of Justice
Milwaukee State Office Building
819 North 6th Street, Room 520
Milwaukee, Wisconsin 53203
(414) 227-4948

Office of Attorney General
123 State Capitol Building
Cheyenne, Wyoming 82002
(307) 777-7841, 6286

Department of Consumer Affairs
Minillas Station, Post Office Box 41059
Santurce, Puerto Rico 00940
(809) 722-7555

Department of Justice
Post Office Box 192
Old San Juan, Puerto Rico 00902
(809) 721-2900

Department of Licensing and Consumer
   Affairs
Property and Procurement Building
Subbase #1, Room 205
St. Thomas, Virgin Islands 00801
(809) 774-3130

EDUCATION

National

Department of Education
400 Maryland Avenue, S.W.
Washington, D.C. 20202
(202) 245-3192

Council of Chief State School Officers
379 Hall of States
400 North Capitol Street, N.W.
Washington, D.C. 20001
(202) 393-8161

State Departments of Education

Department of Education
Gordon Persons Office Building
50 North Ripley
Montgomery, Alabama 36130-3901
(205) 242-9700

Department of Education
801 East 10th Street
Pouch F
Juneau, Alaska 99811
(907) 465-2800

Department of Education
1535 West Jefferson
Phoenix, Arizona 85007
(602) 542-5156

Department of Education
#4 Capital Mall
Little Rock, Arkansas 72201-1071
(501) 682-4204

Department of Education
721 Capitol Mall
Sacramento, California 95814
(916) 445-4338

Department of Education
201 East Colfax
Denver, Colorado 80203-1705
(303) 866-6806

Department of Education
165 Capitol Avenue
305 State Office Building
Hartford, Connecticut 06106
(203) 566-5061

Department of Education
Townsend Building, #279
Post Office Box 1402
Dover, Delaware 19903
(302) 736-4601

Department of Defense
Office of Dependent Schools
2461 Eisenhower Avenue
Alexandria, Virginia 22331-1100
(703) 325-0188

Superintendent of Schools
District of Columbia
415 12th Street, N.W.
Washington, D.C. 20004
(202) 724-4222

Department of Education
The Capitol
Plaza Level 8
Tallahassee, Florida 32399
(904) 487-1785

Department of Education
2066 Twin Towers East
205 Butler Street
Atlanta, Georgia 30334
(404) 656-2800

Department of Education
1390 Miller Street, #307
Post Office Box 2360
Honolulu, Hawaii 96804
(808) 548-6405

Department of Education
650 West State Street
Boise, Idaho 83720
(208) 334-3300

State Board of Education
100 North 1st Street
Springfield, Illinois 62777
(217) 782-2221

Department of Education
100 North Capital Street, Room 229
Indianapolis, Indiana 46204-2798
(317) 232-6665

Department of Education
Grimes State Office Building
East 14th and Grand Streets
Des Moines, Iowa 50319-0416
(515) 281-5294

Department of Education
120 East 10th Street
Topeka, Kansas 66612
(913) 296-3202

Department of Education
1725 Capitol Plaza Tower
Frankfort, Kentucky 40601
(502) 564-4720

Department of Education
626 North 4th Street
Post Office Box 94064
Baton Rouge, Louisiana 70804-9064
(504) 342-3602

Department of Education and Cultural
  Services
State House, Station #23
Augusta, Maine 04333
(207) 289-5800

Department of Education
200 West Baltimore Street
Baltimore, Maryland 21201
(301) 333-2200

Department of Education
Quincy Center Plaza
1385 Hancock Street
Quincy, Massachusetts 02169
(617) 770-7300

Department of Education
608 West Allegan Street
Post Office Box 30008
Lansing, Michigan 48933
(517) 373-3354

Department of Education
712 Capitol Square Building
550 Cedar Street
St. Paul, Minnesota 55101
(612) 296-2358

Department of Education
High Street
Post Office Box 771
Jackson, Mississippi 39205
(601) 359-3513

Department of Education
205 Jefferson, 6th Floor
Post Office Box 480
Jefferson City, Missouri 65102
(314) 751-4446

Department of Education
106 State Capitol
Helena, Montana 59620
(406) 444-3680

Department of Education
301 Centennial Mall, South
Post Office Box 94987
Lincoln, Nebraska 68509
(402) 471-2465

Department of Education
Capitol Complex
400 West King Street
Carson City, Nevada 89710
(702) 885-3100

Department of Education
State Office Park South
101 Pleasant Street
Concord, New Hampshire 03301
(603) 271-3144

Department of Education
225 West State Street
Trenton, New Jersey 08625-0500
(609) 292-4450

Department of Education
Education Building
300 Don Gaspar
Santa Fe, New Mexico 87501-2786
(505) 827-6516

State Education Department
111 Education Building
Albany, New York 12234
(518) 474-5844

Department of Education
Education Building, Room 318
116 West Edenton Street
Raleigh, North Carolina 27603-1712
(919) 733-3813

Department of Education
600 Boulevard Avenue East
State Capitol Building, 11th Floor
Bismarck, North Dakota 58505-0164
(701) 224-2261

Department of Education
65 South Front Street, Room 808
Columbus, Ohio 43266-0308
(614) 466-3304

Department of Education
Oliver Hodge Memorial Education Building
2500 North Lincoln Boulevard
Oklahoma City, Oklahoma 73105-4599
(405) 521-3301

Department of Education
700 Pringle Parkway, S.E.
Salem, Oregon 97310
(503) 378-3573

Department of Education
State Department
333 Market Street, 10th Floor
Harrisburg, Pennsylvania 17126
(717) 787-5820

Department of Education
22 Hayes Street
Providence, Rhode Island 02908
(401) 277-2031

Department of Education
State Department
1006 Rutledge Building
1429 Senate Street
Columbia, South Carolina 29201
(803) 734-8492

Department of Education and Cultural
    Affairs
700 Governors Drive
Pierre, South Dakota 57501
(605) 773-3243

Department of Education
100 Cordell Hull Building
Nashville, Tennessee 37219
(615) 741-2731

Texas Education Agency
William B. Travis Building
1701 North Congress Avenue
Austin, Texas 78701-1494
(512) 463-8985

State Office of Education
250 East 500 South
Salt Lake City, Utah 84111
(801) 538-7510

Department of Education
120 State Street
Montpelier, Vermont 05602-2703
(802) 828-3135

Department of Education
James Monroe Building
Post Office Box 6Q
Richmond, Virginia 23216-2060
(804) 225-2034

Department of Education
State Department
Old Capitol Building
Mail Stop FG-11
Olympia, Washington 98504
(206) 586-6904

Department of Education
1900 Washington Street
Building B, Room 358
Charleston, West Virginia 25305
(304) 348-2681

Department of Education
State Department
125 South Webster Street
Post Office Box 7841
Madison, Wisconsin 53707
(608) 266-1771

Department of Education
Hathaway Building
Cheyenne, Wyoming 82002
(307) 777-7675

Director of Education
American Samoa
State Department
Pago Pago, Tutuila 96799
OS 633-5159

Department of Education
Post Office Box DE
Agana, Guam 96910
OS 671-477-4978

Department of Education
Post Office Box 759
Hato Rey, Puerto Rico 00919
(809) 751-5372

Department of Education
44-46 Kogens Gard
St. Thomas, Virgin Islands 00802
(809) 774-2810

ENVIRONMENTAL PROTECTION AGENCY

National Office

Environmental Protection Agency
401 M Street, S.W.
Washington, D.C. 20460

Regional Offices

Environmental Protection Agency
215 Fremont Street
San Francisco, California 94105

Environmental Protection Agency
999 18th Street
Denver, Colorado 80202

Environmental Protection Agency
345 Courtland Street, N.E.
Atlanta, Georgia 30365

Environmental Protection Agency
230 South Dearborn Street
Chicago, Illinois 60604

Environmental Protection Agency
726 Minnesota Avenue
Kansas City, Kansas 66101

Environmental Protection Agency
John F. Kennedy Federal Building
Boston, Massachusetts 02203

Environmental Protection Agency
26 Federal Plaza
New York, New York 10278

Environmental Protection Agency
841 Chestnut Street
Philadelphia, Pennsylvania 19107

Environmental Protection Agency
1201 Elm Street
Dallas, Texas 75270

Environmental Protection Agency
1200 6th Avenue
Seattle, Washington 98101

FEDERAL TRADE COMMISSION

National Office

Federal Trade Commission
Pennsylvania Avenue at Sixth Street, N.W.
Washington, D.C. 20580
(202) 326-2222

Regional Offices

Federal Trade Commission
11000 Wilshire Boulevard
Los Angeles, California 90024
(213) 209-7890

Federal Trade Commission
901 Market Street
San Francisco, California 94130
(415) 995-5220

Federal Trade Commission
1405 Curtis Street
Denver, Colorado 80202-2393
(303) 844-2271

Federal Trade Commission
1718 Peachtree Street, N.W.
Atlanta, Georgia 30367
(404) 347-4836

Federal Trade Commission
55 East Monroe Street
Chicago, Illinois 60603
(312) 353-4423

Federal Trade Commission
10 Causeway Street
Boston, Massachusetts 02222-1073
(617) 567-7240

Federal Trade Commission
26 Federal Plaza
New York, New York 10278
(212) 264-1207

Federal Trade Commission
668 Euclid Avenue
Cleveland, Ohio 44114
(216) 522-4207

Federal Trade Commission
100 North Central Expressway
Dallas, Texas 75201
(214) 767-5501

Federal Trade Commission
915 Second Avenue
Seattle, Washington 98174
(206) 442-4656

HEALTH AND HUMAN SERVICES, DEPARTMENT OF

National Office

U.S. Department of Health and Human Services
200 Constitution Avenue, S.W.
Washington, D.C. 20201

State Agencies

Department of Public Health
434 Monroe Street, Room 381
Montgomery, Alabama 36130-1701
(205) 261-5052

Department of Health and Social Services
Post Office Box H
Juneau, Alaska 99811-0601
(907) 465-3030

Arizona Department of Health Services
1740 W. Adams Street
Phoenix, Arizona 85007
(602) 255-1024

Department of Health
4815 Markham Street
Little Rock, Arkansas 72205-3867
(501) 661-2111

Department of Health Services
714 P Street, Room 1253
Sacramento, California 95814
(916) 445-1248

Colorado Department of Health
4210 E. 11th Avenue
Denver, Colorado 80220
(303) 331-4601

Department of Health Services
150 Washington Street
Hartford, Connecticut 06106
(203) 566-2038

Department of Health and Social Services
1901 N. DuPont Highway
New Castle, Delaware 19720
(302) 421-6705

Department of Human Services
801 N. Capitol Street, N.E.
Washington, D.C. 20002
(202) 727-0310

State Health Office
1323 Winewood Boulevard
Tallahassee, Florida 32301
(904) 487-2705

Department of Human Resources
47 Trinity Avenue, S.W., Room 522H
Health Building
Atlanta, Georgia 30334
(404) 656-5680

Hawaii Department of Health
Box 3378
Honolulu, Hawaii 96801
(808) 548-6505

Idaho Department of Health and Welfare
450 W. State
Boise, Idaho 83720
(208) 334-5500

Illinois Department of Public Health
535 W. Jefferson Street
Springfield, Illinois 62761
(217) 782-4977

State Board of Health
1330 W. Michigan Street
Box 1964
Indianapolis, Indiana 46206
(317) 633-0100

Department of Public Health
Lucas State Office Building, 3rd and
    4th Floors
Des Moines, Iowa 50319
(515) 281-5605

Kansas Department of Health and
    Environment
Landon State Office Building
Topeka, Kansas 66620
(913) 296-1343

Department for Health Services
275 E. Main Street
Frankfort, Kentucky 40621
(502) 564-3970

Louisiana Department of Health and
    Human Resources
Box 3776
Baton Rouge, Louisiana 70821
(504) 342-6711

Main Department of Human Services
State House, Station 11
Augusta, Maine 04333
(207) 289-3707

Department of Health and Mental Hygiene
201 W. Preston Street
Baltimore, Maryland 21201
(301) 225-6500

Massachusetts Department of Public Health
150 Tremont Street, 10th Floor
Boston, Massachusetts 02111
(617) 727-2700

Michigan Department of Public Health
3500 N. Logan Street
Lansing, Michigan 48909
(517) 335-8000

Department of Health
717 S.E. Delaware Street
Post Office Box 9441
Minneapolis, Minnesota 55440
(612) 623-5000

Department of Health
Felix J. Underwood State Board of
    Health Building
Post Office Box 1700
Jackson, Mississippi 32915
(601) 960-7400

Department of Health
Post Office Box 570
Jefferson City, Missouri 65102
(314) 751-6400

State Department of Health and
    Environmental Sciences
W. F Cogswell Building
Helena, Montana 59620
(406) 444-2544

State Department of Health
301 Centennial Mall, S.
Lincoln, Nebraska 68509
(402) 471-2133

Department of Human Resources
Kinkead Building
505 E. King, Room 600
Carson City, Nevada 89710
(702) 885-4400

Department of Health and Human Services
6 Hazen Drive
Concord, New Hampshire 03301
(602) 271-4685

State Department of Health
CN 360
Trenton, New Jersey 08625
(609) 292-7837

Health and Environmental Department
1190 St. Francis Drive
Post Office Box 968
Santa Fe, New Mexico 87504-0968
(505) 827-0020

State Department of Health
Tower Building
Empire State Plaza
Albany, New York 12237
(518) 474-2011

Department of Human Resources
325 N. Salisbury Street
Raleigh, North Carolina 27611
(919) 733-4534

Department of Human Services
State Capitol
Bismarck, North Dakota 58505
(701) 224-2310

Ohio Department of Health
246 N. High Street
Columbus, Ohio 43266
(614) 466-3543

State Department of Health
1000 N.E. 10th
Oklahoma City, Oklahoma 73152
(405) 271-4200

Oregon State Health Division
1400 S.W. Fifth Avenue
Portland, Oregon 97201
(503) 229-5032

Pennsylvania Department of Health
Health and Welfare Building, Room 802
Harrisburg, Pennsylvania 17120
(717) 787-6436

Department of Health
75 Davis Street
Providence, Rhode Island 02908
(401) 277-2231

Department of Health and Environmental
  Control
2600 Bull Street
Columbia, South Carolina 29201
(803) 734-4880

Department of Health
Joe Foss Building
523 East Capitol
Pierre, South Dakota 57501
(605) 773-3361

Department of Health and Environment
344 Cordell Hull Building
Nashville, Tennessee 37219-5402
(615) 741-3111

Department of Health
1100 W. 49th Street
Austin, Texas 78756
(512) 458-7111

Utah Department of Health
288 North 1460 West
Post Office Box 16700
Salt Lake City, Utah 84116
(801) 538-6101

Vermont Department of Health
60 Main Street
Post Office Box 70
Burlington, Vermont 05402
(802) 863-7280

State Department of Health
109 Governor Street, Room 400
Richmond, Virginia 23219
(804) 786-3561

State Department of Social and Health
  Services
Mail Stop HB-41
Olympia, Washington 98504
(206) 753-4010

State Department of Health
State Office Building #3
1800 Washington Street, E.
Charleston, West Virginia 25305
(304) 348-2971

Department of Health and Social Services
Post Office Box 7850
Madison, Wisconsin 53707
(608) 266-3681

Department of Health and Social Services
Hathaway Building
2300 Capitol Avenue
Cheyene, Wyoming 82002
(307) 777-7656

Department of Public Health and Social
 Services
Post Office Box 2816
Agana, Guam 96910
011-671/734-2083

Puerto Rico Department of Health
Building A, Medical Center
Call Box 70184
San Juan, Puerto Rico 00936

Virgin Islands Department of Health
Box 7309
Charlotte Amalie, St. Thomas,
 Virgin Islands 00801
(809) 774-0117

HEALTH-RELATED
ORGANIZATIONS

Alzheimer's Disease Education and
 Referral Center
Federal Building, Room 6C12
7550 Wisconsin Avenue
Bethesda, Maryland 20892

American Association on Mental
 Retardation
1719 Kalorama Road, N.W.
Washington, D.C. 20009
1-800-424-3688

American Association of Poison Control
 Centers
University of Maryland School of Pharmacy
20 N. Pine Street
Baltimore, Maryland 21201
(301) 528-7604

American Burn Association
202 Goodman Street
Cincinnati, Ohio 45219
(513) 751-3900

American Cancer Society, Inc.
777 Third Avenue
New York, New York 10017
(212) 371-2900

American Chronic Pain Association, Inc.
257 Old Haymaker Road
Monroeville, Pennsylvania 15146
(412) 856-9676

American Cleft Palate Association
University of Pittsburgh
1218 Grandview Avenue
Pittsburgh, Pennsylvania 15211
(412) 481-1376

American Dental Association
211 E. Chicago
Chicago, Illinois 60611
(312) 440-2500

American Diabetes Association, Inc.
1660 Duke Street
Alexandria, Virginia 22314
(703) 549-1500

American Fertility Society
2140 Eleventh Avenue South, Suite 200
Birmingham, Alabama 35205
(205) 251-9764

American Epilepsy Society
33 Hickory Hill
Southington, Connecticut 06489
(203) 246-6566

American Heart Association, Inc.
7320 Greenville Avenue
Dallas, Texas 75231
(214) 706-1446

American Lung Association
1740 Broadway
New York, New York 10019
(212) 315-8700

American Medical Association
535 North Dearborn Street
Chicago, Illinois 60604
(312) 645-5000

**American Occupational Therapy
   Association, Inc.**
1383 Piccard Drive, Suite 300
Post Office Box 1725
Rockville, Maryland 20850-4375
(301) 948-9626

American Orthopaedic Association
222 South Prospect Avenue
Park Ridge, Illinois 20850-4375
(312) 823-7186

American Parkinson Disease Association
116 John Street, Room 417
New York, New York 10038
(212) 732-9550

American Physical Therapy Association
1111 N. Fairfax Street
Alexandria, Virginia 22314
(703) 684-2782

**American Red Cross AIDS Education
   Office**
1730 D Street, N.W.
Washington, D.C. 20006
(202) 737-8300

American Rheumatism Association
1314 Spring Street N.W.
Atlanta, Georgia 30309
(404) 266-0795

**American Speech-Language-Hearing
   Association**
10801 Rockville Pike
Rockville, Maryland 20852
(301) 897-5700

Arthritis Foundation
1314 Spring Street N.W.
Atlanta, Georgia 30309
(404) 872-7100

Association for Retarded Citizens
2501 Avenue J
Post Office Box 6109
Arlington, Texas 76006
(817) 640-0204

**Asthma and Allergy Foundation of
   America**
1717 Massachusetts Avenue, S.W., Suite 305
Washington, D.C. 20036
(202) 265-0265

Autism Society of America
1234 Massachusetts Avenue, S.W., Suite 1017
Washington, D.C. 20005-4599
(202) 783-0125

Blinded Veterans Association
1726 M Street, N.W., Suite 800
Washington, D.C. 20036
(202) 223-3066

Clearinghouse on the Handicapped
U.S. Department of Education
400 Maryland Avenue, S.W.
Switzer Building, Room 3119
Washington, D.C. 20202

Cooley's Anemia Foundation, Inc.
105 E. 22nd Street, Suite 911
New York, New York 10010
(212) 598-0911

Cystic Fibrosis Foundation
6931 Arlington Road
Bethesda, Maryland 20814
(301) 951-4422

**Dwight D. Eisenhower Institute for Stroke
   Research, Inc.**
785 Mamaroneck Avenue
White Plains, New York 10605
(914) 946-3062

Epilepsy Foundation of America
4351 Garden City Parkway
Landover, Maryland 20785
(301) 459-3700

Eye-Bank for Sight Restoration, Inc.
210 E. 64th Street
New York, New York 10021
(212) 838-9211 (24 hours)

Huntington's Disease Society of America, Inc.
140 W. 22nd Street, 6th Floor
New York, New York 10011
(212) 242-1968

Impotence Information Center
Department D, Box 9
Minneapolis, Minnesota 55440

International Eye Foundation
7801 Norfolk Avenue
Bethesda, Maryland 20814
(301) 986-1830

Juvenile Diabetes Foundation International
432 Park Avenue South
New York, New York 10016
(212) 889-7575

Leukemia Society of America, Inc.
733 Third Avenue
New York, New York 10017
(212) 573-8484

March of Dimes Birth Defects Foundation
1275 Mamaroneck Avenue
White Plains, New York 10605
(914) 428-7100

Muscular Dystrophy Association
810 Seventh Avenue
New York, New York 10019
(212) 586-0808

Myasthenia Gravis Foundation, Inc.
53 West Jackson Boulevard, Suite 1352
Chicago, Illinois 60604
(312) 427-6252
1-800-541-5454 (toll free)

National Alliance for the Mentally Ill
1901 N. Fort Myer Drive, Suite 500
Arlington, Virginia 22209
(703) 524-7600

National Association of Children's Hospitals and Related Institutions, Inc.
401 Wythe Street
Alexandria, Virginia 22314
(703) 684-1355

National Association of Patients on Hemodialysis and Transplantation, Inc., American Association of Kidney Patients
211 E. 43rd Street, #301
New York, New York 10017
(212) 867-4486

National Braille Association, Inc.
1290 University Avenue
Rochester, New York 14607
(716) 473-0900

National Council on Alcoholism, Inc.
12 W. 21st Street
New York, New York 10010
(212) 206-6770

National Easter Seal Society
2023 W. Ogden Avenue
Chicago, Illinois 60612
(312) 243-8400

National Foundation for Asthma, Inc.
Post Office Box 30069
Tucson, Arizona 85751-0069
(602) 323-6046

National Foundation for Ileitis and Colitis, Inc.
444 Park Avenue S.
New York, New York 10016-737
(212) 685-3440

National Geriatrics Society
212 W. Wisconsin Avenue
Milwaukee, Wisconsin 53203
(414) 272-4130

National Headache Foundation
5252 N. Western Avenue
Chicago, Illinois 60625
(312) 878-7715

National Head Injury Foundation
333 Turnpike Road
Southborough, Massachusetts 01772
(508) 485-9950
1-800-444-NHIF (toll free)

National Hemophilia Foundation
19 W. 34th Street, Suite 1204
New York, New York 10011
(212) 563-0211

National Kidney Foundation
2 Park Avenue
New York, New York 10016
(212) 889-2210

National Mental Health Association, Inc.
1021 Prince Street
Alexandria, Virginia 22314-2971
(703) 684-7722

National Multiple Sclerosis Society
205 E. 42nd Street
New York, New York 10017
(212) 986-3240

National Organization for Rare Disorders
Post Office Box 8923
New Fairfield, Connecticut 06812
(203) 746-6518
1-800-447-6673 (toll free)

National Society to Prevent Blindness
500 East Remington Road
Schaumburg, Illinois 60173

National Spinal Cord Injury Association
600 West Cummings Park, Suite 2000
Woburn, Massachusetts 01801
(617) 935-2722

National Stroke Association
300 East Hampden Avenue, Suite 240
Englewood, Colorado 80110-2622

Paralyzed Veterans of America
4350 East West Highway, Suite 900
Washington, D.C. 20014
(301) 652-2135

Shriners Hospitals for Crippled Children
Post Office Box 31356
Tampa, Florida 33631-3356
(813) 885-2575

Spina Bifida Association of America
1700 Rockville Pike, Suite 540
Rockville, Maryland 20852
(301) 770-SBAA
1-800-621-3141 (toll free)

The Stroke Foundation, Inc.
898 Park Avenue
New York, New York 10021
(212) 734-3434

United Cerebral Palsy Association, Inc.
66 E. 34th Street
New York, New York 10016
1-800-USA-IUCP

United Ostomy Association, Inc.
36 Executive Park, Suite 120
Irvine, California 92714
(714) 660-8624

United Parkinson Foundation
220 S. State Street, Room 1806-08
Chicago, Illinois 60604
(312) 922-9734

United Way of America
701 N. Fairfax Street
Alexandria, Virginia 22314-2045
(703) 836-7100

Will Rogers Institute
785 Mamaroneck Avenue
White Plains, New York 10605
(914) 761-5550

INSURANCE REGULATORS

Alabama Insurance Department
135 South Union Street
Montgomery, Alabama 36130-3401
(205) 269-3550

Alaska Insurance Department
3601 C Street, Suite 722
Anchorage, Alaska 99503
(907) 562-3626

Arizona Insurance Department
Consumer Affairs and Investigation Division
3030 North Third Street
Phoenix, Arizona 85012
(602) 255-4783

Arkansas Insurance Department
Consumer Service Division
400 University Tower Building
12th and University Streets
Little Rock, Arkansas 72204
(501) 371-1813

California Insurance Department
Consumer Services Division
100 Van Ness Avenue
San Francisco, California 94102
1-800-233-9045
or
600 South Commonwealth Avenue
Los Angeles, California 90005
1-800-233-9045

Colorado Insurance Division
303 West Colfax Avenue, 5th Floor
Denver, Colorado 80204
(303) 620-4300

Connecticut Insurance Department
165 Capitol Avenue
State Office Building, Room 425
Hartford, Connecticut 06106
(203) 566-5275

Delaware Insurance Department
841 Silver Lake Boulevard
Dover, Delaware 19901
(302) 736-4251

District of Columbia Insurance
614 H Street, N.W., Suite 512
Washington, D.C. 20001
(202) 783-3191

Florida Department of Insurance
State Capitol
Plaza Level Eleven
Tallahassee, Florida 32399-0300
(904) 488-0030

Georgia Insurance Department
2 Martin Luther King, Jr., Drive
West Tower, 7th Floor
Atlanta, Georgia 30334
(404) 656-2056

Hawaii Department of Commerce and Consumer Affairs
Insurance Division
Post Office Box 3614
Honolulu, Hawaii 96811
(808) 548-5450

Idaho Insurance Department
Public Service Department
500 South 10th Street
Boise, Idaho 83720
(208) 334-2250

Illinois Insurance Department
320 West Washington Street, 4th Floor
Springfield, Illinois 62767
(217) 782-4515

Indiana Insurance Department
311 West Washington Street, Suite 300
Indianapolis, Indiana 46204
(317) 232-2395

Iowa Insurance Division
Lucas State Office Building
East 12th and Walnut Streets, 6th Floor
Des Moines, Iowa 50319
(515) 281-5705

Kansas Insurance Department
420 S.W. 9th Street
Topeka, Kansas 66612
(913) 296-3071

Kentucky Insurance Department
229 West Main Street
Post Office Box 517
Frankfort, Kentucky 40602
(502) 564-3630

Louisiana Insurance Department
Post Office Box 94214
Baton Rouge, Louisiana 70804-9214
(504) 342-5900

Maine Bureau of Insurance
Consumer Division
State House, Station 34
Augusta, Maine 04333
(207) 582-8707

Maryland Insurance Department
Complaints and Investigation Unit
501 St. Paul Place
Baltimore, Maryland 21202-2272
(301) 333-2792

Massachusetts Insurance Division
Consumer Services Section
280 Friend Street
Boston, Massachusetts 02114
(617) 727-3357

Michigan Insurance Department
Post Office Box 30220
Lansing, Michigan 48909
(517) 373-0220

Minnesota Insurance Department
Department of Commerce
500 Metro Square Building
Junction of 7th and Roberts Streets
St. Paul, Minnesota 55101
(612) 296-4026

Mississippi Insurance Department
Consumer Assistance Division
Post Office Box 79
Jackson, Mississippi 39205
(601) 359-3569

Missouri Division of Insurance
Consumer Services Section
Post Office Box 690
Jefferson City, Missouri 65102-0690
(314) 751-2640

Montana Insurance Department
126 North Sanders
Mitchell Building, Room 270
Post Office Box 4009
Helena, Montana 59604
(406) 444-2040

Nebraska Insurance Department
Terminal Building
941 O Street, Suite 400
Lincoln, Nebraska 68508
(402) 471-2201

Nevada Department of Commerce
Insurance Division
Consumer Section
201 South Fall Street, Room 316
Carson City, Nevada 89701
(702) 885-4270

New Hampshire Insurance Department
169 Manchester Street
Concord, New Hampshire 03301
(603) 271-2261

New Jersey Insurance Department
20 West State Street
Roebling Building
Trenton, New Jersey 08625
(609) 292-4757

New Mexico Insurance Department
Post Office Box 1269
Santa Fe, New Mexico 87504-1269
(505) 827-4500

New York Insurance Department
160 West Broadway
New York, New York 10013
(212) 602-0203 (New York City)
1-800-342-3736 (toll free in New York outside
    New York City)

North Carolina Insurance Department
Consumer Insurance Information
Dobbs Building
Post Office Box 26387
Raleigh, North Carolina 27611
(919) 733-2004

North Dakota Insurance Department
Capitol Building, Fifth Floor
Bismarck, North Dakota 58505
(701) 224-2440

Ohio Insurance Department
Consumer Services Division
2100 Stella Court
Columbus, Ohio 43215
(614) 644-2673

Oklahoma Insurance Department
Post Office Box 53408
Oklahoma City, Oklahoma 73152-3408
(405) 521-2828

**Oregon Department of Insurance and
    Finance**
Insurance Division/Consumer Advocate
21 Labor and Industry Building
Salem, Oregon 97310
(503) 378-4484

Pennsylvania Insurance Department
1326 Strawberry Square
Harrisburg, Pennsylvania 17120
(717) 787-3289

Rhode Island Insurance Division
233 Richmond Street
Providence, Rhode Island 02903-4233
(401) 277-2223

South Carolina Insurance Department
Consumer Assistance Section
Post Office Box 100105
Columbia, South Carolina 29202-3105
(803) 737-6140

South Dakota Insurance Department
500 East Capitol
Pierre, South Dakota 57501
(605) 773-3563

Tennessee Insurance Department
1880 West End Avenue, 14th Floor
Nashville, Tennessee 37219-5318
1-800-342-4031

Texas Board of Insurance
Complaints Division
1110 San Jacinto Boulevard
Austin, Texas 78701-1998
(512) 463-6501

Utah Insurance Department
Consumer Services
Post Office Box 45803
Salt Lake City, Utah 84145
(801) 530-6400

**Vermont Department of Banking and
    Insurance**
Consumer Complaint Division
120 State Street
Montpelier, Vermont 05602
(802) 828-3301

Virginia Insurance Department
Consumer Services Division
700 Jefferson Building
Post Office Box 1157
Richmond, Virginia 23209
(804) 786-7691

Washington Insurance Department
Insurance Building AQ21
Olympia, Washington 98504
(206) 753-7300

West Virginia Insurance Department
2019 Washington Street, East
Charleston, West Virginia 25305
(304) 348-3386

Wisconsin Insurance Department
Complaints Department
Post Office Box 7873
Madison, Wisconsin 537078
(608) 266-0103

Wyoming Insurance Department
Herschler Building
122 West 25th Street
Cheyenne, Wyoming 82002
(307) 777-7401

Guam Insurance Department
Post Office Box 2796
Agana, Guam 96910

Puerto Rico Insurance Department
Fernandez Juncos Station
Post Office Box 8330
Santurce, Puerto Rico 00910
(809) 722-8686

Virgin Islands Insurance Department
Kongens Garde No. 18
St. Thomas, Virgin Islands 00802
(809) 774-2991

INTERNAL REVENUE SERVICE

National Office
Internal Revenue Service
(U.S. Department of the Treasury)
1111 Constitution Avenue, N.W.
Washington, D.C. 20224

Regional Offices

CENTRAL REGION

Internal Revenue Service	Indiana
550 Main Street	Kentucky
Cincinnati, Ohio 45202	Michigan
	Ohio
	West Virginia

MID-ATLANTIC REGION

Internal Revenue Service	Delaware
841 Chestnut Street	Maryland
Philadelphia,	New Jersey
Pennsylvania 19107	Pennsylvania
	Virginia

MIDWEST REGION

Internal Revenue Service	Illinois
1 North Wacker Drive	Iowa
Chicago, Illinois 60606	Minnesota
	Missouri
	Montana
	Nebraska
	North Dakota
	South Dakota
	Wisconsin

NORTH ATLANTIC REGION

Internal Revenue Service	Connecticut
90 Church Street	Maine
New York,	Massachusetts
New York 10007	New Hampshire
	New York
	Rhode Island
	Vermont

SOUTHEAST REGION

Internal Revenue Service	Alabama
275 Peachtree Street, N.E.	Arkansas
Atlanta, Georgia 30043	Florida
	Georgia
	Louisiana
	Mississippi
	North Carolina
	South Carolina
	Tennessee

SOUTHWEST REGION

Internal Revenue Service	Arizona
LB-70	Colorado
7839 Churchill Way	Kansas
Dallas, Texas 75251	New Mexico
	Oklahoma
	Texas
	Utah
	Wyoming

WESTERN REGION

Internal Revenue Service	Alaska
1650 Mission Street	California
San Francisco,	Hawaii
California 94103	Idaho
	Nevada
	Oregon
	Washington

MEDICARE CARRIERS

Medicare/Blue Cross-Blue Shield of
   Alabama (**Alabama**)
Post Office Box C-140
Birmingham, Alabama 35283
(205) 988-2244
1-800-292-8855

Medicare/Aetna Life & Casualty (**Alaska**)
200 S. W. Market Street
Post Office Box 1998
Portland, Oregon 97207-1998
(503) 222-6831
1-800-547-6333

Medicare/Aetna Life & Casualty (**Arizona**)
Post Office Box 37200
Phoenix, Arizona 85069
(602) 861-1968
1-800-352-0411

Medicare/Arkansas Blue Cross and
   Blue Shield (**Arkansas**)
Post Office Box 1418
Little Rock, Arkansas 72203
(501) 378-2320
1-800-482-5525

Medicare/Transamerica Occidental Life
   Insurance Company (**California**)
Box 50061
Upland, California 91785-0061
(213) 748-2311
1-800-252-9020 (counties of Los Angeles,
   Orange, San Diego, Ventura, Imperial,
   San Luis Obispo, Santa Barbara)

Medicare Claims Department
Blue Shield of California
Chico, California 95976
(916) 743-1583
1-800-952-8627 (area codes 209, 408, 415,
   707, 916)

(714) 824-0900
1-800-848-7713 (area codes 213, 619, 714, 805,
818) (rest of state)

Medicare/Blue Shield of Colorado
   (**Colorado**)
700 Broadway
Denver, Colorado 80273
(303) 831-2661
1-800-332-6681

Medicare/The Travelers Insurance
   Company (**Connecticut**)
538 Preston Avenue
Post Office Box 9000
Meriden, Connecticut 06454-9000
1-800-982-6819
(203) 728-6783 (Hartford)
(203) 237-8592 (Meriden area)

Medicare/Pennsylvania Blue Shield
   (**Pennsylvania**)
Post Office Box 890200
Camp Hill, Pennsylvania 17089-0200
1-800-851-3535

Medicare/Pennsylvania Blue Shield
   (**Washington, D.C.**)
Post Office Box 890100
Camp Hill, Pennsylvania 17089-0100
1-800-233-1124

Medicare/Blue Shield of Florida, Inc.
   (**Florida**)
Post Office Box 2525
Jacksonville, Florida 32231
1-800-666-7586 (requests, inquiries,
   explanation, information)
1-800-333-7586 (all other Medicare needs)
(904) 355-3680

Medicare/Aetna Life & Casualty (**Georgia**)
Post Office Box 3018
Savannah, Georgia 31402-3018
(912) 920-2412
1-800-727-0827

Medicare/Aetna Life & Casualty (**Hawaii**)
Post Office Box 3947
Honolulu, Hawaii 96812
(808) 524-1240
1-800-272-5242

EQUICOR, Inc. (**Idaho**)
3150 N. Lakeharbor Lane, Suite 254
Post Office Box 8048
Boise, Idaho 83703-6219
(208) 342-7763
1-800-627-2782

Medicare Claims (**Illinois**)
Blue Cross and Blue Shield of Illinois
Post Office Box 4422
Marion, Illinois 62959
(312) 938-8000
1-800-642-6930

Medicare Part B (**Indiana**)
Associated Insurance Companies, Inc.
Post Office Box 7073
Indianapolis, Indiana 46207
(317) 842-4151
1-800-622-4792

Medicare (**Iowa**)
IASD Health Services, Inc.
(Blue Cross and Blue Shield of Iowa)
636 Grand
Des Moines, Iowa 50309
(515) 245-4785
1-800-532-1285

Medicare/Blue Shield of Kansas City
  (**Kansas**)
Post Office Box 169
Kansas City, Missouri 64141
(816) 561-0900
1-800-892-5900 (counties of Johnson,
  Wyandotte)

Medicare/Blue Shield of Kansas
Post Office Box 239
Topeka, Kansas 66601
(913) 232-3773
1-800-432-3531 (rest of state)

Medicare Part B (**Kentucky**)
Blue Cross and Blue Shield of Kentucky
100 East Vine Street
Lexington, Kentucky 40507
(606) 233-1441
1-800-999-7608

Arkansas Blue Cross and Blue Shield
  (**Louisiana**)
Medicare Administration
Post Office Box 95024
Baton Rouge, Louisiana 70895-9024
1-800-462-9666
(504) 529-1494 (New Orleans)
(504) 272-1242 (Baton Rouge)

Medicare/Blue Shield of Massachusetts/
  Tri-State (**Maine**)
Post Office Box 1010
Biddeford, Maine 04005
(207) 282-5991
1-800-492-0919

Medicare/Pennsylvania Blue Shield
  (**Maryland**)
Post Office Box 890100
Camp Hill, Pennsylvania 17089-0100
1-800-233-1124 (counties of Montgomery,
  Prince George)

Maryland Blue Shield, Inc.
700 East Joppa Road
Towson, Maryland 21204
(301) 561-4160
1-800-492-4795 (rest of state)

Medicare/Blue Shield of Massachusetts, Inc.
  (**Massachusetts**)
1022 Hingham Street
Rockland, Massachusetts 02371
(617) 956-3994
1-800-882-1228

Medicare Part B (**Michigan**)
Michigan Blue Cross and Blue Shield
Post Office Box 2201
Detroit, Michigan 48231-2201
(313) 225-8200 (Detroit)
1-800-482-4045 (in area code 313)
1-800-322-0607 (in area code 517)
1-800-442-8020 (in area code 616)
1-800-562-7802 (in area code 906)

Medicare/The Travelers Insurance
  Company (**Minnesota**)
8120 Penn Avenue South
Bloomington, Minnesota 55431
(612) 884-7171
1-800-352-2762 (counties of Anoka, Dakota,
  Filmore, Goodhue, Hennepin, Houston,
  Olmstead, Ramsey, Wabasha,
  Washington, Winona)

Medicare/Blue Shield of Minnesota
Post Office Box 64357
St. Paul, Minnesota 55164
(612) 456-5070
1-800-392-0343 (rest of state)

Medicare/The Travelers Insurance
  Company (**Mississippi**)
Post Office Box 22545
Jackson, Mississippi 39225-2545
(601) 956-0372
1-800-682-5417 (toll free in Mississippi)
1-800-227-2349 (outside Mississippi)

Medicare/Blue Shield of Kansas City
  (**Missouri**)
Post Office Box 169
Kansas City, Missouri 64141
(816) 561-0900
1-800-892-5900 (counties of Andrew,
  Atchison, Bates, Benton, Buchanan,
  Caldwell, Carroll, Cass, Clay, Clinton,
  Daviess, DeKalb, Gentry, Grundy,
  Harrison, Henry, Holt, Jackson, Johnson,
  Lafayette, Livingston, Mercer, Nodaway,
  Pettis, Platte, Ray, St. Clair, Saline, Vernon,
  Worth)

Medicare/General American Life Insurance
  Company (**Missouri**)
Post Office Box 505
St. Louis, Missouri 63166
(314) 843-8880
1-800-392-3070 (rest of state)

Medicare/Blue Shield of Montana, Inc.
  (**Montana**)
2501 Beltview
Post Office Box 4310
Helena, Montana 59604
(406) 444-8350
1-800-332-6146

Medicare Part B (**Nebraska**)
Blue Cross/Blue Shield of Nebraska
carrier: Blue Shield of Kansas
Post Office Box 3106
Omaha, Nebraska 68103-0106
(913) 232-3773 (customer service site in
  Kansas)
1-800-633-1113

Medicare/Aetna Life and Casualty (**Nevada**)
Post Office Box 37230
Phoenix, Arizona 85069
(602) 861-1968
1-800-528-0311

Medicare/Blue Shield of Massachusetts/
  Tri-State (**New Hampshire**)
Post Office Box 1010
Biddeford, Maine 04005
(207) 282-5991
1-800-447-1142

Medicare/Pennsylvania Blue Shield
  (**New Jersey**)
Post Office Box 400010
Harrisburg, Pennsylvania 17140-0010
1-800-462-9306

Medicare/Aetna Life and Casualty
  (**New Mexico**)
Post Office Box 25500
Oklahoma City, Oklahoma 73125-0500
(505) 843-7771 (Albuquerque)
1-800-423-2925

Medicare/Empire Blue Cross and
  Blue Shield (**New York**)
Post Office Box 100
Yorktown Heights, New York 10598
(212) 490-4444 (counties of Bronx, Kings,
  New York, Richmond)

Medicare/Empire Blue Cross and
  Blue Shield
Post Office Box 100
Yorktown Heights, New York 10598
(212) 490-4444
1-800-442-8430 (counties of Columbia,
  Delaware, Dutchess, Greene, Nassau,
  Orange, Putnam, Rockland, Suffolk,
  Sullivan, Ulster, Westchester)

Medicare/Group Health, Inc.
Post Office Box 1608, Ansonia Station
New York, New York 10023
(212) 721-1770

Medicare/Blue Shield of Western New York
Post Office Box 5600
Binghamton, New York 13902-0600
(607) 772-6906
1-800-252-6550 (rest of state)

EQUICOR, Inc. (**North Carolina**)
Post Office Box 671
Nashville, Tennessee 37202
(919) 665-0348
1-800-672-3071

Medicare/Blue Shield of North Dakota
   (**North Dakota**)
4510 13th Avenue, S.W.
 Fargo, North Dakota 58121-0001
(701) 282-1100
1-800-247-2267

Medicare/Nationwide Mutual Insurance
   Company (**Ohio**)
Post Office Box 57
Columbus, Ohio 43216
(614) 249-7157
1-800-282-0530

Medicare/Aetna Life and Casualty
   (**Oklahoma**)
701 N.W. 63rd Street, Suite 100
Oklahoma City, Oklahoma 73116-7693
(405) 848-7711
1-800-522-9079

Medicare/Aetna Life and Casualty (**Oregon**)
200 S.W. Market Street
Post Office Box 1997
Portland, Oregon 97207-1997
(503) 222-6831
1-800-452-0125

Medicare/Pennsylvania Blue Shield
   (**Pennsylvania**)
Post Office Box 890065
Camp Hill, Pennsylvania 17089-0065
1-800-382-1274

Medicare/Blue Shield of Rhode Island
   (**Rhode Island**)
444 Westminster Mall
Providence, Rhode Island 02901
(401) 861-2273
1-800-662-5170

Medicare Part B (**South Carolina**)
Blue Cross and Blue Shield of South Carolina
Fontaine Road Business Center
300 Arbor Lake Drive, Suite 1300
Columbia, South Carolina 29223
(803) 754-0639
1-800-868-2522

Medicare Part B (**South Dakota**)
Blue Shield of North Dakota
4510 13th Avenue, S.W.
Fargo, North Dakota 58121-0001
(701) 282-1100
1-800-437-4762

EQUICORE, Inc. (**Tennessee**)
Post Office Box 1465
Nashville, Tennessee 37202
(615) 244-5650
1-800-342-8900

Medicare (**Texas**)
Blue Cross and Blue Shield of Texas, Inc.
Post Office Box 660031
Dallas, Texas 75266-0031
(214) 235-3433
1-800-442-2620

Medicare/Blue Shield of Utah (**Utah**)
Post Office Box 30269
Salt Lake City, Utah 84130-0269
(801) 481-6196
1-800-426-3477

Medicare (**Vermont**)
Blue Shield of Massachusetts/Tri-State
Post Office Box 1010
Biddeford, Maine 04005
(207) 282-5991
1-800-447-1142

Medicare/Pennsylvania Blue Shield
   (**Virginia**)
Post Office Box 890100
Camp Hill, Pennsylvania 17089-0100
1-800-233-1124 (counties of Arlington,
   Fairfax; cities of Alexandria, Falls Church,
   Fairfax)

Medicare/The Travelers Insurance
   Company
Post Office Box 26463
Richmond, Virginia 23261
(804) 254-4130
1-800-552-3423 (rest of state)

Direct claims to local Medical Service
   Bureau,

or

Medicare/Washington Physicians' Service
   (Washington)
4th and Battery Building, 6th Floor
2401 4th Avenue
Seattle, Washington 98121
(206) 464-3711
1-800-422-4087 (King county)
(509) 536-4550
1-800-572-5256 (Spokane)
(206) 377-5576
1-800-552-7114 (Kitsap)
(206) 597-6530 (Pierce)
(206) 352-2269 (Thurston)
If out of area call "collect."

Medicare/Nationwide Mutual Insurance
   Company **(West Virginia)**
Post Office Box 57
Columbus, Ohio 43216
(614) 249-7157
1-800-848-0106

Medicare/WPS **(Wisconsin)**
Box 1787
Madison, Wisconsin 53701
1-800-362-7221
(608) 221-3330 (Madison)
(414) 931-1071 (Milwaukee)

Blue Cross/Blue Shield of Wyoming
   (Wyoming)
Post Office Box 628
102 Indian Hills Shopping Center
Cheyenne, Wyoming 82003
(307) 632-9381
1-800-442-2371

Medicare/Hawaii Medical Services
   Association **(American Samoa)**
Post Office Box 860
Honolulu, Hawaii 96808
(808) 944-2247

Medicare/Aetna Life and Casualty **(Guam)**
Post Office Box 3947
Honolulu, Hawaii 96812
(808) 524-1240

Medicare/Seguros De Servicio De Salud De
   Puerto Rico **(Puerto Rico)**
Call Box 71391
San Juan, Puerto Rico 00936
1-800-462-7015
(809) 749-4900

Medicare/Seguros De Servicio De Salud De
   Puerto Rico **(Virgin Islands)**
Call Box 71391
San Juan, Puerto Rico 00936
(809) 778-2665 (St. Croix)
(809) 774-3898 (St. Thomas)

MEDICARE PEER REVIEW ORGANIZATIONS

Alabama Quality Assurance Foundation
   (Alabama)
600 Beacon Parkway West, Suite 600
Birmingham, Alabama 35209-3154
(205) 942-0785

Professional Review Organization for
   Washington **(Alaska)**
10700 Meridian Avenue North, Suite 300
Seattle, Washington 98133
(206) 364-9700

Health Services Advisory Group, Inc.
   (Arizona)
301 East Bethany Home Road
Building B, Suite 157
Post Office Box 16731
Phoenix, Arizona 85102
(602) 264-6382

Arkansas Foundation for Medical Care, Inc.
   (Arkansas)
809 Garrison Avenue
Post Office Box 1508
Fort Smith, Arkansas 72902
(501) 785-2471

California Medical Review, Inc. (California)
60 Spear Street, Suite 500
San Francisco, California 94105
(415) 882-5800

Colorado Foundation for Medical Care
   (Colorado)
1260 South Parker Road
Post Office Box 1730
Denver, Colorado 80231-2179
(303) 321-8642

Connecticut Peer Review Organization, Inc.
   (Connecticut)
100 Roscommon Drive
Middletown, Connecticut 06457
(203) 632-2008

West Virginia Medical Institute, Inc.
   (Delaware)
3412 Chesterfield Avenue, S.E.
Charleston, West Virginia 25304
(304) 925-0461

Delmarva Foundation for Medical Care, Inc.
   (Washington, D.C.)
341 B North Aurora Street
Easton, Maryland 21601
(301) 822-0697

Professional Foundation for Health Care,
   Inc. (Florida)
2907 Bay to Bay Boulevard, Suite 100
Tampa, Florida 33629
(813) 831-6273

Georgia Medical Care Foundation (Georgia)
4 Executive Park Drive, N.E., Suite 1300
Atlanta, Georgia 30329
(404) 982-0411

Hawaii Medical Services Association
   (Hawaii)
818 Keeaumoku Street
Post Office Box 860
Honolulu, Hawaii 96808
(808) 944-3581

Professional Review Organization for
   Washington (Idaho)
10700 Meridian Avenue North, Suite 300
Seattle, Washington 98133
(206) 364-9700

Crescent Counties Foundation for Medical
   Care (Illinois)
350 Shuman Boulevard, Suite 240
Naperville, Illinois 60540
(312) 357-8770

Sentinal Medical Review Organization
   (Indiana)
2901 Ohio Boulevard
Post Office Box 3713
Terre Haute, Indiana 47803
(812) 234-1499

Iowa Foundation for Medical Care (Iowa)
Colony Park, Suite 500
3737 Woodland Avenue
West Des Moines, Iowa 50265
(515) 223-2900

The Kansas Foundation for Medical Care,
   Inc. (Kansas)
2947 S.W. Wanamaker Drive
Topeka, Kansas 66614
(913) 273-2552

Sentinal Medical Review Organization
   (Kentucky)
10503 Timberwood Circle, Suite 200
Post Office Box 23540
Louisville, Kentucky 40223
(502) 339-7442

Louisiana Health Care Review (Louisiana)
9357 Interline Avenue, Suite 200
Baton Rouge, Louisiana 70809
(504) 926-6353

Health Care Review, Inc. (**Maine**)
Henry C. Hall Building
345 Blackstone Boulevard
Providence, Rhode Island 02906
(401) 331-6661

Delmarva Foundation for Medical Care, Inc.
  (**Maryland**)
341 B North Aurora Street
Easton, Maryland 21601
(301) 822-0697

Massachusetts Peer Review Organization,
  Inc. (**Massachusetts**)
300 Bearhill Road
Waltham, Massachusetts 02154
(617) 890-0011

Michigan Peer Review Organization
  (**Michigan**)
40500 Ann Arbor Road, Suite 200
Plymouth, Michigan 48170
(313) 459-0900

Foundation for Health Care Evaluation
  (**Minnesota**)
One Appletree Square, Suite 700
Minneapolis, Minnesota 55425
(612) 854-3306

Mississippi Foundation for Medical Care,
  Inc. (**Mississippi**)
735 Riverside Drive
Post Office Box 4665
Jackson, Mississippi 39296-4665

Missouri Patient Care Review Foundation
  (**Missouri**)
505 Hobbes Lane, Suite 100
Jefferson City, Missouri 65109
(314) 893-7900

Montana-Wyoming Foundation for Medical
  Care (**Montana**)
21 North Main
Post Office Box 5117
Helena, Montana 59601
(406) 443-4020

Iowa Foundation for Medical Care
  (**Nebraska**)
Colony Park Building, Suite 500
3737 Woodland Avenue
West Des Moines, Iowa 50265
(515) 223-2900

Utah Peer Review Organization (**Nevada**)
675 East 2100 South
Salt Lake City, Utah 84106-1864
(801) 487-2290

New Hampshire Foundation for Medical
  Care (**New Hampshire**)
110 Locust Street
Post Office Box 578
Dover, New Hampshire 03820
(603) 749-1641

The Peer Review Organization of
  New Jersey, Inc. (**New Jersey**)
Central Division
Brier Hill Court, Building J
East Brunswick, New Jersey 08816
(201) 238-5570

New Mexico Medical Review Association
  (**New Mexico**)
707 Broadway, N.E., Suite 200
Post Office Box 9900
Albuquerque, New Mexico 87119-9900
(505) 842-6236

Island Peer Review Organization
  (**New York**)
9525 Queens Boulevard, 10th Floor
Rego Park, New York 11374-4511
(718) 896-7230

Medical Review of North Carolina
  (**North Carolina**)
1011 Schaub Drive, Suite 200
Post Office Box 37309
Raleigh, North Carolina 27627
(919) 851-2955

North Dakota Health Care Review, Inc.
  (**North Dakota**)
900 North Broadway, Suite 301
Minot, North Dakota 58701
(701) 852-4231

Peer Review Systems, Inc. (Ohio)
3700 Corporate Drive, Suite 250
Columbus, Ohio 43231-4996
(614) 895-9900

Oklahoma Foundation for Peer Review, Inc.
(Oklahoma)
The Paragon Building, Suite 400
5801 Broadway Extension
Oklahoma City, Oklahoma 73118
(405) 840-2891

Oregon Medical Professional Review
Organization (Oregon)
1220 Southwest Morrison, Suite 300
Portland, Oregon 97205
(503) 279-0100

Keystone Peer Review Organization, Inc.
(Pennsylvania)
777 East Park Drive
Post Office Box 8310
Harrisburg, Pennsylvania 17105-8310
(717) 564-8288

Health Care Review, Inc. (Rhode Island)
Henry C. Hall Building
345 Blackstone Boulevard
Providence, Rhode Island 02906
(401) 331-6661

Medical Review of North Carolina
(South Carolina)
1011 Schaub Drive, Suite 200
Post Office Box 37309
Raleigh, North Carolina 27627
(919) 851-2955

South Dakota Foundation for Medical Care
(South Dakota)
1323 South Minnesota Avenue
Sioux Falls, South Dakota 57105
(605) 336-3505

Mid-South Foundation for Medical Care
(Tennessee)
6401 Poplar Avenue, Suite 400
Memphis, Tennessee 38119
(901) 682-0381

Texas Medical Foundation (Texas)
Barton Oaks Plaza Two, Suite 200
901 Mopac Expressway South
Austin, Texas 78746
(512) 329-6610

Utah Peer Review Organization (Utah)
675 East 2100 South, Suite 270
Salt Lake City, Utah 84106
(801) 487-2290

New Hampshire Foundation for Medical
Care (Vermont)
110 Locust Street
Post Office Box 578
Dover, New Hampshire 03820
(603) 749-1641

Medical Society of Virginia Review
Organization (Virginia)
1606 Santa Rosa Road, Suite 235
Post Office Box K-70
Richmond, Virginia 23288
(804) 289-5320

Professional Review Organization for
Washington (Washington)
10700 Meridian Avenue North, Suite 300
Seattle, Washington 98133-9075
(206) 364-9700

West Virginia Medical Institute, Inc.
(West Virginia)
3412 Chesterfield Avenue, S.E.
Charleston, West Virginia 25304
(304) 925-0461

Wisconsin Peer Review Organization
(Wisconsin)
2001 W. Beltline Highway
Madison, Wisconsin 53713
(608) 274-1940

Montana-Wyoming Foundation for Medical
Care (Wyoming)
21 North Main
Post Office Box 5117
Helena, Montana 59601
(406) 443-4020

Hawaii Medical Services Association
  (**American Samoa/Guam**)
818 Keeaumoku Street
Post Office Box 860
Honolulu, Hawaii 96808
(808) 944-2173

Puerto Rico Foundation for Medical Care
  (**Puerto Rico**)
Merchantile Plaza, Suite 605
Hato Rey, Puerto Rico 00918
(809) 753-6705

Virgin Islands Medical Institute
  (**Virgin Islands**)
Post Office Box 1556
Christiansted
St. Croix, Virgin Islands 00820
(809) 778-6470

OCCUPATIONAL
SAFETY AND HEALTH
ADMINISTRATION

National Office

Occupational Safety and Health
  Administration (OSHA)
(U.S. Department of Labor)
200 Constitution Avenue, N.W.
Washington, D.C. 20210

Regional Offices

Occupational Safety and Health
  Administration
133 Portland Avenue, 1st Floor
Boston, Massachusetts 02114
(617) 656-7159

Occupational Safety and Health
  Administration
201 Varick Street, Room 670
New York, New York 10014
(212) 337-2378

Occupational Safety and Health
  Administration
3535 Market Street
Philadelphia, Pennsylvania 19104
(215) 596-1201

Occupational Safety and Health
  Administration
1375 Peachtree Street, N.E.
Atlanta, Georgia 30367
 (404) 881-3573

Occupational Safety and Health
  Administration
230 S. Dearborn Street
Chicago, Illinois 60604
(312) 357-2220

Occupational Safety and Health
  Administration
555 Griffin Square Building
Griffin and Young Streets
Dallas, Texas 75202
(214) 767-4731

Occupational Safety and Health
  Administration
911 Walnut Street
Kansas City, Missouri 64106
(816) 374-5861

Occupational Safety and Health
  Administration
1961 Stout Street
Denver, Colorado 80294
(303) 844-3061

Occupational Safety and Health
  Administration
450 Golden Gate Avenue
San Francisco, California 94102
(415) 995-5672

Occupational Safety and Health
  Administration
909 1st Avenue
Seattle, Washington 98174
(206) 442-5930

SMALL BUSINESS ADMINISTRATION

National Office
Small Business Administration
Imperial Building
1441 L Street, N.W.
Washington, D.C. 20416

Field Offices
Small Business Administration **(Region I)**
60 Batterymarch, 10th Floor
Boston, Massachusetts 02110
(617) 451-2030

Small Business Administration **(Region II)**
26 Federal Plaza, Room 31-08
New York, New York 10278
(212) 264-7772

Small Business Administration **(Region III)**
475 Allendale Road, Suite 201
King of Prussia, Pennsylvania 19406
(215) 962-3750

Small Business Administration **(Region IV)**
1375 Peachtree Street, N.E., 5th Floor
Atlanta, Georgia 30367
(404) 347-2797

Small Business Administration **(Region V)**
230 South Dearborn Street, Room 510
Chicago, Illinois 60604
(312) 353-0359

Small Business Administration **(Region VI)**
8625 King George Drive, Building C
Dallas, Texas 75235
(214) 767-7643

Small Business Administration **(Region VII)**
911 Walnut Street, 13th Floor
Kansas City, Missouri 64106
(816) 374-5288

Small Business Administration
(Region VIII)
999 18th Street, Suite 701
Denver, Colorado 80202
(303) 294-7001

Small Business Administration **(Region IX)**
450 Golden Gate Avenue
San Francisco, California 94102
(415) 556-7487

Small Business Administration **(Region X)**
2615 4th Avenue, Room 440
Seattle, Washington 98121
(206) 442-5676

SOCIAL SECURITY ADMINISTRATION

National Office
Office of Public Inquiries
Social Security Administration
Department of Health and Human Services
6401 Security Boulevard
Baltimore, Maryland 21235
(301) 965-7700

Regional Offices
BOSTON REGION (I)

Social Security Administration	
Room 1100	Connecticut
John F. Kennedy	Maine
Federal Building,	Massachusetts
Government Center	New Hampshire
Boston, Massachusetts	Rhode Island
02203	Vermont

NEW YORK REGION (II)

The Office of the	New Jersey
Regional Commissioner	New York
Room 40-102	Puerto Rico
26 Federal Plaza	Virgin Islands
New York, New York 10278	

Northeastern Program Service Center
Joseph P. Addabbo Federal Building
1 Jamaica Center Plaza
155-10 Jamaica Avenue
Jamaica, New York 11432-3830
Administrative mail: Post Office Box 4300
Jamaica, New York 11432-3830

PHILADELPHIA REGION (III)

The Office of the Regional
  Commissioner
3535 Market Street
Post Office Box 8788
Philadelphia,
  Pennsylvania 19104

Delaware
District of
  Columbia
Maryland
Pennsylvania
Virginia
West Virginia

Mid-Atlantic Program Service Center
300 Spring Garden Street
Philadelphia, Pennsylvania 19123

ATLANTA REGION (IV)

The Office of the Regional
  Commissioner
101 Marietta Tower,
  Suite 1902
Atlanta, Georgia 30323

Alabama
Florida
Georgia
Kentucky
Mississippi
North Carolina
South Carolina
Tennessee

Southeastern Program Service Center
2001 12th Avenue, North
Birmingham, Alabama 35285

CHICAGO REGION (V)

Chicago Regional Office
105 Adams Street,
  10th Floor
Chicago, Illinois 60603

Illinois
Indiana
Michigan
Minnesota
Ohio
Wisconsin

Great Lakes Program Service Center
Harold Washington Social Security Center
600 West Madison Street
Chicago, Illinois 60606

DALLAS REGION (VI)

Dallas Regional Office
1200 Main Tower
  Building, Room 1440
Dallas, Texas 75202

Arkansas
Louisiana
New Mexico
Oklahoma
Texas

KANSAS CITY REGION (VII)

The Office of the Regional
  Commissioner
Federal Office Building
601 East 12th Street,
  Room 436
Kansas City, Missouri 64106

Iowa
Kansas
Missouri
Nebraska

Mid-America Program Service Center
601 East 12th Street
Kansas City, Missouri 64106

DENVER REGION (VIII)

The Office of the Regional
  Commissioner
Federal Office Building
1961 Stout Street,
  Room 1194
Denver, Colorado 80294

Colorado
Montana
North Dakota
South Dakota
Utah
Wyoming

SAN FRANCISCO REGION (IX)

The Office of the Regional
  Commissioner
75 Hawthorne Street
**San Francisco, California
  94105**

Arizona
California
Guam
Hawaii
Nevada
American
  Samoa

Western Program Service Center
1221 Nevin Avenue
Richmond, California 94802

SEATTLE REGION (X)

The Office of the Regional
  Commissioner
2001 6th Avenue,
  M/S RX-50
Seattle, Washington 98121

Alaska
Idaho
Oregon
Washington

U.S. CUSTOMS SERVICE

National Office

U.S. Customs Service
(U.S. Department of the Treasury)
1301 Constitution Avenue, N.W.
Washington, D.C. 20229

District Directors

Anchorage, Alaska 99501	(907) 271-4043
Baltimore, Maryland 21202	(301) 962-2666
Boston, Massachusetts 02109	(617) 565-6147
Buffalo, New York 14202	(716) 846-4374
Charleston, South Carolina 29402	(803) 724-4312
Charlotte Amalie, St. Thomas, Virgin Islands 00801	(809) 774-2530
Chicago, Illinois 60607	(312) 353-6100
Cleveland, Ohio 44114	(216) 522-4284
Dallas/Ft. Worth, Texas 75261	(214) 574-2170
Detroit, Michigan 48226	(313) 226-3177
Duluth, Minnesota 55802	(218) 720-5201
El Paso, Texas 79985	(915) 534-6799
Great Falls, Montana 59401	(406) 453-7631
Honolulu, Hawaii 96806	(808) 541-1725
Houston/Galveston, Texas 77052	(713) 226-2334
Laredo, Texas 78041-3130	(512) 726-2267
Los Angeles/Long Beach, California 90731	(213) 514-6001
Miami, Florida 33131	(305) 536-4101
Milwaukee, Wisconsin 53202	(414) 291-3924
Minneapolis, Minnesota 55401	(612) 348-1690
Mobile, Alabama 36601	(205) 690-2106
New Orleans, Louisiana 70130	(504) 589-6353

New York, New York New York Seaport area, New York, New York 10048	(212) 466-5817
Kennedy Airport area Jamaica, New York 11430	(718) 917-1542
Newark area Newark, New Jersey 07114	(201) 645-3760
Nogales, Arizona 85621	(602) 287-3637
Norfolk, Virginia 23510	(804) 441-6546
Ogdensburg, New York 13669	(315) 393-0660
Pembina, North Dakota 58271	(701) 825-6201
Philadelphia, Pennsylvania 19106	(215) 597-4605
Port Arthur, Texas 77642	(409) 724-0087
Portland, Maine 04112	(207) 780-3326
Portland, Oregon 97209	(503) 221-2865
Providence, Rhode Island 02903	(401) 528-5080
St. Albans, Vermont 05478	(802) 524-6527
St. Louis, Missouri 63105	(314) 425-3134
San Diego, California 92189	(619) 557-5360
San Francisco, California 94126	(415) 556-4340
San Juan, Puerto Rico 00903	(809) 723-2091
Savannah, Georgia 31401	(912) 944-4256
Seattle, Washington 98174	(206) 442-0554
Tampa, Florida 33602	(813) 228-2381
Washington, D.C. 20041 Washington Dulles Int'l Airport Chantilly, Virginia 22021	(202) 566-8511
Wilmington, North Carolina 28401	(919) 343-4601

PRECLEARANCE OFFICES

Montreal	(514) 636-3875
Toronto	(416) 676-2606
Winnipeg	(204) 774-5391
Calgary	(403) 250-0693
Edmonton	(403) 955-8186
Vancouver	(604) 278-1825
Bermuda	(809) 293-0353
Nassau	(809) 327-7126
Freeport	(809) 352-7256

CUSTOMS ASSISTANCE ABROAD

Bangkok	011/662/252-5040*
Bonn	011/49/228/339-2207
Brasilia	011/55/61/223-0120, Ext. 459
Brussels	011/32/2/513-44-50, Ext. 2770
Hong Kong	011/852/5/239-011
Karachi	011/92/21/515081
London	011/44/1/493-4599
Mexico City	(905) 211-0042, Ext. 3687*
Ottawa	(613) 238-5335*
Panama City	011/507/271-777
Paris	011/33/1/4296-1202, Ext. 2392
Rome	011/39/6/4674-2475 or 2489
Rotterdam	011/31/10/117560
Tokyo	011/81/3/583-7141, Ext. 7205
Vienna	011/43/222/31-55-11

U.S. GOVERNMENT OFFICES

The White House Office
1600 Pennsylvania Avenue, N.W.
Washington, D.C. 20500
(202) 456-1414

U.S. Senate
The Capitol
Washington, D.C. 20510
(202) 224-3121

The House of Representatives
The Capitol
Washington, D.C. 20510
(202) 224-3121

The Supreme Court of the United States
United States Supreme Court Building
1 First Street, N.E.
Washington, D.C. 20543
(202) 479-3000

U.S. Government Printing Office
North Capitol and H Streets, N.W.
Washington, D.C. 20401
(202) 275-2051

Library of Congress
101 Independence Avenue, S.E.
Washington, D.C. 20540
(202) 707-5000

U.S. Department of Agriculture
14th Street and Independence Avenue, S.W.
Washington, D.C. 20250
(202) 447-2791

U.S. Department of Commerce
14th Street Between Constitution Avenue
  and E Street, N.W.
Washington, D.C. 20230
(202) 377-2000

U.S. Department of Defense
The Pentagon
Washington, D.C. 20301-1155
(202) 545-6700

U.S. Department of Education
400 Maryland Avenue, S.W.
Washington, D.C. 20202
(202) 245-3192

U.S. Department of Energy
1000 Independence Avenue, S.W.
Washington, D.C. 20585
(202) 586-5000

* Disregard 011 and area code numbers when calling within the city.

U.S. Department of Health and Human Services
200 Independence Avenue, S.W.
Washington, D.C. 20201
(202) 245-6296

U.S. Department of Housing and Urban Development
451 7th Street, S.W.
Washington, D.C. 20410
(202) 755-5111

U.S. Department of the Interior
1800 C Street, N.W.
Washington D.C. 20204
(202) 343-3171

U.S. Department of Justice
Constitution Avenue and 10th Street, N.W.
Washington, D.C. 20530
(202) 633-2000; (202) 633-1888 (TDD number for Hearing Impaired)

U.S. Department of Labor
200 Constitution Avenue, N.W.
Washington, D.C. 20210
(202) 523-8165

U.S. Department of State
2201 C Street, N.W.
Washington, D.C. 20520
(202) 647-4000

U.S. Department of Transportation
400 7th Street, S.W.
Washington, D.C. 20590
(202) 366-4000

U.S. Department of the Treasury
1500 Pennsylvania Avenue, N.W.
Washington, D.C. 20220
(202) 566-2000

U.S. Department of Veterans Affairs
810 Vermont Avenue, N.W.
Washington, D.C. 20420
(202) 233-2300

INDEPENDENT GOVERNMENT ORGANIZATIONS
ACTION
1100 Vermont Avenue, N.W
Washington, D.C. 20525
(202) 634-9380

Central Intelligence Agency
Washington, D.C. 20505
(703) 482-1100

Commission on Civil Rights
1121 Vermont Avenue, N.W.
Washington, D.C. 20425
(202) 376-8177

Consumer Products Safety Commission
5401 Westbard Avenue
Bethesda, Maryland 20207
(301) 492-6580

Equal Employment Opportunity Commission
1801 L Street
Washington, D.C. 20507
(202) 634-6036
1-800-USA-EEOC (toll free)

Federal Aviation Administration
Department of Transportation
800 Independence Avenue, S.W.
Washington, D.C. 20591
(202) 267-3484

Federal Bureau of Investigation
Department of Justice
9th Street and Pennsylvania Avenue, N.W.
Washington, D.C. 20535
(202) 324-3000

Federal Communications Commission
1919 M Street, N.W.
Washington, D.C. 20554
(202) 632-7000
(202) 632-6999 (TDD number for hearing impaired)

Federal Deposit Insurance Corporation
550 17th Street, N.W.
Washington, D.C. 20429
(202) 393-8400

Federal Election Commission
999 E Street, N.W.
Washington, D.C. 20463
(202) 376-3120
1-800-424-9539 (toll free)

Federal Emergency Management Agency
500 C Street, S.W.
Washington, D.C. 20472
(202) 646-4600

Federal Reserve System
20th Street and Constitution Avenue, N.W.
Washington, D.C. 20551
(202) 452-3000

Interstate Commerce Commission
12th Street and Constitution Avenue, N.W.
Washington, D.C. 20423
(202) 275-7119

**National Aeronautics and Space
  Administration**
600 Independence Avenue, S.W.
Washington, D.C. 20546
(202) 453-1000

**National Archives and Records
  Administration**
7th Street and Pennsylvania Avenue, N.W.
Washington, D.C. 20408
(202) 523-3218

National Endowment for the Arts
1100 Pennsylvania Avenue, N.W.
Washington, D.C. 20506
(202) 682-5400

National Science Foundation
1800 G Street
Washington, D.C. 20550
(202) 357-5000

National Transportation Safety Board
800 Independence Avenue, S.W.
Washington, D.C. 20594
(202) 382-6600

Nuclear Regulatory Commission
Washington, D.C. 20555
(301) 492-7000

Peace Corps
1990 K Street, N.W.
Washington, D.C. 20526
(202) 254-5010

Postal Rate Commission
1333 H Street, N.W.
Washington, D.C. 20268-0001
(202) 789-6800

Securities and Exchange Commission
450 5th Street, N.W.
Washington, D.C. 20549
(202) 272-3100

Selective Service System
National Headquarters
Washington, D.C. 20435
(202) 724-0820

Small Business Administration
Imperial Building
1441 L Street, N.W.
Washington, D.C. 20416
(202) 653-7561
1-800-368-5855 (toll free)

Smithsonian Institution
1000 Jefferson Davis Drive, S.W.
Washington, D.C. 20560
(202) 357-1300

United Nations
New York, New York 10017
(212) 963-1234

United States Postal Service
475 L'Enfant Plaza, S.W.
Washington, D.C. 20260-0001
(202) 268-2000

U.S. PASSPORT SERVICES

National Office

Passport Services
Bureau of Consular Affairs
1425 K Street, N.W.
Room G-62
Washington, D.C. 20524
(202) 523-1355

Field Offices

Passport Services
11000 Wilshire Boulevard
Los Angeles, California 90024-3615
(213) 209-7075

Passport Services
525 Market Street
San Francisco, California 94105-2773
(415) 974-9941

Passport Services
1 Landmark Square
Stamford, Connecticut 06901
(203) 325-3530

Passport Services
1425 K Street, N.W.
Washington, D.C. 20524-0002
(212) 647-0581

Passport Services
Federal Office Building
Miami, Florida 33130
(305) 536-4681

Passport Services
Federal Building
Honolulu, Hawaii 96850
(808) 541-1918

Passport Services
Federal Building
Chicago, Illinois 60604
(312) 353-7155

Passport Services
701 Loyola Avenue
New Orleans, Louisiana 70130
(504) 589-6161

Passport Services
Thomas P. O'Neill Federal Building
Boston, Massachusetts 02222
(617) 565-6990

Passport Services
Rockefeller Center
New York, New York 10111-0031
(212) 541-7710

Passport Services
Federal Building
Philadelphia, Pennsylvania 19106
(215) 597-7482

Passport Services
1919 Smith Street
Houston, Texas 77002
(713) 653-3158

Passport Services
Federal Building
Seattle, Washington 98174
(206) 442-7945

UTILITY COMMISSIONS

Public Service Commission
Post Office Box 991
Montgomery, Alabama 36101
(205) 261-5207
1-800-392-8050 (toll free in Alabama)

Public Utilities Commission
420 L Street, Suite 100
Anchorage, Alaska 99501
(907) 276-6222

Corporation Commission
1200 West Washington Street
Phoenix, Arizona 85007
(602) 542-3935
(602) 255-2105 (TDD)

Public Service Commission
1000 Center Street
Little Rock, Arkansas 72202
(501) 682-1453
1-800-482-1164 (toll free in Arkansas)

Public Utilities Commission
505 Van Ness Avenue, Room 5207
San Francisco, California 94102
(415) 557-2444
(415) 557-0798 (TDD)

Public Utilities Commission
1580 Logan Street
Logan Tower, Office Level 2
Denver, Colorado 80203
(303) 894-2021
1-800-888-0170 (toll free in Colorado)

Department of Public Utility Control
1 Central Park Plaza
New Britain, Connecticut 06051
(203) 827-1553
1-800-382-4586 (toll free in Connecticut)

Public Service Commission
1560 South DuPont Highway
Post Office Box 457
Dover, Delaware 19903
(302) 736-4247
1-800-282-8574 (toll free in Delaware)

Public Service Commission
450 5th Street, N.W.
Washington, D.C. 20001
(202) 626-5110

Public Service Commission
101 East Gaines Street
Tallahassee, Florida 32399-0850
(904) 488-7001
1-800-342-3552 (toll free in Florida)

Public Service Commission
244 Washington Street, S.W.
Atlanta, Georgia 30334
(404) 656-4556
1-800-282-5813 (toll free in Georgia)

Public Utilities Commission
465 South King Street, Room 103
Honolulu, Hawaii 96813
(808) 548-3990

Public Utilities Commission
State House
Boise, Idaho 83720
(208) 334-3427

Commerce Commission
527 East Capitol Avenue
Post Office Box 19280
Springfield, Illinois 62794
(217) 782-7295
(217) 782-7434 (TDD)

Utility Regulatory Commission
913 State Office Building
Indianapolis, Indiana 46204
(317) 232-2701

State Utilities Board
Lucas State Office Building
Des Moines, Iowa 50319
(515) 281-5979

State Corporation Commission
Docking State Office Building
Topeka, Kansas 66612
(913) 296-3324
1-800-662-0027 (toll free in Kansas)

Public Service Commission
730 Schenkel Lane
Post Office Box 615
Frankfort, Kentucky 40602
(502) 564-3940

Public Service Commission
One American Place, Suite 1630
Post Office Box 9115
Baton Rouge, Louisiana 70825
(504) 342-4404
1-800-228-9368 (toll free in Louisiana)

Public Utilities Commission
State House Station 18
Augusta, Maine 04333
(207) 289-3831
1-800-452-4699 (toll free in Maine)

Public Service Commission
231 East Baltimore Street
Baltimore, Maryland 21202
(301) 333-6000
1-800-492-0474 (toll free in Maryland)

Department of Public Utilities
100 Cambridge Street, 12th Floor
Boston, Massachusetts 02202
(617) 727-3500

Public Service Commission
6545 Mercantile Way
Post Office Box 30221
Lansing, Michigan 48909
(517) 334-6445
1-800-292-9555 (toll free in Michigan)
1-800-443-8926 (toll free TDD in Michigan)

Public Utilities Commission
780 American Center Building
160 East Kellogg Boulevard
St. Paul, Minnesota 55101
(612) 296-7124
(612) 287-1200 (TDD)
1-800-852-8747 (toll free in Minnesota)

Public Service Commission
Post Office Box 1174
Jackson, Mississippi 39215
(601) 961-5400

Public Service Commission
Post Office Box 360
Jefferson City, Missouri 65102
(314) 751-3234
1-800-392-4211 (toll free in Missouri)

Public Service Commission
2701 Prospect Avenue
Helena, Montana 59620
(406) 444-6199

Public Service Commission
300 The Atrium
1200 N Street
Post Office Box 94927
Lincoln, Nebraska 68509
(402) 471-3101

Public Service Commission
727 Fairview Drive
Carson City, Nevada 89710
(702) 687-6000

Public Utilities Commission
8 Old Suncook Road
Building No.1
Concord, New Hampshire 03301
(603) 271-2431
1-800-852-3793 (toll free in New Hampshire)

Board of Public Utilities
Two Gateway Center
Newark, New Jersey 07102
(201) 648-2027
(201) 648-7983 (TDD)
1-800-824-0241 (toll free in New Jersey)

Public Service Commission
Post Office Box 2205
Santa Fe, New Mexico 87504
(505) 827-6940

Public Service Commission
3 Empire State Plaza
Albany, New York 12223
(518) 474-7080

Complaints: 1-800-342-3377 (toll free in
New York)

Utilities Commission
Post Office Box 29510
Raleigh, North Carolina 27626
(919) 733-4249

Public Service Commission
State Capitol Building
Bismarck, North Dakota 58505
(701) 224-2400
1-800-932-2400 (toll free in North Dakota)

Public Utilities Commission
180 East Broad Street
Columbus, Ohio 43266-0573
(614) 466-3016
(614) 466-8180 (TDD)
1-800-282-0198 (toll free in Ohio)

Corporation Commission
Jim Thorpe Office Building
Oklahoma City, Oklahoma 73105
(405) 521-2264
1-800-522-8154 (toll free in Oklahoma)

Public Utility Commission
300 Labor and Industries Building
Salem, Oregon 97310
(503) 378-6611
1-800-522-2404 (toll free in Oregon)

Public Utility Commission
Post Office Box 3265
Harrisburg, Pennsylvania 17120
(717) 783-1740
1-800-782-1110 (toll free in Pennsylvania)

Public Utilities Commission
100 Orange Street
Providence, Rhode Island 02903
(401) 277-3500 (voice/TDD)
1-800-341-1000 (toll free in Rhode Island)

Public Service Commission
Post Office Drawer 11649
Columbia, South Carolina 29211
(803) 737-5100
1-800-922-1531 (toll free in South Carolina)

Public Utilities Commission
500 East Capitol Avenue
Pierre, South Dakota 57501
(605) 773-3201

Public Service Commission
460 James Robertson Parkway
Nashville, Tennessee 37219
(615) 741-2904
1-800-342-8359 (toll free voice/TDD in
  Tennessee)

Public Utility Commission
7800 Shoal Creek Boulevard, Suite 400N
Austin, Texas 78757
(512) 458-0100
(512) 458-0221 (TDD)

Public Service Commission
160 East 300 South
Post Office Box 45585
Salt Lake City, Utah 84145
(801) 530-6716

Public Service Board
State Office Building
120 State Street
Montpelier, Vermont 05602
(802) 828-2358
1-800-622-4496 (toll free in Vermont)

State Corporation Commission
Post Office Box 1197
Richmond, Virginia 23209
(804) 786-3608
1-800-552-7945 (toll free in Virginia)

Utilities and Transportation Commission
1300 Evergreen Park Drive South
Olympia, Washington 98504
(206) 753-6423
1-800-562-6150 (toll free in Washington)

Public Service Commission
Post Office Box 812
Charleston, West Virginia 25323
(304) 340-0300
1-800-344-5113 (toll free in West Virginia)

Public Service Commission
4802 Sheboygan Avenue
Post Office Box 7854
Madison, Wisconsin 53707
(608) 266-2001

Public Service Commission
700 West 21st Street
Cheyenne, Wyoming 82002
(307) 777-7427

Public Service Commission
Call Box 870
Hato Rey, Puerto Rico 00919-0870
(809) 751-5050

Public Services Commission
Post Office Box 40, Charlotte Amalie
St. Thomas, Virgin Islands 00804
(809) 776-1291

VETERANS AFFAIRS

National Office
U.S. Department of Veterans Affairs
810 Vermont Avenue, N.W.
Washington, D.C. 20420

Regional Offices
VA Regional Office
474 South Court Street
Montgomery, Alabama 36104

VA Regional Office
235 East 8th Avenue
Anchorage, Alaska 99501

VA Regional Office
3225 North Central Avenue
Phoenix, Arizona 85102

VA Regional Office
Post Office Box 1280
North Little Rock, Arkansas 72155

VA Regional Office
11000 Wilshire Boulevard
Los Angeles, California 90024

VA Regional Office
44 Union Boulevard
Denver, Colorado 80225

VA Regional Office
450 Main Street
Hartford, Connecticut 06103

VA Regional Office
1601 Kirkwood Highway
Wilmington, Delaware 19805

VA Regional Office
941 North Capitol Street, N.E.
Washington, D.C. 20421

VA Regional Office
Post Office Box 1437
St. Petersburg, Florida 33731

VA Regional Office
730 Peachtree Street, N.E.
Atlanta, Georgia 30308

VA Regional Office
Post Office Box 50188
Honolulu, Hawaii 96850

VA Regional Office
550 West Fort Street
Boise, Idaho 83724

VA Regional Office
Post Office Box 8136
Chicago, Illinois 60680

VA Regional Office
575 North Pennsylvania Street
Indianapolis, Indiana 46204

VA Regional Office
210 Walnut Street
Des Moines, Iowa 50309

VA Regional Office
901 George Washington Boulevard
Witchita, Kansas 67211

VA Regional Office
600 Federal Plaza
Louisville, Kentucky 40202

VA Regional Office
701 Loyola Avenue
New Orleans, Louisiana 70113

VA Regional Office
31 Hopkins Plaza
Baltimore, Maryland 21201

VA Regional Office
John F. Kennedy Federal Building
Boston, Massachusetts 02203

VA Regional Office
477 Michigan Avenue
Detroit, Michigan 48226

VA Regional Office and Insurance Center
Bishop Henry Whipple Federal Building,
   Fort Snelling
Post Office Box 1820
St. Paul, Minnesota 55111

VA Regional Office
100 West Capitol Street
Jackson, Mississippi 39269

VA Regional Office
1520 Market Street
St. Louis, Missouri 63103

VA Regional Office
Fort Harrison, Montana 59636

VA Regional Office
100 Centennial Mall North
Lincoln, Nebraska 68508

VA Regional Office
245 East Liberty Street
Reno, Nevada 89520

VA Regional Office
275 Chestnut Street
Manchester, New Hampshire 03103

VA Regional Office
20 Washington Pl.
Newark, New Jersey 07102

VA Regional Office
500 Gold Avenue, S.W.
Albuquerque, New Mexico 87102

VA Regional Office
111 West Huron Street
Buffalo, New York 14202

VA Regional Office
252 7th Avenue at 24th Street
New York, New York 10001

VA Regional Office
251 North Main Street
Winston-Salem, North Carolina 27102

VA Regional Office
Fargo, North Dakota 58102

VA Regional Office
1240 East 9th Street
Cleveland, Ohio 44199

VA Regional Office
125 South Main Street
Muskogee, Oklahoma 74401

VA Regional Office
1220 S.W. 3rd Avenue
Portland, Oregon 97204

VA Regional Office and Insurance Center
5000 Wissahickon Avenue
Philadelphia, Pennsylvania 19101
(Mail: Post Office Box 8079)

VA Regional Office
1000 Liberty Avenue
Pittsburgh, Pennsylvania 15222

VA Regional Office
380 Westminster Mall
Providence, Rhode Island 02903

VA Regional Office
1801 Assembly Street
Columbia, South Carolina 29201

VA Regional Office
2501 West 22nd Street
Post Office Box 5046
Sioux Falls, South Dakota 57117

VA Regional Office
110 9th Avenue S.
Nashville, Tennessee 37203

VA Regional Office
2515 Murworth Drive
Houston, Texas 77054

VA Regional Office
1400 North Valley Mills Drive
Waco, Texas 76799

VA Regional Office
125 South State Street
Salt Lake City, Utah 84147

VA Regional Office
White River Junction, Vermont 05001

VA Regional Office
210 Franklin Road, S.W.
Roanoke, Virginia 24011

VA Regional Office
915 2nd Avenue
Seattle, Washington 98174

VA Regional Office
640 4th Avenue
Huntington, West Virginia 25701

VA Regional Office
Post Office Box 6
Milwaukee, Wisconsin 53295

VA Regional Office
2360 East Pershing Boulevard
Cheyenne, Wyoming 82001

VA Regional Office
Barrio Monacillos
G.P.O. Box 4867
San Juan, Puerto Rico 00936

OTHER ORGANIZATIONS
Military Discharge Review Boards
Air Force Manpower and Personnel Center
Attention: MPCDOA1
Randolph Air Force Base, Texas 78150-6001

Army Discharge Review Board
Attention: SFMR-RBB, Room 200A
1941 Jefferson Davis Highway
Arlington, Virginia 22202-4504

Coast Guard
Attention: GPE1
Washington, D.C. 20593

Navy Discharge Review Board
801 North Randolph Street, Suite 905
Arlington, Virginia 22203

EMPLOYMENT
National Personnel Records Center
9700 Page Boulevard
St. Louis, MO 63132-5199

U.S. Office of Personnel Management
Federal Job Information Center
1900 "E" Street, N.W.
Washington, D.C. 20415

OTHER
American Battle Monuments Commission
Room 5127, Pulaski Building
20 Massachusetts Avenue, N.W.
Washington, D.C. 20314

FORMS OF ADDRESS

Using the correct title or designation when addressing someone in a letter is not just courteous; it is also a way of letting that person know that you respect him or her. This evidence of respect will lay the groundwork for a timely and polite reply.

This section of the appendix is designed to help you find the appropriate forms of address. It is divided into six categories: Government, Diplomats, Armed Services, Education, Clergy, and Professions. Within each category, the positions (first column) have been listed alphabetically. In the second (middle) column, when you see the word "name," use your recipient's full name, for example, the Honorable William A. Rodgers. In the third (last) column, when you see the word "name," use your recipient's surname (last name) unless otherwise designated, for example, Dear Ms. Johnston.

POSITION	INSIDE ADDRESS	SALUTATION
Government		
Assemblyman/woman	The Honorable (name of assemblyman/woman)	Dear Mr./Ms. (name):
Associate justice, U.S. Supreme Court	Mr./Madam Justice (name of justice) The Supreme Court of the United States	Dear Mr./Madam Justice:
Attorney general	The Honorable (name of attorney general) Attorney General of the United States	Dear Mr./Madam Attorney General:
Cabinet officers	The Honorable (name of secretary) Secretary of (Department)	Dear Mr./Madam Secretary:
Chief justice, U.S. Supreme Court	The Chief Justice of the United States, The Supreme Court of the United States	Dear Mr./Madam Chief Justice:
Governor of a state	The Honorable (name of governor) Governor of (name of state)	Dear Governor (name):
Judge, federal	The Honorable (name of judge) Judge of the United States District Court for the (area) District of (state)	Dear Judge (name):
Judge, state or local	The Honorable (name of judge) Judge of the Court of (name of state, county, or town)	Dear Judge (name):
Lieutenant governor	The Honorable (name of lieutenant governor) Lieutenant Governor of (name of state)	Dear Mr./Ms. (name):

POSITION	INSIDE ADDRESS	SALUTATION
Mayor of a city or town	The Honorable (name of mayor) Mayor of (name of city or town)	Dear Mayor (name):
President	The President The White House	Dear Mr. President:
President of Board of Commissioners	The Honorable (name of president), President Board of Commissioners of City or County of (name of city or county)	Dear Mr./Ms. (name):
Representative, state	The Honorable (name of representative) House of Representatives	Dear Mr./Ms. (name):
Representative, United States	The Honorable (name of representative) House of Representatives	Dear Mr./Ms. (name):
Senator, state	The Honorable (name of senator) The State Senate	Dear Senator (name):
Senator, United States	The Honorable (name of senator) United States Senate	Dear Senator (name):
Speaker of the House of Representatives	The Honorable (name of Speaker) Speaker of the House of Representatives	Dear Mr./Madam Speaker:
Vice president, U.S.	The Vice President of the United States	Dear Mr. Vice President:

Diplomats

POSITION	INSIDE ADDRESS	SALUTATION
Ambassador, United States	The Honorable (name of ambassador) American Ambassador to (name of country)	Dear Mr./Madam Ambassador:
Ambassador to the United States	His/Her Excellency (name of ambassador) Ambassador of (name of country)	Dear Mr./Madam Ambassador:
Charge d'Affaires, United States	The Honorable (name of charge d'affaires) United States Charge d'Affaires	Dear Mr./Ms. (name):
Consul, United States	(name of consul), Esq. United States Consul	Dear Mr./Ms. (name):

POSITION	INSIDE ADDRESS	SALUTATION
Minister, United States	The Honorable (name of minister) American Minister to (name of country)	Dear Mr./Madam Minister:
Foreign minister to United States	The Honorable (name of minister) Minister of (name of country)	Dear Mr./Madam Minister:
Secretary general, United Nations	His/Her Excellency (name of secretary general) Secretary General of the United Nations	Dear Mr./Madam Secretary General:
U.N. representative (foreign)	His/Her Excellency (name of representative) Representative of (name of country) to the United Nations	Dear Mr./Madam (name):
U.N. Representative, United States	The Honorable (name of representative) United States Representative to the United Nations	Dear Mr./Ms. (name):

Armed Services

Military and naval officers	(Full rank) name of officer), USA (for Army), USN (for Navy), USCG (for Coast Guard), USAF (for Air Force), USMC (for Marine Corps)	Dear (full rank) (name):

Education

Dean, college or university	Dean (name of dean) (name of college or university)	Dear Dean (name):
President, college or university	Mr. (name of president) President (name of college or university)	Dear President (name):
President, college or university (with a doctorate)	(Name of president), (abbreviation for degree) President (name of college or university)	Dear Dr. (name):
Professor, college or university	Professor (name of professor) (name of college or University)	Dear Professor (name):

POSITION	INSIDE ADDRESS	SALUTATION
Professor, college or university (with a doctorate)	(Name of professor), (abbreviation for degree) (name of college or university)	Dear Dr. (name of professor):

Clergy

POSITION	INSIDE ADDRESS	SALUTATION
Abbot	The Right Reverend (name of abbot) Abbot of (name of abbey) Abbey	Dear Father Abbot:
Archbishop or Bishop, Eastern Orthodox or Roman Catholic	The Most Reverend (name of archbishop or bishop) Archbishop or Bishop of (name of city)	Dear (Archbiship or Bishop) (name):
Archdeacon, Episcopal	The Venerable (name of archdeacon) Archdeacon of (name of city)	Dear Archdeacon (name):
Bishop, Episcopal	The Right Reverend (name of bishop) Bishop of (name of city)	Dear Bishop (name):
Bishop, other Protestant	The Reverend (name of bishop) (denomination) Bishop	Dear Bishop (name):
Brotherhood, Roman Catholic	Brother (name of brother)	Dear Brother (first name of Brother):
Brotherhood, Superior of	The Very Reverend (Director name of superior)	Dear Father Superior:
Cardinal, Roman Catholic	His Eminence (first name of cardinal) Cardinal (last name of cardinal) Archbishop of (name of city)	Dear Cardinal (name):
Clergyman/woman, Protestant	The Reverend (name of clergyman/woman) (name of church)	Dear Mr./Ms. (name):
Dean of a cathedral, Episcopal	The Very Reverend (name of dean) Dean of (name of cathedral)	Dear Dean (name):
Monsignor, Roman Catholic	The Right Reverend Monsignor (name of monsignor)	Dear Monsignor (name):
Patriarch, Greek Orthodox	His All Holiness Patriarch (first name of patriarch)	Your All Holiness:

POSITION	INSIDE ADDRESS	SALUTATION
Patriarch, Russian Orthodox	His Holiness the Patriarch of (name of place)	Your Holiness:
Pope, Roman Catholic	His Holiness The Pope Vatican City	Your Holiness:
Priest, Roman Catholic	The Reverend (name of priest), S.J. (name of church)	Dear Father (name):
Rabbi, man or woman	Rabbi (name of rabbi)	Dear Rabbi (name):
Sisterhood, Roman Catholic	Sister (name of sister)	Dear Sister (first name of sister):
Sisterhood, Superior of	The Reverend Mother Superior (name of convent)	Dear Reverend Mother:

Professions

Attorney	Mr./Ms. (name of attorney), Attorney at Law	Dear Mr./Ms. (name):
Dentist	(name of dentist), D.D.S.	Dear Dr. (name):
Physician	(name of physician), M.D.	Dear Dr. (name):
Veterinarian	(name of veterinarian), D.V.M.	Dear Dr. (name):

U.S. POSTAL SERVICE

Once your letter has been written, you must next select the proper way to send it. Urgency, value, and destination will influence your choice of the service most appropriate for your needs. If your message requires an immediate reply, or if you are attempting to send a parcel of nonstandard size to a domestic or foreign destination, several options are available.

This section provides a brief overview of mailing methods offered by the U.S. Postal Service to local, regional, national, and international locations.

As technology brings people and nations of the world closer together, our need to communicate continues to increase. The demand for faster and more efficient means of dispatch promotes ongoing changes in fees, services, and methods of transportation. If you have questions regarding a particular service or rate schedule, contact your local post office.

EXPRESS MAIL

Express Mail is the method available through the U.S. Postal Service system to rush high-priority items to destinations throughout the United States and selected foreign countries. It is available 7 days a week, 365 days a year for items that weigh up to 70 pounds and do not exceed 108 inches in combined length and girth.

Services include insurance, shipment receipt, and record of delivery at the destination post office. The Postal Service will refund, upon application to the originating office, postage for any such shipments not meeting the service standard, with the exception of those delayed due to strike or work stoppage.

Express Mail Next-Day Service is perhaps the service used most frequently by individuals. Each designated Express Mail facility has established schedules to receive your items to guarantee next-day delivery. Assuming that your letter or package reaches your local post office by the deadline, your shipment should reach your addressee by 3:00 P.M. the following day, or the addressee may call for it at the designated post office as early as 10:00 A.M. the following business day. Contact the facility nearest you for their deadline.

Express Mail Custom-Designed Service operates on a scheduled basis between specific locations. A service agreement designating place and date of shipment is required. This arrangement is more advantageous to businesses and organizations that need such services on a regular basis.

Express Mail Same-Day Airport Service is available for items requiring same-day delivery. Mailable items must be taken to a designated airport by a specified time to guarantee same-day delivery. Arrangements should be made for pickup at the designated airport at the point of destination.

FIRST CLASS MAIL*

This form of mailing features local next-day service and third-day service nationwide. It is restricted to items weighing less than 12 ounces and provides a one-year forwarding service and return of unclaimed mail. Items dispatched by this method may not be opened for postal inspection. (When sending a first class letter with parcels being shipped by a different class, you must indicate "First Class Letter Enclosed" on the parcel and be prepared to pay first class postage for the letter in addition to the required fee for the parcel.)

ITEMS RECOMMENDED FOR FIRST CLASS MAILING

Letters and copies
Wedding announcements
Invitations
Checks (personal/canceled)
Personal tapes and cassettes
Nonnegotiable bonds
Nonnegotiable stock certificates

Payments on accounts
Birth announcements
Greeting cards
Copies of documents (of no real or usable value)
Typed reports/papers

Registered First Class

Registered First Class is designed to offer maximum expediency and protection for shipment of valuable items to domestic and foreign destinations. Registered items are tracked as they travel from the point of origination to their intended destination. Fees are based upon item value and provide proof of mailing and delivery. For additional fees, the sender may restrict delivery and obtain a return receipt verifying to whom the item was delivered. Such items are covered up to $25,000.

ITEMS RECOMMENDED FOR REGISTERED FIRST CLASS MAILING

Negotiable bonds
Certified checks
Jewelry
Letters for restricted delivery

Negotiable stock certificates
Checks endorsed in blank
Signed original documents (with real or usable value)

Certified First Class

This particular class provides the sender with information regarding proof of mailing and delivery of items not considered to have real or usable value. For an additional fee, the sender can restrict delivery domestically. Unlike Registered First Class Mail, **Certified First Class** offers no protection against loss or damage and applies only to domestic mail.

---

* Businesses and organizations should consult their local postmaster for information regarding Presort First Class Mail and ZIP + 4 First Class Mail.

ITEMS RECOMMENDED FOR CERTIFIED FIRST CLASS MAILING

Nonnegotiable bonds   Documents with no real or usable value
Letters delivered to addressee only   Other documents requiring proof of delivery

First Class Zone Rated (Priority) Mail

First Class Zone-Rated Mail applies to first class items weighing more than 12 ounces, with rates based upon zoned distances. The maximum weight allowance is 70 pounds, and size is limited to 108 inches combined length and girth (with the exception of items shipped to APOs and FPOs). For additional fees, First Class Zone-Rated (Priority) shipments may be sent registered, insured, C.O.D., or special delivery.

SECOND CLASS MAIL*

Second Class Mail service pertains primarily to delivery of newspapers and periodicals that must meet content, production, subscriber, and specified postal requirements.

THIRD CLASS MAIL*

Third Class Mail service is available for dispatch of business or organizational advertising mail and merchandise that weighs less than 16 ounces. These items are subject to postal inspection; however, the sender may seal the items by indicating "THIRD CLASS (MAGAZINE/PRINTED)" on the outside or wrapper. With few exceptions (such as autographs), other instructions, inscriptions, and messages are not permitted. Consult your local postmaster for clarification.

ITEMS RECOMMENDED FOR THIRD CLASS MAILING

Manuscripts (to 16 ounces)   Photographs
   (with accompanying proof sheets)   Printed matter (to 16 ounces)
Circulars   Catalogs
Books   Cuttings
Seeds   Roots
Bulbs   Plants
Scions

---

* Nonprofit organizations should contact their local postmaster for information regarding special mailings and nonprofit rates.

* Businesses and nonprofit organizations should consult their local postmaster for information concerning Bulk Rate Third Class Mailing.

FOURTH CLASS MAIL (PARCELS)*

Parcels exceeding 1 pound (up to 70 pounds and 108 inches in combined length and girth) may be sent **Fourth Class Mail** to most domestic locations. Sealed items are subject to postal inspection. The sender should identify contents and indicate "MAY BE OPENED FOR POSTAL INSPECTION" on the package. Articles being returned for repair may include sales slips. If other forms of correspondence are enclosed, the sender should indicate "FIRST CLASS MAIL ENCLOSED" and pay the appropriate fee for First Class in addition to the Fourth Class rate for the parcel.

Fourth Class Mail may receive the same handling as First Class Mail, with the exception of special delivery at the point of destination, if the sender pays the appropriate fees for special handling.

OTHER IMPORTANT SERVICES

C.O.D. (COLLECT ON DELIVERY) services permit the sender (who must guarantee return postage) to ship an item that has not been paid for. The recipient is required to pay the price of the item, up to $500.00, plus the cost of postage. Protection against loss or damage is available for C.O.D. shipments. The service is restricted to domestic mail.

Insurance is available for most First, Third, and Fourth Class items, providing up to $500.00 in coverage for loss or damage to merchandise. Restricted Delivery and Return Receipts are available on merchandise insured in excess of $25.00.

Postal Money Orders are available through all post offices in amounts up to $700.00 They may be redeemed at all post office locations, as well as banks and many businesses.

Special Delivery can be obtained for all classes of mail with the exception of Express Mail and Bulk Rate Third Class Mail. Consult your local post office regarding delivery restrictions at point of destination.

Special Handling applies to Third and Fourth Class Mail items, and fees are based on item weight and class of mail. While it provides for special dispatch and method of transportation, it does not allow for special delivery at the point of destination.

Additional services are available through the U.S. Postal Service. Individuals may contact their local post offices for information concerning seasonal deadlines, nondelivery on recognized holidays, locations and services available through self-service postal centers, lockbox and caller services, and items and services of interest to stamp collectors. Domestic postal rate charts as well as information concerning international mail rates, restrictions, and procedures are available through most postal outlets.

---

* Due to the variance in rates and requirements in this category, senders should contact their local post office for information and instructions.

STATE ABBREVIATIONS

Alabama	AL	Missouri	MO
Alaska	AK	Montana	MT
Arizona	AZ	Nebraska	NE
Arkansas	AR	Nevada	NV
California	CA	New Hampshire	NH
Colorado	CO	New Jersey	NJ
Connecticut	CT	New Mexico	NM
Delaware	DE	New York	NY
District of		North Carolina	NC
Columbia	DC	North Dakota	ND
Florida	FL	Ohio	OH
Georgia	GA	Oklahoma	OK
Hawaii	HI	Oregon	OR
Idaho	ID	Pennsylvania	PA
Illinois	IL	Rhode Island	RI
Indiana	IN	South Carolina	SC
Iowa	IA	South Dakota	SD
Kansas	KS	Tennessee	TN
Kentucky	KY	Texas	TX
Louisiana	LA	Utah	UT
Maine	ME	Vermont	VT
Maryland	MD	Virginia	VA
Massachusetts	MA	Washington	WA
Michigan	MI	West Virginia	WV
Minnesota	MN	Wisconsin	WI
Mississippi	MS	Wyoming	WY

"WHAT THEY MEAN WHEN THEY SAY . . ."
Glossary of Business Terms and Abbreviations

AARP (Senior Services) The American Association of Retired Persons. An organization dedicated to the enhancement of opportunities and protection of rights and privileges specifically related to citizens 50 years of age and older.

ACCOUNTS PAYABLE (Finance/Credit) Accounts that businesses or organizations pay for products or services billed to them by other businesses, organizations, or individuals.

ACCOUNTS RECEIVABLE (Finance/Credit) Payments due from other businesses, organizations, and individuals for products or services rendered by the billing company.

ACTION (Senior Services) A nationwide network of volunteers, with headquarters in Washington, D.C., that assists with programs designed to meet basic human needs and support self-improvement efforts of low-income communities and individuals.

ADJUSTER (Insurance) A state-licensed individual contracted or employed by insurance companies to assess the extent of a policyholder's loss and recommend appropriate reimbursement from the insurance company, within policy guidelines.

AFFIRMATIVE ACTION (Veterans Affairs) Federal legislation designed to prevent contractors or subcontractors operating under federal contracts of $10,000 or more to engage in employment practices that discriminate against Vietnam era and certain other disabled veterans. Such contractors and subcontractors are encouraged to actively secure placement and promote qualified veterans.

AGENT (Insurance) An individual licensed by the state and employed by an insurance company to offer clients protection against economic loss through the sale and management of appropriate insurance coverages.

AMORTIZATION (Real Estate) A schedule of mortgage payments reflecting dates payments are due, the amount of each payment, and the amount of principal and interest to be applied against the outstanding balance for the term of the loan.

ANNUITY (Insurance) An investment or contract designed to provide income for a specified period of time or a lifetime.

APPRAISAL (Insurance/Real Estate) The estimated value of an item or property based upon age, condition, demand, known comparables, and market value at a given time.

ASSESSMENT (Credit/Finance/Insurance/Real Estate) An evaluation of current status, contributing circumstances, economic impact, or value.

ASSIGNMENT (Insurance/Real Estate) (Insurance) The transfer of one's interest in an insurance policy to another individual, for example, a homeowner's insurance policy to a new owner. (Medicare) A physician's or provider's agreement to accept what Medicare deems appropriate as payment in full. Generally, Medicare pays 80% of the approved charge, and the patient pays the remaining 20%.

ASSUMABLE (Real Estate) A mortgage provision that allows a borrower to transfer an existing mortgage to another qualified borrower.

ATTACHMENT (Business Correspondence) An additional item attached to a letter that together constitute the whole of a correspondence package. Also referred to as "enclosure."

BCC (Business Correspondence) A designation affixed to the sender's copy of his or her correspondence indicating copies were sent to other interested parties without the addressee's knowledge.

BENEFICIARY (Insurance) An individual (s) or organization entitled to receive a specified benefit amount upon the death of the insured, as set forth in the provisions of the life insurance policy.

BETTER BUSINESS BUREAU (Consumer) A nonprofit organization sponsored by local businesses to investigate consumer complaints and provide information regarding businesses and organizations.

BINDER (Insurance/Real Estate) A temporary contract that validates or "binds" an agreement until a permanent document can be issued.

BROKER (Insurance/Finance/Real Estate) An individual licensed by the state in which he or she conducts business to act on behalf of another individual or organization in contractual or financial transactions, in exchange for a commission or fee.

CARRIER (Medicare/Transportation) (Medicare) An insurance company contracted by the federal government to handle claims from physicians, providers, and suppliers for Medicare patients. Each state has a designated Medicare carrier. (Transportation) A method of transport or courier.

CASH SURRENDER VALUE (Insurance) The actual amount of money available to a policy holder who elects to terminate a policy before it matures.

CC (Business Correspondence) Designation indicating that the writer intends to supply other individuals or organizations with a copy of the original document, with the addressee's knowledge.

C.E.O. (Any business or organization) The chief executive officer or senior official of a company or organization.

CERTIFICATE OF INSURANCE (Insurance) A form issued to an individual covered under a group policy outlining coverages and other considerations that comprise the whole of the contract.

CIA (Government) The Central Intelligence Agency, headquartered in Washington, D.C., helps to safeguard national security through the compilation, evaluation, and dissemination of political, military, economic, and scientific information worldwide.

C.O.D. (U.S. Postal Service) Collect on Delivery. An arrangement that allows a manufacturer or supplier to ship an item that has not been paid for, authorizing the postal or courier service to collect the actual cost of the item, plus shipping and handling fees, from the recipient at the time of delivery.

COINSURANCE (Insurance/Health Care/Medicare) That portion of a medical fee that the insured is responsible for. The difference between the amount charged and the insurance company's (carrier's) liability according to the terms and conditions of the policy.

CONSUMER PROTECTION OFFICE (Consumer) Located throughout the United States, this organization is responsible for providing consumer protection against fraudulent activities.

CONVERSION PRIVILEGE (Insurance) A contractual provision that allows a group policy holder to convert, upon termination of employment, his or her group coverage to an individual policy without proof of insurability.

CREDIT LIFE (Finance/Credit) Coverage sold through a lender that provides repayment of any unpaid balance in the event of the borrower's death.

CREDIT REPORTING AGENCY (Credit) An organization that collects data on individuals who have established a credit history and disburses this information to businesses and organizations with authorized access.

DEDUCTIBLE (Insurance) The amount an insured must pay "up front" against a loss in addition to what the insurance company is required to pay in accordance with the terms and conditions of the policy.

DEFAULT (Finance/Real Estate) Failure to honor an agreement, as in repayment of a loan.

DEFERRED PAYMENTS (Finance) Payments that, for valid and approved reasons, may be postponed for a specified period of time or the borrower may be required to pay only the interest for the duration of the deferment.

DEPRECIATION (Finance/Real Estate) A decline in value due to aging, normal wear and tear, obsolescence, natural disaster, or malicious intent.

DIAGNOSIS RELATED GROUP (DRG) (Medicare) The amount Medicare determines to be an average cost for treatment of patients with similar conditions.

DOCUMENTARY STAMPS (Finance/Real Estate) A state tax stamp applied to contracts, deeds, and mortgages when a titled property passes from one owner to another.

ENTITLEMENT (Veterans Affairs/Social Security/Medicare) A determination of eligibility under prescribed terms and conditions.

EQUITY (Real Estate) An unencumbered and indisputable financial interest in an item of value or real estate, generally the difference between established market value and the amount owed.

ESCROW (Finance/Real Estate) Funds held in trust by one party for another, to be released at a set time under specified terms and conditions.

FAA (Government/Travel) The Federal Aviation Administration, operating under the jurisdiction of the U.S. Department of Transportation, regulates air commerce to promote development and safety and fulfill the requirements of national defense.

FBI (Government) The Federal Bureau of Investigation, headquartered in Washington, D.C., is subject to the jurisdiction of the U.S. Department of Justice and is charged with the responsibility of gathering facts, locating witnesses and compiling evidence in cases involving federal intervention.

FDIC (Finance) The Federal Deposit Insurance Corporation. Headquarted in Washington, D.C., this independent government agency was established to protect the nation's money supply by providing insurance coverage for bank deposits and overseeing operations of state-chartered banks that are not members of the Federal Reserve System.

FEMA (Government) The Federal Emergency Management Agency is charged with the responsibility of emergency preparedness at federal, state, and local levels, coordinating planning of relief operations and recovery assistance in times of disaster.

FORECLOSURE (Real Estate) Repossession of property by the lender as a result of the borrower's failure to pay.

FTC (Government/Consumer) The Federal Trade Commission is committed to the task of overseeing competitive trade practices and protects consumer rights through the investigation and prosecution of those engaged in fraudulent activities.

GRACE PERIOD (Insurance) A period of time, usually 30 days, in which an overdue premium may be paid without penalty or interruption of coverage.

GUARANTOR (Finance/Credit) One who guarantees a financial obligation will be paid; a cosigner on the personal note or a contract of another individual.

HCFA (Medicare) Operating under the jurisdiction of the Department of Health and Human Services, the Health Care Financing Administration oversees the management of Medicare, Medicaid and other federal medical care quality control staffs.

HMO (Health Care/Medicare) Health Maintenance Organizations are designed to provide a variety of medical services for a fixed monthly fee. Unlike standard plans, the members of HMOs may be restricted to their choice of physicians and acute care facilities, finding themselves limited to utilizing only those that are approved by their HMO.

HUD (Government) The U.S. Department of Housing and Urban Development focuses upon the nation's housing needs, development and preservation of the nation's communities, and the provision of equal housing opportunities for individuals.

ICC (Government/Travel) The Interstate Commerce Commission regulates interstate surface transportation to ensure such carriers provide the public with rates and services that are fair and reasonable.

INDEMNITY (Insurance) Compensation for a loss, financial protection against an unexpected occurrence.

LIEN (Finance/Real Estate) A claim one may place against the property of a business or individual who fails to meet a financial obligation.

LESSEE (Real Estate) A tenant who temporarily occupies or takes possession of property owned by another.

LESSOR (Real Estate) One who leases his property to another under specified terms and conditions.

MAJOR MEDICAL (Insurance) Insurance protection designed to pay a prescribed portion of expenses associated with a major illness, including hospitalization and specified services by physicians, suppliers, and other related care givers.

MEDICARE (Medicare) A federal program designed to provide medical expense coverage for qualified persons age 65 and over and those who qualify due to permanent and total disability or suffer from end-stage renal disease.

MEDIGAP INSURANCE (Insurance) A type of policy designed to supplement Medicare coverage.

MORTGAGEE (Finance/Real Estate) A borrower who contracts to purchase real estate.

MORTGAGOR (Finance/Real Estate) The lender who finances the purchase of real estate.

OSHA (Employment/Government) The Occupational Safety and Health Administration, under the jurisdiction of the U.S. Department of Labor, is responsible for the development and compliance of safety and health standards in the workplace.

PARTICIPATING PHYSICIAN (Medicare) A physician who agrees to accept assignment, the amount Medicare deems appropriate, as payment in full for services rendered to Medicare patients.

PEER REVIEW ORGANIZATION (PRO) (Medicare) An investigative group of physicians, under contract to the Health Care Financing Administration, responsible for evaluating services to Medicare beneficiaries. Each state has its own peer review organization.

P.I.T.I. (Real Estate) Principal, interest, taxes and insurance payments.

POLICY TERM (Insurance) The time period covered under an existing policy, from inception date to termination date.

PREEXISTING CONDITION (Insurance) A physical or psychological condition that exists at the time a policy is purchased, and for which the company may decline to cover or require a specified waiting period before coverage becomes effective.

PRORATE (Finance) To assess, or divide equally among a given number of individuals, as in prorating someone's share of the total cost of an item.

QUITCLAIM DEED (Real Estate) A legal document in which one individual may relinquish claim to property to another individual.

REINSTATEMENT (Consumer/Finance/Insurance/Real Estate) To return to a previous condition, such as paying the overdue premium on a policy to restore protection to the insured after a notice of cancellation has been issued.

SBA (Self-employed) The Small Business Administration promotes and protects the interests of small businesses in matters of government purchases, contracts, loans, and catastrophic occurrences that cause economic injury and acts in a regulatory and licensing capacity.

TERM INSURANCE (Insurance) A life insurance policy in which benefits are paid to a beneficiary should the policyholder die within the prescribed policy period.

TITLE INSURANCE (Real Estate) Protects the buyer against defects in the title should it later be discovered unknown encumbrances existed at the time of the sale of the property.

UTILIZATION REVIEW COMMITTEE (Health Care) A committee of physicians responsible for ensuring patients' treatment or lengths of stay in a hospital are based upon medical necessity.

VENDOR (Self-employed) A manufacturer, supplier, or representative of a company who contracts to supply other businesses with a specific product.

VETERANS PREFERENCE (Veterans Affairs) A method by which qualified veterans receive special consideration with reference to federal employment.

VISA (Travel) An endorsement affixed to a passport by an appropriate official granting permission for a visitor to enter the official's country.

WAIVER (Employment/Insurance/Finance/Education) To relinquish, or set aside, existing restrictions based upon acceptable reasons or alternatives.

WARRANTY (Consumer) A performance or repair guarantee.

WORKERS' COMPENSATION (Employment) Protection for an employee who suffers a loss due to work-related injury or occupational disease. Benefits are administered through a government regulated system, to which employers contribute.

Index

A

Account in collections, health-care-related, 82-83
Acknowledgments, 163-65
  gift arrived, 164
  information received, 164
  met your friend, 165
  payment received, 164
Administration on Aging, requesting information
    from, 120-21
Affirmative action, 332
Aging:
  organizations, 261
  state agencies, 258-61
  See also Social Security Administration
Air carrier, medical clearance, 147-48
American Association of Retired Person (AARP):
  definition, 332
  membership information request, 128
Anniversary:
  of business partnership, 246
  of employment, apology for overlooking, 174
Announcements, 167-72
  birth/adoption, 168
  class reunion, 169
  engagement, 168-69
  graduation of son/daughter, 168
  humanitarian event, 170
  moved to new location, 171
  new associate/employee, 171
  special interest group/club, forming, 171-72
  volunteers, seeking, 170
  wedding of son/daughter, 169
Apologies, 173-78
  anniversary of employment, overlooked, 174
  for bounced check, 177
  for damage to property, 178
  diffusing an unpleasant situation, 175-76
  for failure to supply information, 178
  for forgetting special event, 174
  for impulsive statement, 175
  for late payment, 177
  "sorry I haven't written," 175
  unable to attend function, 177
  for unseemly behavior of guest, 176
  for withdrawing voluntary commitment, 176
Armed services, forms of address, 322
Auto insurance discounts, requesting, 94-95

B

Back order, notification of, 55
Banking authorities, 261-64

Bankruptcy rebuttal, 27
Baptism, 247
Bar/bat mitzvah, 247
Beneficiary, changing, 93
Bereavement travel, 142
Better Business Bureaus:
  definition, 333
  local bureaus, 264-73
  national bureau, 264
Birth/adoption, announcement of, 168
Birthday:
  children, 181
  party invitation, 220
  of son/daughter, 246
Bounced check, apology for, 177
Broadcast networks, 273
Business clubs/organizations:
  announcing a special event, 12
  invitation to join, 10
  letters to, 9-13
  recruiting volunteers (blanket letter), 13
  refusing a donation, 12
  rejecting membership application, 11
  requesting payment of membership dues, 11-12
  thanking volunteers, 13
  welcoming new member, 10-11
Business letters:
  about consumer products/services, 15-21
  about environment, 57-60
  about financial matters, 61-68
  about health care, 79-85
  about hobbies/special interests, 87-90
  about taxes, 135-39
  about veterans affairs, 149-56
  closing, 5
  conclusion, 4
  content, 4
  copies to other, 5
  credit, 23-29
  dates, 3
  education, 31-35
  employment, 37-50
  failure to respond, 5
  first impressions, 3
  insurance-related, 91-96
  layout guide, 7-8
  media-related business letters, 97-102
  reference or subject lines, 4
  return address, 3
  return to source, 6
  salutation/greeting, 4
  sample letter, 8
  self-employment, 51-56
  senior services, 119-22